THE POLITICAL POTENTIAL OF SORTITION

The Luck of the Draw:
SORTITION AND PUBLIC POLICY

Series Editor: Barbara Goodwin
University of East Anglia

A major new series on the
use of randomisation
in education, politics
and other areas of public policy

The Political Potential of Sortition, Oliver Dowlen
978-1845401375 (cloth)
978-1845401795 (pbk.)

The Athenian Option, Anthony Barnett and Peter Carty
978-1845401399 (pbk.); 978-1845401405 (cloth)

The Nature and Use of Lotteries, Thomas Gataker (ed. Conall Boyle)
978-1845401177 (pbk.)

A People's Parliament, Keith Sutherland
A Citizen Legislature, Ernest Callenbach and Michael Phillips
978-1845401085 (pbk.); 978-1845401382 (cloth)

Justice by Lottery, Barbara Goodwin
1845400259 (pbk)

imprint-academic.com/sortition

THE POLITICAL POTENTIAL OF SORTITION

A STUDY OF THE RANDOM SELECTION OF CITIZENS FOR PUBLIC OFFICE

Oliver Dowlen

ia

imprint-academic.com

Published in the UK by Imprint Academic
PO Box 200, Exeter EX5 5YX, UK

Published in the USA by Imprint Academic
Philosophy Documentation Center
PO Box 7147, Charlottesville, VA 22906-7147, USA

ISBN 9 781845 401375 (cloth)
ISBN 9 781845 401795 (pbk.)

A CIP catalogue record for this book is available from the
British Library and US Library of Congress

Contents

Preface

The origins of this book lie back in 1994 in a proposal made by the *Labour Committee for the Democratic Accountability of Secret Services*, a grouping to which I then belonged. The proposal, which was not followed up with any organisational detail, was that secret services should be monitored for abuses of human rights, and that the monitors who undertook the task should be selected randomly. The idea was the brainchild of Dr Keith Nilsen whose general orientation was that the modern political arena was so dominated by covert factionalism that fundamental values such as truth and integrity were under serious threat. His solution lay in establishing institutions whose impartiality was not open to question.

While I understood the reasoning behind this and other similar projects advanced by Dr Nilsen, I felt that advocacy was not enough and that further investigation of the question of random selection was necessary to discover its full potential. Nor was I entirely happy with Dr Nilsen's claim that the anti-factional capacity of sortition was a self-evident truth.[1] Truths can certainly be understood from practice, but in the case of a largely discontinued practice such as sortition they have to be argued for anew and evidence (old and new) presented in support of those arguments. My main motivation for this study lay in the idea that a broadly-based and open discourse on the potential of sortition was a good thing. Such a discourse, I felt, could be taken forward by a thorough exploration of how sortition had been used and a principled analysis of the properties of the lottery process.

In 2002 I was fortunate enough to study the subject for a doctorate at New College Oxford under the supervision of Mark Philp and, initially, Elizabeth Frazer. Through the internet group of scholars

---

[1] Nilsen (2004). Nilsen also made proposals for the use of sortition in Iraq, details of which can be found in Nilsen (2007). He also founded the *Society for Democracy including Random Selection* in South London in 2000.

organised by Conall Boyle (aptly named the *Kleroterians*) my completed thesis then reached the attention of Keith Sutherland of Imprint Academic who was planning a series on sortition. I was delighted to be asked to be part of this exciting initiative and to be in the good company of other contributors to the subject, including, of course, Thomas Gataker.

This book is, in all essentials, a re-working of my doctoral thesis; but there are some important changes of emphasis that need to be noted. Extra emphasis is placed on the importance of the 'active context' and the 'constitutional context' of each application or proposed application of sortition. This is to help the reader to see how the level of detail advanced during the historical narratives links into the arguments about what sortition can bring to the political community. I have also added a glossary and a number of diagrams in order to help the less specialist reader to get a clearer idea of the schemes and contexts where lot was used or advocated. I have placed bibliographical notes at the end of every chapter save the last. These are designed to give the reader an overview of the main sources that I used in the research. They also give some indication of the selection of background literature that I used that would not otherwise be indicated in the footnotes. They also include details of the location of some primary documents.

In addition I have included a brief appendix on the decline of sortition. Because this question was not part of my original study plan I thought it best to make a clear separation between this short, somewhat speculative, section and the main body of the book.

I would like to acknowledge the role of Keith Nilsen in introducing me to the subject of sortition; the help of Mark Philp in keeping me on track during my thesis preparation; the help of Miriam Ronzoni and Tizziana Torresi in the translation of Guicciardini's *Del modo di eleggere…*; and the help of Antoine Vergne in tracing the documentary evidence for the French split legislature proposal of 1793.

My thanks also go to Rachel Hammersley for pointing me in the direction of the Lesueur/Rutledges draft constitution of 1792, and to Dr O. Murray for indicating how lot was used for deciding inheritance in Ancient Athens. In addition I would like to thank my (younger) fellow students at the Politics Department of Oxford University for their enthusiasm and encouragement; Conall Boyle for bringing us students of sortition together; Keith Sutherland for his initiative in bringing out the series; Barbara Goodwin for editing this work; and my wife Berenice for her help and support.

Introduction

This is the study of one particular aspect of government: the random selection of political officers by sortition or lot. Sortition was widely used in Ancient Athens and in the city republics of Italy in the late medieval and renaissance periods. There has therefore been a considerable investment in this form of selection during periods of great importance in the development of our political ideas and practices. With the notable exception of jury selection, however, it is largely absent from today's electoral politics. Despite this there has been a recent revival of interest in sortition both from academic writers and from those involved in practical politics. Much of this has been a response to perceived problems with liberal democracy such as the growing gulf between citizen and professional politician and the exclusion of significant minority groups from the political process.

In the 1970s and 80s there was a growing interest in community politics and randomly-selected citizens' juries were seen as a means of advancing the ideas of a truly participatory democracy. Although the citizens' jury models of this period advocated lot as the means by which citizens were to be selected to serve, there was little attention given to the exact contribution that sortition was to make. From the later 1980s and 1990s, however, a number of more ambitious sortive schemes began to surface, some of which sought to find a closer match between the qualities of sortition and the purpose for which it was to be deployed. These included schemes for the selection of one or other chamber of the UK parliament by lot,[1] a proposal to elect a truly representative Citizen's Legislature for the United States by drawing members randomly from the citizen body,[2] and a

---

[1] Barnett and Carty (1998/2008); Sutherland (2004; 2008).
[2] Callenbach and Phillips (1985/2008).

scheme for randomly selected monitors for secret services.[3] This coincided with a debate, mainly amongst political theorists and philosophers, which explored the proposition that the lotteries could provide a just means of distributing social goods.[4]

In 2007, however, the French presidential candidate Ségolène Royal went to the polls with a manifesto that included setting up citizens' juries, selected by lot, to oversee the work of elected representatives. This indicates that sortition might be about to escape from the realms of theory and that very soon selection of citizens for public office by lot could once again become part of our day-to-day political practice.

While this book should be seen as a contribution to an expanding discourse on the subject, I do not advocate any particular scheme, nor, indeed, do I present arguments to persuade the reader that the modern re-introduction of lot would necessarily be a good thing. I am not entirely sure that we are ready for it—lotteries are not a regular part of our current political culture and we lack any practical knowledge of how lottery-based schemes could actually operate within the political arena. My contribution is accordingly based on the premise that a certain amount of theoretical and historical ground-clearing is required in order that a principled and informed framework for understanding the political value of sortition might be established. While I make some suggestions about how we could approach the modern application of sortition in my concluding chapter, I leave open the question of whether such a re-introduction is necessary.

I therefore set out with the straightforward aim of identifying what benefits the random selection of political officers could bring to the political community. This is simply defined by the book's title *The Political Potential of Sortition*, but some aspects of this task are far from simple. By applying the term 'potential' to the project I address the idea that there is a special power or capacity inherent in the lottery that is absent from other forms of selection or decision-making. It also suggests that there are some circumstances, contexts or lottery schemes that will realise this and bring it to fruition, others that will not, and others that will do so only partially or incompletely. To investigate how this operates our starting point has to be the lottery procedure itself—or, to be more accurate, the relationship between lottery form (what a lottery is) and its function (what task it is being

[3] Nilsen (2007).
[4] Goodwin (2005); Elster (1989); Duxbury (1999).

asked to perform). I attend to this analytical task in Chapter One where I identify the defining feature and chief operating characteristic of all lotteries as the 'blind break'. This is the zone at the centre of the lottery from which all rational activity is deliberately excluded. I therefore characterise the blind break as 'arational' to distinguish it from the operations of both the rational *and* the irrational. It is in this central feature that the potential of sortition lies, and once this is identified it is then possible to talk of applications that make a positive virtue of the blind break, and those that, for whatever reason, do not. We can then assess any application by asking (and hopefully answering) the question 'is lot being asked to do what lot does best?' The identification of the blind break also helps me to make a critical appraisal of the role of lot in probability theory and sampling methods and to investigate the nature of weighted lotteries.

Another device that I employ in order to help discuss and define the action of a lottery is what I call the 'box of possible epithets'. This follows from the indisputable fact that a lottery is a mechanical decision-making process. If we wish to describe the qualities of a decision made by a lottery, then the epithet, or adjective we use must denote a non-human quality — in other words a quality that does not pertain to the human act of making a decision. To help simplify this I imagine a box containing all possible non-human epithets. All of these can be used to describe a lottery decision; we then have to ask which is the most useful for any given analytical task. In Chapter One I present this idea and explain why I single out the term 'arational' as the most important of these possible terms of description.

This chapter is then followed by five chapters in which I attempt to apply these findings to the past practice of sortition in the political arena. To define the 'political' my starting-point is political practice. My focus throughout this study is on the concept of the political community and the process by which people have utilised whatever means they thought necessary to establish efficient, inclusive government and to defend it against dangers such as factional fragmentation or arbitrary oppression. It is in the application of these rule-governed procedures and institutions and in the habits of collective behaviour they create that we find the subject matter of politics. In broader terms I would describe politics as the 'art of the city' in which the term 'city' applies to a community of people rather than merely an urban geographical location. It is also a fitting description because, historically, many of the most significant innovations in the western political tradition took place in cities and it was here that the culture of conscious citizenship was born.

My five historical chapters therefore track the role of sortition against the background of this type of 'struggle for politics'. They are case studies in the application and advocacy of sortition, but they also attempt to portray political practice in its process of development. In some accounts, such as the story of political consolidation in Ancient Athens in Chapter Two, the detailed discussion of the defence of the Second Florentine Republic in Chapter Four and the final historical chapter on the French Revolution, the sense of struggle is immediate and palpable. In nearly all of the contexts I explore, however, the problem of bringing different factions or parties into the same political process or under the same constitution is present in some form or another.

Because all these case studies or historical narratives show what happens when sortition is used or advocated within the cut-and-thrust of political endeavour, they can render a more thorough, all-round account of its potential than if the exploration was based solely on theory and argument. Together they tell the story of the pressures and tensions that attend the decisions to introduce lottery schemes, how they were supported or opposed, and how they performed in practice. Above all they show how lotteries were used or advocated in response to very real problems or crises.

While I am keen to place every scheme in its immediate *active* context, I also try to present the different *constitutional* environments in which sortition operated. In the first instance this enables me to compare the use of lot with other measures designed to produce the same result or contribute to the same ends. On a more general level, however, it also allows me to make comparisons between different forms of government in a particularly pointed manner. This is directly related to the question of modern advocacy. If we are to advance sortition as a solution to modern problems and in the context of modern political systems, we should be aware of the differences between our current arrangements and those where sortition was more widely practised. We cannot rebuild Ancient Athens or renaissance Florence in the twenty-first century, but if we are aware of the constitutional context of any lottery scheme we can then make an intelligent appraisal of how well a similar scheme might address similar needs in the modern polity.

The attention given to the constitutional context of sortition in this study also allows us to understand the part played by random selection in our political inheritance. By comparing different governmental arrangements we can begin to see sortition against a broad panorama of political ideas and practices leading towards the present. Furthermore, if we look at a number of political communities, some of which have had a considerable impact on our own, we can begin to formulate a concrete understanding of the 'political community' in a general sense.

An additional benefit of exploring the use of lot by using historical case studies can be found in the idea of problem solving. In each historical chapter certain problems or questions presented themselves as being more important or significant than others. In Chapter Two the problem or question that demanded the greatest attention was the relationship between sortition and democracy in Ancient Athens. Was sortition, as suggested by Aristotle and others, a defining feature of democracy as a polity type, or are there other ways that the story of their unfolding relationship could be told? My approach to this was to look at the role of lot in what I call 'political consolidation'. This is the process by which the authoritative institutions and rule-governed procedures necessary for consensual government were established. It was in this process that sortition played a pivotal role and the rational political order it helped to create enabled the *demos* to participate fully in public affairs. In this chapter I had deliberately to 'de-couple' lot from its close association with the developed democracy of fifth century Athens in order to investigate how its earlier use fostered the conditions that made democracy possible.

The main subject of Chapter Three is the comparison between two lottery-based schemes for election from the late medieval communes and republics of northern Italy. The earlier form, the *brevia*, is an essentially public form of choosing electors by lot; the later form, the *scrutiny*, was practised in Florence and a few other city republics. It consisted of the election of a pool of candidates whose names were then drawn out at regular intervals to fill political posts as they fall vacant in rotation. Many parts of this scheme were private or secret and this feature contrasts pointedly with the earlier *brevia*. Both lottery schemes are designed to inhibit factional intrigue and electoral irregularity, but operate in very different ways and with differing constitutional objectives. The main problem was to determine the precise function of sortition in each case.

In Chapter Four the focus narrows to deal with events in Florence in 1465-6 and in 1497-9. In both these short periods lot was used to defend the popular republican institutions of the city — in the first against the arbitrary rule of the Medici dynasty, in the second against the threat to the new republic posed by an invigorated aristocratic faction. As well as exploring how lot figured in the political defence of popular Florentine republicanism, this chapter looks at contemporary works by Machiavelli and Guicciardini in which they both advocate and criticise the use of sortition. The fall of the Second Florentine republic in 1530 sees the end of this particular popular republican model in Europe in which lot traditionally played an important role. A scheme put forward by Machiavelli in 1520 is very much within this tradition. The more aristocratic Guicciardini, however, advocates a new form of popular republic in which preference election plays a major part. He also revisits and re-writes the Florentine debates of 1497–9 in three different works, the most significant being a pair of dramatised speeches, one for and one against the use of lot. He is one of the few writers in the European tradition to take the issue seriously and in this chapter I advance various reasons why I think he does this and what it tells us about the changes in political thinking that were taking place at this time.

The final two chapters look at the practice and advocacy of sortition in contexts where its political use was less widespread. My main aim here is to investigate how its political potential was understood and realised in such circumstances. Chapter Five tells how James Harrington's *Oceana* advances ideas for a republican constitution for Britain based on the Venetian model — which makes widespread use of sortition. His ideas are then taken up in some of the experimental constitutions of the American colonies. The only form in which it is consistently adopted, however, is the randomly selected jury. This first makes its appearance in South Carolina in 1682. The jury plays an important part in the struggle for press freedom that occurs during the latter part of the eighteenth century in both England and America, and within this context there are some attempts to see sortition as a means of embedding justice in the community. In this chapter I trace some of these developments and look briefly at the relationship between the secret ballot and sortition. Both were originally part of the same integrated elective model practised in Venice, but in this period the secret ballot begins to be used without its sortive element. In addition to these general themes the chapter looks at a range of 'stand alone' lottery schemes and explores how the special problem-solving potential of sortition operates outside the context of its systematic political usage.

In the final historical chapter I look at how the political actors in the French Revolution understood the political potential of sortition. As the body politic began to creak and groan under the pressure of competing factions, a number of lottery-based schemes were adopted. The effects, however, were short-lived and they were, in some cases, counter-productive. Here I examine the role of practical experience in the design and implementation of lottery schemes and raise the question why the French were unable to draw from the success of Italian republicanism in this area.

The key feature of this study, however, is not the historical detail or the historical problems it raises, but the combination of political practice with analysis of lottery form and function. A few words need therefore to be said about how this combination operates. Because I identify the blind break as the central component of the lottery, I can then divide applications between 'strong' uses, which make a positive virtue of the blind break, and 'weak' uses, which do not. This distinction enables me to address a very particular and very important problem. While there are many historical and theoretical accounts that testify to the use of lot for the selection of political officers, there is a distinct shortage of surviving accounts that explain *why* it was used. This situation is further complicated by the fact that where discussion of sortition exists, it is more often than not in the writings of its detractors. These accounts tend to downplay or avoid mention of the possible benefits of using lot, portraying it as irrational, unstable or contrary to the principle of picking the best person for the job in hand.

To understand exactly what sortition might be bringing to any of the political systems we investigate and to assist in the general case of determining the political potential of lot we therefore need to adopt a process of intelligent reconstruction. This, of course, can be significantly assisted if we bring information from the active context and the constitutional context of any application into the equation. But we can also get a clearer idea of exactly why lot was used in any instance by actively searching for significant reasons why using an arational process could be advantageous, and how these might outweigh any disadvantages that might accrue from using this method of choice.

In the first instance this enables us to distinguish between the action of the arational lottery process itself and those consequences of using a lottery that are in fact the result of rational design decisions—such as might concern the size and nature of the pool. The idea that the use of lot to select political officers increases citizen participation in government is an example of this. The *main* reason why lottery schemes can achieve high levels of citizen participation is because the pool is opened to all citizens, not because an arational mechanism is used for their selection. In our search for the political potential of sortition it is important that we understand which part of the lottery process is doing what.

In our process of reconstruction it is also important that we are able to separate minor reasons why lot might have been introduced from more significant reasons why it might have been used. The idea that lot forms a 'logical' or 'convenient' means of establishing a rotational system could have been the reason that many sortive schemes were introduced—lot is, after all, quick and easy to administer once established.[5] This, however, does not take us to the heart of what lot, as a specifically arational means of making decisions, contributes to the process of selecting public officers. To be convenient or logical does not require arationality. The distinction between strong and weak applications of lot therefore helps to keep the general aims of the enquiry in focus, and helps us to assess the value of particular examples or explanations.

I end this introduction, paradoxically, with a sort of conclusion. It concerns the nature of the subject itself, the lottery. This conclusion is that the lottery is a complex phenomenon. It is multi-sided in the sense that it has many functions or aspects; these often come into operation at the same time and invariably seem to be of equal importance. A lottery decision is impartial, unpredictable, amoral, arational, unemotional, anonymous—to take but a few items from the 'box of possible epithets'. It is a social phenomenon, in the sense that it is a human invention that is used in a social setting and, usually, in the pursuit of social ends. At the same time, however, it denies the operation of the human qualities of thought, intention, will and morality. It is linked to the idea that there are some times when choices can (perhaps should) be taken out of our own hands, and as such stands at the threshold of some of the most profound areas of human speculative thought. It is also used for some of the most frivolous of human pastimes: those of gambling and games of chance.

Despite this complexity, it is also a commonplace in human culture. It is simple to operate, is universally used, and its benefits and risks intuitively grasped by young and old. My aim in this study is to make inroads into one particular application of the lottery and to see what it reveals of itself when subjected to a rigorous, but I hope not too abstract, framework of inquiry. I also aim to explore what possible benefits it can produce if its capacity is understood well

---

[5]   See Manin (1997), p. 31 and Hansen (1999), p. 236.

and applied appropriately. So saying, I do not suppose this will be the last word on the subject — the lottery is too elusive to be pinned down for any length of time. During the course of my investigation I have seen this beguilingly simple mechanism throw up many surprises — and I fully expect this to continue.

Bibliographical notes

For the newcomer to the subject the classic contributions are Headlam's 1891 *Election by Lot at Athens* (Headlam, 1933) and Gataker's *Of the Nature and Use of Lot* of 1619 (Gataker, 1627). Both of these have recently been republished: the Headlam by Kessinger in their Legacy Reprint Series, the Gataker by Imprint Academic (2008). The third important historical contribution is Guicciardini's *Del modo di eleggeri gli uffici nel Consiglio Grande*, which is unfortunately not readily available and has not yet been published in English. Of the more recent historical accounts Bernard Manin (1997) devotes a considerable portion to the use of lot, both in Ancient Athens and elsewhere. He does this, however, largely as a preliminary to his evaluation of representative government.

The second half of the twentieth century offered up a flurry of political writers who advocated the use of lot as an element in their new democratic participatory packages. In this group I include Dahl (1970), Barber (1984), Burnheim (1985), Callenbach and Phillips (1985, republished 2008), and those who promoted the 'Citizens' Jury' initiatives in the 1970s and 80s — particularly Crosby in Crosby, Kelly and Schaefer (1986), and Dienel in Dienel (1989) and Dienel and Renn (1995). As a general rule these writers advocate rather than explore sortition. Carson and Martin's solid *Random Selection in Politics* (1999) chronicles these developments well. For the reform of the House of Lords see Barnett and Carty (2008; originally 1998), and for a similar scheme in a different political context see Sutherland (2004; 2008). Nilsen's contributions can be found on the web sites www.sortition.com and www.sortition.org.uk (Nilsen, 2007).

In addition to the major contributions mentioned above, see also journal articles by: Amar (1984); Aubert (1959); Boyle (1998); Coote, Stewart, Kendall (1997); Eckhoff (1989); Engelstad (1988); Fishburn (1977); Frienberg, (1971); Greely (1977); Hofstee (1990); Kuper (1996); Mueller, Tollinson, Willett (1972); Mulgan (1984); Sher (1980); Stone (2007 and 2007b) and Zeckhauseur (1969).

There have also been a number of recent writers within the general orbit of political theory and philosophy who have shown an interest in lot. The best of these are the full-length works of Elster (1989), Goodwin (2005) and Duxbury (1999), along with some notable short works by Broome (1984, 1991). Of these Goodwin adopts a more consistent political orientation in her exploration of the relationship between justice and the lottery. A notable contribution with a different starting point can be found in Gobert (1997). This looks at random selection for political office from the perspective of its surviving institution, the jury, and is a further exploration of the ideas found in the short but important article 'Upon the Country ... ' by Maurice Pope (1989).

Discussion of lotteries also forms a sub-section of rational and social choice literature. Zeckhauseur (1969) is responsible for bringing the lottery into this area of discourse on the ground made fertile by Arrow, von Neumann and Morganstern. This is followed up in Fishburn (1977).

Chapter One

The Blind Break and its Implications

In this chapter I look at how we can best understand the use of lotteries. The aim is to find what models or frameworks for understanding will best serve us in the later task of examining the political potential of lot. Throughout the chapter, and in fact throughout the book as a whole, I approach the lottery as if it was a tool. It is a human invention similar to fire or the wheel, designed to fulfil certain tasks. It has a number of characteristics and potentialities that are very useful in certain applications and less useful in others. My aim is to show how these potentialities operate, and to develop a consistent approach with which I can investigate a wide range of applications of sortition. To do this, I advance two devices or ways of looking at the lottery process, both of which place the idea of arationality at its centre. They do this in slightly different ways: the first is a simple procedural description of how a lottery works, and the second enables us to approach the problems of lottery application from a more qualitative perspective. This is based on the idea that a lottery is a mechanical or 'non-human' process and brings to the act of choice a range of specifically non-human qualities, the most important of which is arationality.

On the basis of these devices or viewpoints I define two distinct types of application of lot. The first I call a strong application. This is where the arational nature of lot is regarded as a positive virtue. The second is a weak or weaker form of application and can be identified where lot is used but where arationality is not required, or is less than an essential requirement. We can also understand this as where the arational nature of lot is contradicted by other aims or ideas within the application.

Two devices for examining the use of lotteries

A lottery is a form of mechanical decision-making developed as a tool for solving particular problems. Those who decide to use a lottery usually do so because they calculate that this type of choice will be more useful to them than the type of choice that relies on human reason. The decision to use a lottery is an active, rational decision, but it has a calculated arational element within that rational context.

By a rational decision I mean a decision that is taken by means of the application of human reason and which involves the judging, or weighing, of options against each other to decide which is viable or preferable. I think of an irrational decision as a human decision in which the faculty of reason is overwhelmed by other human faculties, such as passion, instinct or emotion. I use the term arational to mean a decision that is made neither by the human faculty of reason, nor by any other human faculty—hence it is neither rational nor irrational. In applying the term 'rational' to a decision I do not imply that the decision is necessarily a good, or a well-made decision, but merely one which involves the weighing of ideas and options.

Apart from the decision to use lot, any lottery also involves preliminary structural choices about the size and nature of the pool and what the draw is to be for. With the notable exception of lottery games, which I believe should form a category of their own, lot is often used for the type of decision that previously, or in other circumstances, would have been taken by reason. Lotteries therefore operate within the type of purposeful context that pertains to rational choice.

Although I describe a lottery choice as mechanical, an actual lottery draw is often undertaken by a human agent. When this happens the action of this agent is made as arbitrary and mechanical as possible. The symbolic objects—balls, tickets etc.—are made to look or feel identical, and every effort is made to exclude differentiation by human sense or reason. The agent who makes the draw is, consequently, playing the part of a machine or a 'non-human'.

While we often talk about a lottery choice as having been made by chance, I avoid this term because it suggests some sort of external agency to the process, and detracts from the overall rational context in which most lotteries exist. When we talk about a chance encounter or a chance event we are usually talking about a process which is subject to a far wider range of variable factors than a lottery and is subject to far fewer controls.

My first device is a means of describing the central arational component in the midst of its rational context. It also describes the procedural features common to all lotteries. It can be illustrated as follows:

■ │ │ □
│ │
■ │ │
│ │
■ │ │
│ │
■ │ │

───────────────▶

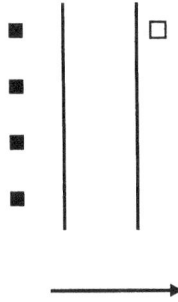

On the left is the pool of options. I show these after they have been arbitrarily equalised into symbols. If a human agency makes the draw, these symbols are designed so they are identical to the senses. If a machine is used they have identical physical characteristics so that every symbol is subject to the same treatment. On the right is the option that is chosen. In the middle the two vertical parallel lines represent where the choice is made. This configuration I call the 'blind break' and it describes the state of deliberate discontinuity in the chain of rationality that is central to the procedure. The arrow is to indicate that this is a time-based process that leads from the pre-sentation of a number of options to the choice of one of these as the outcome or result.

We can think of the pre-lottery decisions as belonging mainly on the left of the diagram. These would include the decision to use a lottery, decisions concerning the size of the pool and the entrance qualifications for it, and general decisions about the outcome. The general nature of the outcome — the nature of the office in question, for example — is usually known before the lottery is undertaken. The draw is to decide which of the options qualifies for this pre-decided status.

We can also think of the 'devaluation' of the options as taking place on the left of the diagram. This is the process by which differ-ent options, all of which have different values and qualities, are con-verted into symbols which appear equal to the person or machine that makes the choice, but also bear a hidden indication as to which option they stand for. After the winning symbol is selected this hid-den value is revealed and rational choices are made as to how the consequences of the result are to be pursued.

The central feature of this device is the arational blind break. It represents a break in the chain of reasoned, planned thought and action that accompanies most decision-making procedures. Embodied in the lottery, therefore, is the idea of discontinuity or disconnection. We can think of a lottery decision as taking place in a special zone where it is insulated from the qualities that exist around it and which take place before and after it.

The temporal nature of this device mirrors the sequence of events of a lottery and defines its procedures and its essential features. All lotteries follow this basic pattern, but the mechanics of the draw and the arrangements for ensuring the choice is 'blind' and arational vary. If the blind break is compromised by sleight of hand, or any other form of trickery, we can no longer classify the procedure as being a proper lottery. The blind break must remain blind. I therefore regard it as the most central, essential or defining feature of the lottery.

Two other features of the lottery need to be noted at this juncture. The first is the fact that although lotteries are designed and implemented by specific individuals or groups of individuals, a lottery has no identifiable agent who can be held responsible for its particular outcome. The other is the fact that a lottery offers an equal opportunity to every option or member of the pool. As we shall see, these features bear an important relationship to the question of arationality.

My second device is closely associated with the fact that a lottery is a mechanical form of decision-making. It also derives from the blind break and is a way of understanding what happens in the blind break and what are the consequences of its operation. If the first approach addresses the general shape, essential features and operations of the lottery procedure, the second is based on the questions, 'What sort of decision is a lottery decision?' and, 'How are we to understand its qualities?' The answer that a lottery decision is a mechanical decision starts us off in the right direction, but it does not answer the second question. I would suggest that the best way of assessing the qualities and potential inherent in a lottery is to think of it primarily as a *non-human* process. The qualities of a lottery choice, therefore, have to be understood negatively — as precisely those that do *not* belong to a choice made by a conscious human being.

This device takes the form of an imaginary box containing all these 'non-human' qualities applicable to a lottery choice. If we need to describe a lottery decision we can be certain that every word in the box will provide an accurate epithet — one that actually pertains to the lottery decision. The supply of qualities in the box is, of course, very large because it contains the negative of every human attribute. It is useful for us to think of it this way, at least initially because it helps us to understand what a lottery decision is, and what it is not. We can illustrate this concept as follows:

A lottery decision is a(n)

> **impartial**
> amoral
> *alogical*
> non-discrimininating
> **unemotional**
> non-prejudiced
> *non-thinking*
> **arational**
> *unpredictable*
> ***non-creative***
> non-wilful
> *non-passionate*
> un-ambitious
> *non-calculating*
> etc …

… … decision

Because there is an almost inexhaustible supply of possible (accurate) epithets in the box we can, and, of course, should, pick those that best suit our purposes. But in doing so we should be clear about what we are doing and bearing in mind the range of qualities inherent in a lottery decision. In the arena of political decision-making the non-human epithets that most concern us are the non-human equivalents of the terms that usually pertain to the making of decisions. Of these I would argue that the most useful is the term *arational*. In the first instance it marks a distinction between the use of reason, which plays an important part in normal decision-making, and the denial of the rational facility in lot-based decisions. To lose rationality from a decision-making process is a major loss, which would not be suffered without a good reason. Secondly, the loss of reason from a lottery is the point of departure for the loss of other reason-related qualities such as discrimination, morality and predictability. Because there is no weighing of good and bad, a lottery decision is also amoral; it is also, by the same token, non-discriminating. Where there can be no rational discrimination, there can be no logic — but equally there can be no passion, no prejudice, no faulty reason, no reason driven by desire, or by fear or favour. A lottery decision is impervious to the action of will— good or bad. There is no love in a lottery decision, but no hate either. Because there is no weighing of options, no one can predict a lottery decision beyond the simple question of probability based on the number in the draw. A lottery is not a horse race; there is no form that can be studied. Compared to other types of decision-making there can be no pooling of ideas or viewpoints in a lottery decision — but also no argument, contention or persuasion. A lottery decision is, for this reason, direct, unmediated and quick.

Because a decision to use a lottery involves the consideration and rejection of other decision-making methods, looking at these alternatives is a useful means by which we can see what a lottery can bring to a given situation that other methods might not. While I would argue that the term 'arational' is the most useful way to distinguish a lottery from non-lottery decisions, recognising that it is just one from the box of possible epithets helps us to extend our understanding of the advantages of using lotteries. We do not have to look at everything in the box, but the idea of the box defines the potential of lot at its broadest.

With this new device we can now return to the first 'blind break' figuration with a richer set of auxiliary qualities to employ in our analysis if necessary. In both arationality is central. The relationship between these two models is that the blind break view of the lottery procedure can give us the quickest access to what is happening in any given case, but the 'box of possible epithets' is useful if we need to explore further. We can see how this works as we start to examine how well lotteries can be applied to the problems they are meant to solve.

Strong and weak applications of lot

If we think of a lottery as a tool that is used to serve a purpose, we can also discuss whether a good match is made between the tool and the task to which it is put. In this respect identifying the blind break as the central part of the lottery procedure and arationality as the most important quality from the box of epithets is important. A tool is best applied to a task that is commensurate with its most essential qualities. Lot is therefore best applied when its primary quality, arationality, is required to solve the problem at hand. We can also express this by saying that in these cases a positive virtue is made of the arational blind break. When this takes place we can talk of a 'strong' application or use of lot.

An example of a strong use of lot is when a study sample of twenty people of similar physique is selected for a drug trial. Ten of these are selected by lot to take a placebo, and the remaining ten are given the drug. Who was given which remains undisclosed to both participants and observers until the end of the trial. Here a positive use is made of the blind break in so far as the random selection is central to the whole trial. It ensures that there is no possible rationale to link the subjects together or link any one of them to the dose that they end up receiving. In terms of the 'non-human' values, the key quality that is required is that the choice should be unbiased, it should not be subject to human judgement in case that judgement is biased or prejudiced. Because it is not a qualitative human decision, another trial that uses lot will be comparable because it will be subject to the same basic condition—it will not be variable in human terms. This objective quality can also be expressed in a more politically charged way: that the use of lot prevents anyone involved in the experiment from manipulating or fixing the outcome. Both expressions, the general value of the lack of human bias, and the more pointed prevention of wilful manipulation, are indications of the same essential strong use: both require an arational process. In fact, although the blind break appears to do more work when the process is under greater wilful threat, it still acts in a preventative capacity where no such direct threat exists.

The weak use of lot is more complex. A weak application of lottery can occur when a decision needs to be rational, but due to expediency, lot is used because a rationally made outcome is too difficult to achieve. An example of this is when a choice between two strong candidates for a particular job is settled by lot (e.g., by flipping a coin) simply because it is too hard to choose between them by weighing up rational criteria. Here there are no positive reasons for using an arational method of choice. We could argue that lot is used here as a surrogate or substitute for rational judgement.[1]

An example of weak use in a second sense would be when, as a power-sharing arrangement, three senior executive members are chosen by lot from an assembly of eighty which is split thirty–fifty between two rival parties. Here the use of lot has some advantages. Compared to preference elections it prevents the majority from necessarily dominating the executive. The polity can be seen as impartial, and corruption can be inhibited because there is no one to be bribed or threatened in respect to the appointment. On the other

[1]   See Broome (1991) p. 98.

hand if lot is used *with the express purpose* of creating some idea of balance or proportion, then this constitutes a weak use because such a task does not require arationality. In these circumstances there is a contradiction between the *arational*, random lottery, and the idea of *ratio* expressed in the general notion of power-sharing.

If proportionality is required here it would be better to use a directly rational or ratio-based system where, for instance, the minority party could chair the executive for three out of five of its meetings. This is also an example of a weighted lottery because it is 'weighted' in favour of the larger group, and relies on this in its appeal to both parties. I discuss this form of lottery in greater detail later in the chapter.

We should not think of weak and strong applications of lot as mutually exclusive, however. One of the problems with the application of lot is that even if only one of its qualities is required, the process is not flexible enough to produce that one quality alone but will contain the whole range of arational and non-human qualities. In any application the vast majority of these will be neutral, but some will assume the status of unwanted side effects. Arationality might be valuable in respect to some aspects of the application, but problematic for others. In such cases we have to assess whether the application is weak or strong in its main function. This is not always easy to do, but a useful method is to compare the use of a lottery with other possible means of achieving the same ends. I did this with the power-sharing aspect of the last example.

A weak use of lot might not be a wholly inappropriate use, and can solve problems effectively, especially in a one-off situation. More prolonged use is likely to expose the contradictions between the essential qualities of the mechanism and the use to which it is put. A lottery is also at its 'purest' when its arational essence is put to appropriate use, but it can become corrupted by misuse or use in the wrong context. An example of this would be the consistent use of calculation and manipulation to undermine the unpredictability of a lottery. This can happen more readily in a weighted lottery than in a normal lottery. As a working proposition I suggest that as the blind break becomes less blind, so the lottery ceases to be a lottery. This can also be expressed by the idea that as more human qualities become part of a lottery process, or associated with that process, that process becomes corrupted.

Every serious decision to employ a lottery involves a trade off between the value gained from *excluding* certain human qualities from the decision and the value lost because a lottery decision is an arational decision. With a strong use of lot this exclusion is purposeful and is intrinsically linked to the context in which the lottery is to operate. With weak or weaker uses of lot this trade off is mismanaged and the arationality becomes a nuisance or an impediment. Problems that arise in this way often mean that other elements have to be introduced into the lottery design to compensate for the unwanted effects of the lottery.

The lottery as a process without a responsible agent and as a process which acts equally

There are two formal qualities of the lottery process that I now need to look at briefly. First is the idea that a lottery decision is one that cannot be attributed to a single person; second is the relationship between the lottery and equality. At first glance it would seem as though these two ideas operate outside the frame of analysis supplied by the blind break and the box of possible epithets. On closer inspection, however, they can be seen to concur with the general viewpoint that I am advancing in this chapter.

A lottery might be employed primarily because it takes the decision out of the hands of an individual, and makes no one responsible either for the choice or the outcome. This 'non-subject' or 'non-agent' status of the lottery thus appears as an essential, even defining, aspect of the lottery process. If we look at this scenario from the point of view of the box of non-human values, however, it is clear that a decision which has no active subject must also be bereft of all the values that a subject can bring to the making of a decision. The decision to use lot to appoint, say, a judge is a decision that cannot be motivated by greed, ambition or personal preference for or against any party. It is impartial because it does not include the human quality of preference or partiality. There is no conscious preferential judgement involved, and by the same token subconscious preference is also excluded. As we shall see later in the study, this non-agent characteristic of lot is a very important aspect of its application in the political sphere, but it does not exist outside the framework of lot as an essentially arational means of making decisions. A lottery choice is an anonymous choice, but it is also a choice made in the absence of all the qualities possessed by a human decision-maker. In our examination of lot systems, however, we must distinguish between the non-agent aspect of the particular lottery process, and the idea that someone, or some body of people, has rationally instigated the process as a whole. This 'organising sub-ject' can be very significant in the political use of lot.

A similar, but slightly more complex, problem is presented by the formal characterisation of a lottery as a means of making a decision that gives all in the pool an equal chance of featuring in the outcome. First we have to ask exactly what is meant by the term 'equal' when we use it in respect to the workings of a lottery. Certainly in terms of the mechanics of the process, the balls or tickets are made to look alike, to look equal and to stand an equal chance of being picked. On closer analysis, however, what is meant by this is that the lottery, whether drawn by a mechanical or human agency, will choose in a way that does not discriminate between the options on the basis of any quality that they might or might not possess. A lottery choice is therefore an 'e-quality' or 'non-quality' choice because it denies the rational human tendency to discriminate or choose according to quality. We can therefore view the equality of opportunity pre-sented by a lottery choice as an outcome of its essential arationality.

In practice a lottery is often used to prevent quality-based advan-tage or disadvantage becoming a factor in any choice that is to be made. Once the lottery pool is decided upon, all within the pool have the same stake in the outcome irrespective of their personal qualities or how those qualities might be judged. A lottery will not create equality for its participants — its outcome involves choosing one winner, not dividing the prize between all the members of the pool — nor does it make all in the pool equal in all aspects of their lives. What it does is create a highly artificial situation in which the qualitative differences between all in the pool are temporarily sus-pended in respect to the decision to be made by the lottery.

Proportionality and the lottery

The best point of entry for a consideration of the relationship between the idea of proportion and the lottery is by means of a prac-tical example. I have been given a ticket to a football match, but find I cannot go. I have five friends who are keen on football so I hold a lottery to decide who gets the ticket. They all know that this is taking place and that the draw is between five candidates.

Within this lottery, as with all lotteries, a fundamental relationship exists between the number of winners and the number in the pool. In the example this can be expressed by the ratio 1:5. In probability law this ratio is used to define the probability or likelihood of winning the ticket from the point of view of each of the friends. Each friend has a one in five chance, or a one-fifth probability, of winning the ticket. This is achieved by dividing the number of actual outcomes by the number of possible outcomes.

What, then, does this ratio contribute to the lottery process itself and the way we understand it? The first point in answer to this question is that while this ratio is integral to all lotteries, it derives, not from the arational procedure itself, but from the rational decisions that precede the operation of the lottery. There is no contradiction, therefore, between this ratio and the arational nature of the draw. The size of the pool and the number of winners can be thought of as the basic ingredients to which the mechanism of the lottery is applied.

Problems in how we understand the lottery process can, however, arise, if we give this ratio a status in the operation of a lottery that it does not actually possess. In the case of my five friends, the fact that each has a one in five chance of winning the ticket is less important that the fact that they all have an equal chance, a chance not influenced by my personal opinion of their qualities. Where the ratio might become important, however, is if a comparison needs to be made between this lottery and another one with a smaller or larger pool. But it cannot tell any of my friends anything they do not already know about the operation of the lottery or its potential outcome.

Similarly, the idea expressed in the law of large numbers, that each of my friends might win approximately one fifth of the draws if I were to hold repeated lotteries over a long period of time, is of little direct use. It does not answer the question of who gets this particular ticket. If a lottery is to make a positive virtue of its essential arationality, it must operate in the short term, and be based on the uncertainty of the immediate result. A lottery can be employed on the grounds that it will produce some form of proportional outcome in the longer term, but such cases are weak applications because they do not require or utilise the arational blind break.

I need to end this consideration of the relationship between proportionality and the lottery with a few words on the role of lot in probability theory. One of the key areas of activity from which probability theory emerged was the study of unfinished card games.[2] Its early founders addressed the problem of how to divide the stake amongst the individual players according to the advantages inherent in the cards they held and the possible permutations of play had

[2]   See Todhunter (1865) and Bork (1967), particularly in respect to the work of De Moivre, Bernoulli and Montmort.

it continued. To do this the fundamental ratio between the number in the pool and the number of outcomes in a simple lottery was incorporated as a basic tool, datum, or yardstick. This enabled complex comparisons to be made on an objective, mathematical basis, and similarly enabled lottery-like configurations in the world at large to be examined by comparison to the control model of the simple lottery form. In this way the simple lottery operates in the service of a more complex system of calculation and it is valuable in this role because it is wholly impartial and objective.

We can characterise this as a special form of strong application of lot — it consists of the application of the practical model of the lottery to a theory. It is strong in a general sense because the blind break excludes subjective judgement, but it then becomes part of a general formula that is applied to particular non-lottery or lottery-like configurations as a means of comparison. We can therefore think of it as applying the qualities of a lottery to a given problem rather than applying a lottery itself. Probability theory can help us to understand how a number of lotteries, or lottery-like configurations can operate in respect to each other, but if we then re-apply it to the simple lottery it can only tell us certain things. It can express the relationship between the possible outcomes and one particular outcome as a ratio, and it can tell us that if the lottery is repeated a large number of times, the results will approximate to that ratio. According to the law, if I hold repeated lotteries for the football ticket each of my friends will get about one fifth of the total of tickets made available in this way.

To summarise: the arationality of the lottery process is incompatible with human ideas of ratio, proportion or balance. It cannot, therefore, produce an outcome that reflects these qualities. Where a lottery is used to try to do this, it constitutes a weak application and will produce randomness, not ratio. The fundamental ratio between the numbers in the pool and the number of outcomes is part of the rational pre-context of every lottery. It defines the numerical content of each particular draw, expressed as a ratio, but it cannot bring to the lottery anything beyond this basic information, and the idea that in the long term the outcomes might be evenly spread amongst those in the pool.

Sampling, the weighted lottery, and the independent result

If probability theory uses lot as a datum from which to explore other random contexts, the use of lot, or attempted use of lot, to explore proportional problems or create proportional outcomes is a more complex proposition. Sampling the population by lot for survey purposes is an obvious example. At first sight it seems as if random sampling, with a large enough sample, will produce a proportionate relationship between the pool and the sample. The sample will then be the pool 'in miniature'. I do not wish to contest this claim directly, but I feel it ssneeds to be tempered by a number of considerations that are pertinent to our concerns.

Because such use does not require or place a positive value on the blind break, it constitutes a weak use of lot. The act of sampling itself indicates that some form of proportionate or comparative measurement is being sought and there is thus a contradiction between the essential arational characteristic of the form of the lot-tery and the function that it is asked to perform. There are uses for an entirely random sample — but I would argue that such uses are limited. Moreover, sampling practice indicates that other methods, or combinations of methods, give more useable data.

One widely used method is stratified sampling. This amounts to a 'rationalisation' of the random process where the pool is con-sciously divided into separate strata and samples are then taken randomly from each stratum. An example of this is when respon-dents are recruited at random from different demographic sectors of the population. The use of this method suggests that lot on its own is too haphazard to produce data in the categories, or ratios, required for such survey purposes.[3]

V. Barnett clarifies this issue when he claims that simple random sampling is used because it is 'easy to operate from a statistical viewpoint'.[4] Conformity with probability theory is essential and '… we are compelled to introduce an element of "randomness" into sampling procedures and to draw our samples according to some imposed probability mechanism.'[5] This is characterised as *epsem*, or the 'equal probability selection method'. Sampling by quota (with no random element) is representative but prone to subjective judge-

---

[3]   See Conway (1967) p. 129. 'Stratified samples have smaller sampling errors than simple random samples of the same size.'

[4]   Barnett (1974) p. 22.

[5]   *Ibid*. p. 14.

ment.[6] We are drawn to the conclusion that lot is used because it eliminates human bias and acts as an objective yardstick rather than because it can deliver any form of proportionality or 'representativeness'.[7] Representation, proportion and ratio all come from the rational, pre-lottery elements, rather than the arational, lottery element in effective sampling.

Where this discussion on sampling helps the development of our analysis of sortition, however, is in its relation to the weighted lottery. I would describe the weighted lottery as an application of the standard lottery form that attempts to mix randomness and proportion. In the form of a draw, rather than, for instance, a weighted die or coin, its characteristic feature is that before the options are converted into equal symbols, they are grouped or considered as a ratio between one type of option and another (or others). It is this intention to group the options and to measure the outcome in terms of these groupings which defines this type of application.[8] It is a weighted lottery in the sense that a member of the larger or largest grouping in the pool is more statistically likely to be chosen. It can be illustrated as follows:

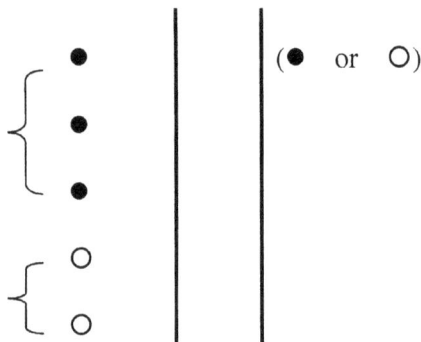

[6] *Ibid.* pp. 14, 131.

[7] *Ibid.* p. 14. See also Jackson and Brashers (1986), 'In general random factors are brought into experimental designs to reduce threats to validity.'

[8] Amar's proposal for lottery voting, a scheme which involves choosing the office holder at random from the bag, or box of votes cast, is, in fact, a weighted lottery. It is designed to present the respective parties in the field a chance of election in proportion to the votes cast for them. See Amar (1984). On the subject of weighted lotteries see also Stone (2007b) p. 16.

Here three black balls and two white balls of identical size and weight are placed in a bag and one is drawn out. Any of the five individual balls can be drawn, but the interest or objective is not to pick an individual winner, but to pick a ball of one colour or the other. While it is more likely that a black ball will be chosen, there is also a possibility that the ball drawn will be white. The chances of each can be expressed in terms of statistical probability, and a deliberately weighted lottery (such as our example) is often specifically designed to produce some sort of balance between the results and the ratio between the groups in the pool based on the idea of proportionality.

Thus if a parliament, which is divided between party A and party B by a ratio of 60:40 members respectively, holds a lottery to select, say, the seventh member of a commission which would otherwise contain three from each party, this would constitute a weighted lottery. Party A would have an advantage in the lottery, which would therefore be 'weighted' in their favour. This weighting, however, only operates because the pool is divided into two parties and to the extent that the result is interpreted in terms of the parties, and not in terms of the individuals selected.

Because the winner (black or white ball, member of party A or party B) is judged primarily by colour, or group, and not by its status as an individual entity, the winner is not independent from the set to which he, she or it originally belonged. In other words it is still rationally or logically connected to the value sets on the other side of the blind break. The blind break is therefore being deliberately compromised, and is being compromised by the notion of proportionality inherent in the idea that each option belongs or conforms to a pre-existing group.

A weighted lottery operates by virtue of two principles: the law of large numbers (without which we cannot understand the respective chances of the groups in the pool) and the conformity of the members of the pool to their respective groups. If the members of these groups are considered, measured, or act as individuals and not as group members, the lottery ceases to operate as a weighted lottery. It would then lose its element of comparative proportionality, and becomes a simple process of random selection.

There is a sense, therefore, in which there are elements of a weighted lottery within a direct lottery where common properties exist amongst the options in the pool. Similarly there are elements of a direct lottery within a weighted lottery because there are members of the pool that are independent of any grouping. The key feature that defines the weighted lottery of this draw type, compared to a truly random process of selection, however, is the extent to which the outcomes are considered only in respect to their groupings in the pool. These outcomes are then dependent on—i.e., not independent of—those groupings.

Although it is a curious hybrid of ratio and chance, the weighted lottery helps us to understand the relationship of strong randomness, or sortition in a strong application, to the idea of groups and the conformity to groups.[9] I would argue here that a weighted lottery is not only a weak use of sortition, but that the principle of grouping, or weighing, options undermines the fundamentals of random selection itself.

If we look at the weighted lottery from the point of view of the box of non-human values, the picture that emerges is one of the non-human qualities of the lottery itself standing in direct opposition to the rational human organisation of the groupings in the pool. As the pool becomes more organised into groups, and the outcome more and more interpreted according to groups, the lottery becomes more predictable, more subject to ratio and less and less arational. While our example, which deals with coloured balls, illustrates how a simple grouping of a simple object operates in a weighted lottery, a weighted lottery operating between groups of people is a far more complex proposition. Grouping according to likeness is an important function of human rationality. The formation of groups of people involves a high level of rational preference and discrimination, and stands in contradiction to the arational disconnection and independence (literally non-dependence) that arises from a true direct act of random selection.

This would suggest that the idea of conformity to a group, or dependence on a group, is incompatible with the strong, arational operation of a lottery. Those selected by a lottery are random, or disconnected from each other. They have been selected in the absence of the grouping capacity of the human mind. Their only deliberate commonality is their status of belonging to the same pool. This is important because it begins to show sortition in its essential form and strongest application as antithetical to notions of ratio, proportionality and group conformity. If the essential feature of lottery

---

[9] This also helps us to understand the function of those lotteries which operate as weighted lotteries without being specified or designed as such. Sher (1980) p. 204, discusses the idea that the status of a lottery changes with our knowledge of it.

form, or procedure, is the blind break, its ideal product is random because it is independent of any proportion, set, or ratio that precedes the blind break. For a further critique of this notion of randomness as independence I shall enlist the help of a mathematician.

In the late 1980s, G.J. Chaitin and A.N. Kolmogorov began to formulate a mathematical definition of randomness within the domain of algorithmical information theory. Deriving from the application of computer programming methodology to the broader questions concerning the way we understand numbers, Chaitin's definition of randomness is that a random element or number cannot be compressed into a programme (or string of bits) shorter than itself.[10] A non-random sequence, on the other hand, can be compressed into a shorter programme because that programme follows rational rules in which one operation can be described in terms of another.

Mathematical and statistical notions of randomness have, in general, focused on the idea of independence or non-dependence. In mathematics two propositions are independent if they do not derive from each other—i.e. neither is the logical entailment of the other. Likewise, statistical thought defines randomness in terms of independent events: events that have no bearing on each other. These are good working definitions,[11] but Chaitin's 'deep' explanation of randomness is of an altogether different order.[12] It is at once more precise and more practical. It is also more dynamic and capable of further development. Writing in 2001 Chaitin extends his definition:

> Something is random if it is algorithmically incompressible or irreducible. More precisely, a member of a set of objects is random if it has the highest complexity possible within this set. In other words, the random objects in a set are those that have the highest complexity.[13]

The great virtue, or one of the great virtues, of this definition is that it is derived from practice. It is a combination, in Chaitin's words, of 'deep philosophy and clever hacking.'[14] What is more important, however, is that this type of information theory is applicable beyond its discipline of origin. It can be easily incorporated into genetic biology, robotics and cognitive neuro-science, for

---

[10] Chaitin (1988) p. 52.
[11] See Brock (1990) p. 234.
[12] Chaitin (2001) p. 162.
[13] *Ibid.* p. 111.
[14] *Ibid.* p. 163.

example. At the same time it is couched in the vernacular — we only have to know the most elementary concept of programming to understand it — and thus it can be easily incorporated into general forms of discourse without any great loss to its fuller meaning.

Its application to the design of political procedures is a natural consequence of this potential. The notion of randomness as complex independence offered by Chaitin is entirely congruous with the general direction of my analysis of lottery form and function — it is a welcome addition because it arrives at the same place from a very different direction. It switches our focus from the process or procedure of lottery towards the product of that process, and in doing so changes our perspective on sortition. From this vantage point we can begin to understand randomness as an essential and ubiquitous part of both natural and human developmental processes.[15] It is thus a positive virtue rather than a product of chance that has somehow to be contained. True randomness as complex independence can be best created or encouraged by strong sortive processes, which are, by definition, uncompromised by logical connections, proportionate relations or conformity to set or group.

Conclusion

In this chapter I hope to have laid the analytical foundations for the historical studies that follow. Inevitably real contexts and events throw up new configurations and combinations that cannot be foreseen or understood in advance. Nonetheless this chapter gives us a precise but flexible critical language with which to face these challenges. Central to this language is the notion of arationality. The argument that the essence of a lottery lies in its arationality is most clearly demonstrated by the identification of the blind break — the point in the procedure that is distinguished by its insulation from human reason — as the central defining component of a lottery.

The two devices of the blind-break procedure and the box of non-human epithets or qualities enable me to adopt a twin-track approach with which to assess different applications of lot. The blind break provides a quick means of understanding the lottery procedure and the extent that arationality features in any application. The 'box' on the other hand gives us a wider, more qualitative

---

[15] Dennett (2003) equates our development of freedom from our biological limitations with the concept of evasion or 'evitability'. This can be seen as a propensity to step out of previous conformity parallel with Chaitin's positive rendering of randomness.

approach in which many values have the potential to come to the fore. The box proved invaluable for sorting out how to understand the relationship between equality and the lottery, and the 'non-subject' quality of the lottery process.

These two devices allow me to distinguish between two different applications of lot. In strong applications of lot the arational is regarded as a positive asset to the task in hand, while in weak, or weaker, applications this arationality is either used as a substitute for reason, or compromised by other objectives in the application. My brief explorations of the relationship between ratio and lot, the role of lot in probability theory, sampling by lot and the weighted lottery follow from these premises. Lot has its greatest potential when its most essential characteristic is used positively in a manner commensurate with the desired ends — when lot does what lot does best.

My conclusion that the weighted lottery is a weak use of lot and could ultimately undermine many of the values of a direct lottery led me to a consideration of the question of groupings in a lottery pool. In this my intuition that such groupings establish a mode of operation based on ratio and prediction that is contrary to the notion of disconnection, or independence, inherent in a lottery concurs with some aspects of modern information theory on the complexity of the random.

At the core of the chapter, however, lies the notion of arationality. Although it is just one of a very large box of non-human values that can be used to describe a lottery decision, it is the most important of these for our purposes. Not only does it underpin a wider range of values, such as unpredictability and impartiality, inherent in the operation of a lottery, but it is also the point of maximum contrast between a decision made by lot and a decision made by other means.

As we begin to apply these principles to the use of lot in the political sphere, the distinction between weak and strong applications of lot assumes increasing importance. Significantly it enables us to see past the modern preoccupation with representative sampling and focuses our attention on exactly what the essential arationality of the lottery process has the potential to bring to any application.[16]

---

[16] This preoccupation is reflected in a number of modern proposals such as Callenbach and Phillips (2008) and Mueller *et al.* (1972).

Bibliographical notes

The most revealing works that I used in the research for this chapter are those that deal with the histories and development of disciplines that involve random selection. The best of these is definitely Todhunter's *A History of the Mathematical Theory of Probability from the time of Pascal to that of Laplace* (1865). Hacking's short paper of 1988, 'Telepathy: origins of randomness in experimental design', *Isis* 79, which explores the use of random controls in the experiments of the Society for Psychical Research, is also very revealing, as is R.A. Fisher's *The Design of Experiments*, first published 1935. These works enabled me to understand exactly how and why random procedures were first used and were therefore more valuable than those that approached lottery selection as a given methodological component. On sampling, Conway (1967), Deming (1950), Fox and Tracy (1986) and Jackson and Brashers (1986) were useful because they explained the actual role taken by lot in the various sampling techniques in current use. Shewhart's 1931 classic *Economic Control of Quality of Manufactured Product* helped me to approach the use of lot in quality control at an early stage in the development of the discipline. Chaitin's major work is his 2001 *Exploring Randomness*. My overall view of the notion of 'complex independence' was also tempered by Dennett's *Freedom Evolves* (2003).

Chapter Two

Sortition and Political Consolidation in Ancient Athens

The most significant historical example of the political use of sortition is that of Ancient Athens. By the fifth century BCE the Athenian polity employed lot comprehensively — in three out of its four major governmental institutions. Moreover, although the eligibility for office varied, the main criterion for political participation was that of citizenship. Athens therefore provides us with a unique paradigm: the citizen-lot polity.

The Athenian lot-polity developed through several distinct stages over a period of nearly three hundred years from the archonship of Solon in 594 BCE to the fall of Athenian democracy to Macedonia in 322 BCE.[1] During this period Athens changed from a minor city-state trying to find a framework through which to solve basic problems of land tenure and collective defence, to a major regional power with a complex cosmopolitan society and a diverse trading economy. Parallel with this path — sometimes leading, sometimes following — was the development of subtle, interdependent and inclusive institutions of government. This essentially public and multi-sided nature of the process of governmental decision-making generated the term *politei* — the forerunner of our 'politics'. *Politeia* can be narrowly translated as 'constitution',[2] but is better understood in terms of the activity of the citizen body as a whole in the public affairs of the city or *polis*.[3] From the perspective of the western political tradition, therefore, Athens during this

---

[1] Even under aristocratic rule many of the randomly-selected institutions continued into the 3rd century BCE. See Dow (1939).

[2] Aristotle (1946) p. 99 [*Pol.*, III. 1276b 1–2].

[3] Barker in Aristotle (1946) lxvi; Hansen (1999) p. 65.

period constitutes one of the most significant examples of how a political community is forged or consolidated.

The aim of this chapter is to look at the practical role of sortition in the process of political consolidation in Ancient Athens. I preface my exploration with a brief discussion of the relationship between lot and religion. I then give a description of how lot was used at the time when it was applied most consistently and comprehensively: during the late fifth and early fourth centuries BCE. This gives us a snapshot of the lot-polity in its most highly developed form. I then turn my attention to the historical process of political consolidation. I do this initially by examining the most significant link in this chain — the reforms of Kleisthenes that took place in 507 BCE. I then look forwards and backwards to assess their impact. While this tells us *how* lot was used and something of the active process that it was part of, it does not address the question of *why* it was used and what special qualities it brought to the political community. The main sources for this period, unfortunately, give us little help in this area.[4]

To address this question, therefore, I have to rely on political analysis and informed reconstruction. By coupling a broad understanding of the geo-political pressures facing the *polis* with a realistic appraisal of the options facing the (named or unnamed) political actors, we can use the existing source material to its best advantage. An understanding of the diverse potential of sortition, particularly the difference between strong and weak applications of lot, can then help us to reconstruct possible motives for its use. I investigate this in the form of three case studies in which I examine the three Athenian institutions in which lot was most extensively used: the *boule* or Council; the *dikasterion* or People's Courts:[5] and the magistrates — the vast majority of whom were selected by sortition.[6] This helps us to understand the range of diverse potential of sortition but they also indicate aspects of its more general potential. In the conclusion of this chapter I consider the importance of lot in promoting and defending the key features of the Athenian polity as it moved towards democracy. My orientation throughout is that too close an

---

[4]   The main sources are Herodotus' *Histories*, particularly the speech by Otanes in book III, which identifies the rule of the people with magistrates appointed by lot (III.80.6, Herodotus (1998) p. 205; Herodotus (1954) p. 210); the *Ath. Pol.* or *Constitution of Athens* attributed to Aristotle; and Aristotle's *Politics*.

[5]   This includes the *nomothetai* or legislative body which was introduced in the fourth century.

[6]   600 out of the 700 or so magistrates were selected by lot.

identity between lot and democracy can mask its complex and subtle role in the earlier political consolidation of the *polis*. If we adopt a more general political orientation, however, the use of lot can be seen, not as an egalitarian consequence of democracy, but as a factor that contributed to its rise.

Lot and religion in Ancient Athens

Lot itself was certainly not a new idea in fifth-century Athens, and, as with most ancient societies, it would have been known and understood as a means of solving particular types of problems. It was also intrinsically connected to religion and was seen as a means by which the gods could intervene in human affairs. In ancient Athens, therefore, we can see sortition as existing, as it were, on the cusp between the sphere of belief and the sphere of concrete practical endeavour.

Lot was used in the Delphic Oracle,[7] and was used to appoint priests.[8] In Book Seven of the *Iliad*, Agamemnon arranges a lottery among his comrades to determine who will fight Hector. The process, and hence the outcome, is accepted as being the will of the gods, but it is also a useful political means by which the matter can be settled.[9] On the other side of the equation, an important practical example of the use of lot in Athens relates to the distribution of estates. In the absence of a system of primogeniture the inheriting sons would agree on the division of the estate into parts of equal value. Lots would then be cast to determine who would have which part. This was a simple form of distribution in which the uncertain outcome of lot was used to prevent self interest from dominating the original division.[10]

In the nineteenth century the debate over the use of lot in ancient Athens revolved around the issue of its religious function. N. D. Fustel de Coulanges in *The Ancient City* stresses the idea that lot was an indication of divine will.[11] The city therefore 'believed that in this manner it received its magistrates from the gods.' He also cites a short passage from Plato's *Laws* in support of this. Here the 'seventh

---

[7] See Robbins (1916). See also Andrewes (1982) p. 386. Apparently, priestesses were also chosen by lot from all Athenian women. Palmer (1996) p. 126.

[8] Headlam (1933) p. 5.

[9] Homer (1987) p. 109 [*The Iliad* VII 161 ff]. Also Andrewes (1982) p. 386.

[10] I am grateful to Dr. O. Murray for this point.

[11] Fustel De Coulanges (1864) p.182; Curtius (1857–67) vol. II p. 619; and Holm (1898) p. 101.

title to authority' is that public office should have the 'favour of the gods' and be blessed by fortune. The passage, a dialogue between an Athenian and Cleinias, goes on: '… we tell him that the fairest arrangement is for him to exercise authority if he wins, but be subject to it if he loses'. This would suggest that while lot could encourage the highly practical acceptance of political authority, the idea that the process itself represented a higher authority, whether in the divine form, or in the form of the abstract 'general good', was never far away.[12] In contrast, J. M. Headlam, while aware of the religious origins of sortition, is keen to stress the practical role of lot in Athens and link it securely to democracy.[13] He argues consistently against the idea that lot performed a solely religious function and sees sortition as a necessary means by which democracy was defended.[14]

Clearly we should not draw too sharp and modern a division between the sacred and the secular into the Athens of the fifth century BCE.[15] Lot was certainly acceptable to the Athenians as signifying the will of the gods. But while it was recognised as a useful means by which political problems could be solved, this function was not, of itself, devoid of supernatural resonance. Use of lot meant that officers were not chosen by any individual, or set of individuals. This lack of a palpable subject left a gap that could be filled by the idea of a supernatural will. Although such a notion presents sortition as fulfilling a largely rhetorical role, such rhetoric could also be important politically, and should not, therefore, be ignored. I would also suspect that a citizen selected to political office by lot would be expected to adopt an attitude of political piety not dissimilar from that of his religious counterpart: a sense of being 'called' by the *polis*. I would, however, be wary of approaching the study of lot in ancient Athens exclusively from the perspective of religious belief. Headlam's general orientation—that we should start by examining the practical rationale for the employment of sortition —seems to me to offer the best way forward.[16]

---

[12] Plato (1970) p. 138 [*The Laws* III. 690 vi 759].
[13] Headlam (1933) p. 12.
[14] *Ibid.* p. 31.
[15] Democracy, after all, enjoyed cult status in the fourth century. See Hansen (1999) p. 83.
[16] Headlam (1933), pp. 2–10.

A snapshot of the Athenian lot-polity

If we look at the Athenian polity during the period of 441 until 397 BCE, that is, ten years on either side of the Peloponnesian war, we can get the best idea of the extent of the use of sortition in the context of developed democracy. Lot was used to select the *boule* or Council of 500, the *dikastai* who passed judgement in the People's Courts in numbers of up to 2,501, and 600 out of the executive body of approximately 700 magistrates. The major exception to this method of selection was the 100 or so members of the magisterial body who were directly elected by the Assembly on the grounds that their work required specialist skills or experience. The most significant of these was the board of ten *strategoi* or generals, but other elected posts included some of the most important financial officers, magistrates in charge of the Eleusinian Mysteries, and the officers in charge of the water supply.[17] In the fourth century a new legislative body, the *nomothetai*, was instituted. This mirrored the *dikasterion* in that every new law had to be approved by similarly large numbers of randomly-selected *dikastai* in a courtroom setting.

All non-elected magisterial and *bouleutic* offices were subject to strict annual rotation. No citizen could hold the same magisterial office more than once, and *boule* membership could only be held twice in any citizen's lifetime. No officer selected by lot could hold office of any sort during consecutive years. An exception to this principle was made in the case of the generals and the other elected magistrates who could hold the same office for as long as they could continue to be elected to it.

During this period, sovereignty lay with the Assembly and the Courts. The older aristocratic council, the *areopagos*, still existed but its duties had been severely curtailed. The role of the *boule* was to prepare items for the Assembly and receive instructions from that body. It also had charge of foreign affairs, and was responsible for some judicial functions, especially those concerning the conduct of its own members. It was, moreover, the political and administrative heart of the *polis* and the institution that the oligarchs first sought to control when they took power in 411 and 403.[18]

---

[17] Hansen (1999) p. 233.

[18] See Headlam (1933) pp. 45–6; Sinclair (1988) p. 102-3; Stockton (1990) p. 148; and particularly Gomme (1962), who states, 'The Council is so important that it is indispensable; it is the lynch-pin of the democracy; it is the first object of attack by the enemies of democracy …' p. 186.

Decisions in the Courts were made by very large numbers of *dikastai* who were selected by lot from a pre-selected pool on the day of the trial. The role of the *dikastai* is analogous to those of a modern jury, but we should be careful not to take this comparison too far. The Courts had a far greater political or public interest role than under the modern system of separation of powers, involved a much higher level of public participation, and had a higher public profile. Private lawsuits were judged by 201 or 401 *dikastai*, depending on the sum at stake. Most public prosecutions were heard by 501, but for more serious political cases panels of 1001, 1501, 2001 and 2501 were used.[19] After hearing equally-timed presentations from the two contending parties, the *dikastai* would vote by secret ballot, without deliberation.[20] By the early fourth century any citizen was entitled to challenge an Assembly decision through the Courts on the grounds that it was unconstitutional or against the interests of the *polis*.[21] This was known as the *graphe paranomon*.[22]

The notion of citizenship was fundamental to Athenian political practice. Citizenship was granted to all male Athenians on reaching the age of eighteen, but *metics* (foreigners) and slaves were excluded.[23] Citizenship was hereditary and not based on property ownership or social class. There were therefore both rich and poor citizens—an important difference between the Athenian *polis* and the city republics of Renaissance Italy. Although all citizens who had completed their military service were entitled to attend the Assembly, qualification for political office was more restricted. Only Athenian citizens above the age of thirty could hold office, and since life expectancy for men was around the age of twenty-five, this meant that government office was restricted to the most senior sector of society. Qualification for office also generally followed class lines, but there were important exceptions.

Since the time of Solon, Athenian citizens were divided into four economic classes: the *pentakosiomedimnoi*, mainly consisting of aristocrats and the wealthiest landowners; *hippeis*, or cavalrymen, those

---

[19] Hansen (1999), p. 187.

[20] *Ibid.* pp. 164–9.

[21] The citizen bringing the action was known as *ho boulemenos*, 'anyone who wishes'. This did not only apply to those bringing court cases but to any political initiative such as putting one's name forward for public office. Hansen (1999) pp. 266–8.

[22] See Yunis (1988).

[23] Many of those who made up this category were rich and influential. They often married into the local aristocracy to attempt to gain citizen status.

able to afford a horse; the *zeugitai*, based on the light infantrymen or *hoplites*; and the *thetes* or labourers.[24] *Dikastai* could be drawn from any economic class, and while the *thetes* were officially excluded from all other offices, by the end of the fifth century this had become a dead letter and the offices of magistrate and Councillor were *de facto* open to all citizens over the age of thirty. The only exceptions to this were the board of treasurers who had to be members of the *pentakosiomedimnoi*, and the *archons*, who (until 403 BCE) had to come from the top two classes. All office-holders were required to take oaths before taking their posts. In the case of the *dikastai*, 6,000 citizens were first selected by lot; these then swore the *Helliastic Oath*. Panels were then drawn from who presented themselves as available on the day of the hearing.

It seems to have been a general principle that only those who wished to hold office came forward to become part of their respective lottery pool. There was a very strong ethos of public service, and those able but unwilling to put their names forward did not generally command the respect of their fellow citizens.[25] Because Athens was a very close-knit, localised society there is no doubt that encouragement would have been given to would-be volunteers by their local *deme* (local ward) or tribe members, or by members of the other family or religious groupings to which most citizens belonged.

Before taking office, selected candidates would be subject to a *dokimasia* or scrutiny.[26] This was held by the Courts, in the case of magistrates, and the *boule*, in the case of its own members and the nine *archons*, or chief magistrates. The *dokimasia* was primarily to check the selected officer's status as a citizen and to ask a number of questions such as whether he honoured his parents or performed his required religious devotions. This gives the appearance that it was a mere formality, but after the restoration of democracy in 403 BCE it was used to exclude supporters of the previous tyrannical regime from office.[27] Since exactly the same format was used in the

---

[24] Sinclair (1988) p. 2; Hansen (1999) pp. 106–9. When Athens became a sea power this gave a military role to the *Thetes* who were the oarsmen in the fleet. This role did not entail any personal expenditure on equipment.

[25] See Thucydides (1972) p. 147 [II. 40] '... we do not say that a man who takes no interest in politics is a man who minds his own business; we say he has no business here at all'.

[26] Adelege (1983); Staveley (1972) pp. 56–60.

[27] This is the principal claim of Adelege (1983).

case of elected magistrates, the *dokimasia* does not seem to have been designed to counteract the random nature of the lottery.[28]

The accounts of every councillor and magistrate would be rigorously checked during the year after he had office to ensure that no embezzlement had taken place. Any citizen was also entitled to mount a court action against an individual magistrate on similar grounds, or for more serious acts against the *polis*. This latter measure, the *eisangelia*, largely replaced the older practice of ostracism — the sending of a named individual into voluntary exile by popular vote — and served a similar function in making powerful individuals accountable to the people.[29] These measures meant that although the threshold to office was low, constant checks and legislation linked to severe sanctions ensured a high standard of behaviour in public office.[30]

Since the Kleisthenic re-organisation of Attica in 507 BCE the administration of the city and surrounding area was divided into two tiers: 139 *demes* or local wards and ten tribes.[31] Each *deme* was allocated a quota of Councillors to be selected annually. The lotteries for the Council originally took place at *deme* level but were later held centrally under the auspices of the appropriate tribe. Magistrates, who operated in boards of ten, were selected centrally.

The tribes were totally artificial groupings, and were made up of three sections, called *trittyes*, each from a different region of Attica. Each tribe had its own special meeting place in the city where information was exchanged and various religious devotions held.[32] The *boule* was divided into ten *prytaneis* on a tribal basis, and each *prytany* would form a special executive committee in rotation for one tenth of a year each.[33] The order of rotation of the *prytaneis* was instigated by lot, and one member of the *prytany* in office would then be chosen by lot every day to be the nominal head of state for that day only. He would hold the keys to the treasury and undertake other ceremonial duties. The selection of *dikastai* was organised so as to produce equal numbers from each tribe as far as this was possible, and after 403 the *archons* were selected by double sortition, each

[28] Hansen (1999) pp. 218–20; Sinclair (1988) p. 77.
[29] See Thomsen (1972).
[30] On penalties see Hansen (1999) pp. 222–3.
[31] See Traill (1975); and Whitehead (1986).
[32] Hansen (1999) p. 105.
[33] See Hansen (1999) pp. 250, 265, 314. Up to 400 the *prytaneis* would preside over Council and Assembly meetings, after that, nine *proedroi*, were selected by lot to take that role.

tribe selecting ten candidates by lot to go into the final pool. The army and the navy were also organised on a tribal basis. The tribe and the *deme* structure can be described as the organisational glue that held Athenian society together. They linked the Athenian citizen with the political process on a daily basis.[34]

Lotteries were apparently first held by drawing black and white beans from a bag. By the fourth century, however, special machines or *kleroteria* were in operation.[35] These were particularly useful for selecting the *dikastai* simply because the large numbers of citizens who presented themselves as candidates on the mornings when the Courts were in session would render lot-drawing by hand impracticable.[36] All sworn *dikastai* would have a bronze name ticket, which would also have a letter inscribed on it. On arrival at the court, a candidate for the day's proceedings would place his ticket in a box marked with that letter. At a fixed point in the proceedings the name tickets would be drawn from the box and placed in rows on a slotted stone block. At the side of the rows of names was a tube down which black or white tokens would fall randomly from a funnel. If a white token emerged first, the first row of names would be selected, and so on until the required number was reached. Once inside the court a further draw would be held to allocate each *dikastes* to his respective courtroom. A strict rotational scheme governed the daily appointment of the officials who presided over the lotteries.[37]

One aspect that is striking about the constitutional arrangements in Athens during this period is the extremely high level of participation in the political institutions of the city. Out of a total citizen population of around 30,000,[38] the Assembly was regularly attended by around 6,000. As we saw, a similar number would have sworn the

---

[34] In addition there were numerous other organisations to which an Athenian citizen might belong. These included the *gens*, or family groupings, *phratria*, or brotherhood associations, religious and cult groups. Citizens were registered by their original *deme* name even if they lived in a different part of Attica. See Hansen (1999) pp. 47, 101; and Whitehead (1986).

[35] This usage was identified by S. Dow in 1937 for a number of slotted stone stelae which had been excavated from the agora in Athens. See Dow (1939) and Kroll (1972).

[36] Before Dow's attribution the description of the process in the *Ath Pol* LXIII–LXV (Aristotle, 1986, pp. 202–4) made little sense. Bronze allotment plaques also indicate that this process was also used for magistrates and other offices in the fourth century.

[37] A fuller description of the *klerolerion* and its use can be found in Dow (1939) and in J.M. Moore's commentary. Aristotle (1986) pp. 303–8.

[38] Gomme (1933); Hansen (1999) pp. 90–4.

Helliastic Oath, which entitled them to sit as *dikastai*. Rotation in office meant that large numbers of citizens would have taken part in the administrative processes of government on a regular basis. We must also remember, however, that the notion of public service in government was closely linked to the notion of military service, which was compulsory. It would have been understood that a *polis* which was well-organised politically was also stronger militarily.

Participation was not always forthcoming however, and incentives proved necessary. In the fifth century payment was introduced, not only for office holders, but also for attendance at the Assembly and Courts. Contemporary sources indicate that not all posts could be filled.[39] Each *deme* had to select both Council members and reserves for each seat, and if no more than two candidates came forward, the lottery might be merely to decide which of two candidates took which role.[40] Some magisterial posts were less prestigious than others and evidence suggests that in some cases there was difficulty in making up a full board of ten. These problems were exacerbated by the fall in population due to the plague and the Peloponnesian war.

Another remarkable aspect of the Athenian polity, and one pertinent to our investigation of the use of lot, was the total lack of anything resembling a body of professional bureaucrats. The 700 magistrates covered all administrative and organisational tasks required by the *polis*, from naval requisition to overseeing the water supply and sanitation. Athens therefore had no state apparatus in the modern sense of the word, and because all offices were subject to sortition and rotation, or re-election, there was no such thing as a permanent post.

The overall picture revealed in this snapshot is of a rationally organised political society capable of flexibility and adjustment that incorporated a wide range of inventive institutions designed to combat perceived ills—such as corruption and concentrations of political power. The nature of its institutions and procedures indicates, moreover, that Athenian political society championed and promoted ideas of freedom and fairness. The system and its values were maintained and enhanced by unprecedented, (and, I would suggest, unsurpassed) levels of citizen participation in government. Within this constitutional context there was considerable investment in sortition as a means of selecting political officers and, it

[39] See Staveley (1972) p. 40; and Whitehead (1986) p. 267.
[40] Staveley (1972) pp. 49–51.

seems, considerable commitment, if not enthusiasm, for these arrangements on the part of the citizenry at large.

Political consolidation: the key role of the Kleisthenic revolution

In this section my aim is to look at the process of political development or political consolidation that took place in Ancient Athens between the period of Solon in the early sixth century and the fall of democracy in 322 BCE.[41] I start in at the point of maximum change: the events of the Kleisthenic revolution of 508–7 and the programme of constitutional reforms that followed. From there I look briefly backward and then forward to the period of developed democracy in the late fifth and fourth centuries.

Athens between 561 and 510 was under the rule of a tyrannical dynasty consisting of the popular tyrant Peisistratos followed by his despotic son Hippias. When this was brought to a close, with Spartan help, a power struggle ensued between two aristocratic contenders, Isagoras and Kleisthenes, a member of the powerful Alkmaeonid family who had recently returned from exile.[42] Kleisthenes, we are told, lost out when Isagoras was elected *archon*.[43] Herodotus then describes how Kleisthenes 'allied himself with the common people' and 'took the demos into his faction' in order to resolvesss this impasse.[44] It is difficult to know exactly what this means, or exactly how it happened. Given the circumstances, however, we can be fairly sure that some sort of bargain was struck to ensure that the arrangement could not be reversed after the succession had been achieved. We can also surmise that the *demos* itself was sufficiently organised to respond to whatever Kliesthenes put on offer. The upshot of this was what can only be described as a revolutionary situation.[45] Isagoras called for the help of the Spartan

---

[41] The main sources for this are the *Histories* of Herodotus, Book 5; and the *Ath.Pol.* sections XX–XXII (Herodotus, 1954, pp. 334–7; Aristotle, 1986, pp. 163–6). It is highly likely that the latter relies on the former. See Hansen (1999) pp. 27–54 for a succinct summary of these historical developments.

[42] See Ostwald (1988) p. 304 on the anti-Peisistraid measures such as bans and proscriptive lists that followed the overthrow of the dynasty. This adds weight to the idea that political division in Attica was an on-going and serious problem.

[43] Aristotle (1986) p. 164 [*Ath. Pol* XX. 1] states that he lost power in the *hetaireiai* or aristocratic political clubs.

[44] Herodotus (1998) p. 327 [*Hist*. V. 66].

[45] Ober (1998) p. 228 gives a particularly good account of this.

Kleomenes, and Kleisthenes, along with 700 others, was forced into exile. Kleomenes tried to dissolve the *boule* and set up Isagoras as a puppet oligarch.[46] The *boule*, however, stood firm, and the *demos* forced the Spartans up to the Acropolis, besieging them there for two days. When the Spartans capitulated, Kleisthenes and his supporters were recalled from exile.[47] These events show how the *demos* was brought onto the political stage and how it responded immediately and decisively to usher in the new order.

But what was this new order to consist of? There could be no going back to tyranny – even popular tyranny – or to the instability of aristocratic factional struggle. Nor could the fragile state be put into the hands of the politically inexperienced *demos*.[48] We can begin to get some idea of what sort of bargain was made by looking at the nature of the reforms carried out by this new partnership. If the original agreement and the independent action of the *demos* gave them a political role, the radical programme that followed gave them the political organisation and structure necessary to carry out that role – literally to learn the 'art of the city'.

Under Kleisthenes the population of Attica was divided into ten new tribes in such a way as to break up local allegiances. As we saw earlier in the chapter, these tribes formed the basic political and military infrastructure of the state, but they also encouraged new loyalties since tribe members from different parts of the peninsular would now live and fight together on military campaigns. Kleisthenes was also responsible for setting up the *deme* structure and for organising the new *boule* of 500 based on a quota of members from each *deme*. Significantly the reforms stipulated that the registration of citizens should take place at *deme* level and that every citizen registered in this way should have a *deme* name in addition to his family names. This *deme* identity would apply even when citizens took up residence in other parts of Attica.

The initial effect of these measures was to take local power away from the *gens*, (family groups) the *phratria* (brotherhood associations) and the aristocratic clubs or *hetaireia*, which had previously controlled the membership of the tribes and hence admission to the Council.[49] The longer term effect was the creation of a new unit in

---

[46] Aristotle (1986) p. 163 [*Ath.Pol.* XX. 3]; Herodotus (1954) p. 337 [*Hist.*V. 72]. See also Ober (1998) p. 219.

[47] Aristotle (1986) pp. 163–4 [*Ath.Pol.* XX. 3–4]; Herodotus (1954) p. 337 [*Hist.* V. 72–3].

[48] Hignett (1952) p.125 describes the Kleisthenic reforms as a 'leap in the dark'.

[49] Hansen (1999) p. 400; Murray (1988) p. 15.

which the relationship of the parts to the whole and the individual citizen to the parts could be described as 'political' in so far as they were exclusively concerned with the running of the *polis*. It was a defining act of political consolidation and introduced a structure that remained unchanged for 300 years.

Kleisthenes is also credited with the introduction of ostracism.[50] While this measure has often attracted criticism on the grounds that it was used in the cause of personal rivalry, and while it was later superseded by more flexible and focussed procedures, ostracism is perfectly understandable in the context of an agreement between an aristocratic leader and the *demos*. It is above all a measure to combat oligarchy or tyranny—it could even have been introduced to assuage fears about the ambitions of Kleisthenes himself.

While we must recognise the importance of these events, Solon, who held office immediately before Peisistratos, had taken the first steps in creating a unified citizenry when he abolished debt enslavement and created fixed bands or classes based on wealth. It is measures such as these that first place the *demos* on the Athenian political stage. The abolition of debt-enslavement could be particularly singled out as the key moment in the consolidation of the idea of a distinct citizen body.[51] He had also established a Court of Appeal, which had the effect of strengthening the economic position of the poorer members of Attic society. These actions mark a distinct step in the formation of a strong 'hoplite' class which became the backbone of the Athenian military in the period leading up to the mid fifth century. We should therefore read the Kleisthenic reforms as part of a much longer process of political development.

Despite the entrance of the *demos* onto the political stage of 507–8 we cannot characterise the Athenian *polis* of Kleisthenes as democratic since overall political power still lay in the hands of the old aristocratic council or *areopagos*.[52] Nonetheless we should recognise that the advent of full democracy in 462 was only possible because forty years earlier Kleisthenes had defined the political arena and had given the citizenry practical political responsibility.

----

[50] This measure does not seem to have been used until 487. Hansen (1999) p. 35; Ostwald (1988) p. 309. Its advocacy by Kleisthenes is commensurate with the general thrust of his reforms and the circumstances of their introduction. For an assessment of the value of these reforms as a whole see Murray (1990) pp. 13–14.

[51] Hignett (1952) p. 119.

[52] *Ibid.* p. 156.

One of the most significant factors influencing the next qualitative change in the Athenian political system was the decision of 483/2 to turn Athens into a major sea power. This brought a new military class, the *thetes* or oarsmen, into existence and gave them an important role in the defence of the *polis*. Soon they demanded a greater political voice. [53] In 462, with the fleet in the harbour and the hoplites away on campaign, Ephialtes and the young Perikles moved the Assembly to deprive the *aereopagos* of the majority of its powers. This ushered in what is often called the golden age of Athenian democracy. It was marked by extraordinary prosperity, an expanding empire and unchallenged power in the Aegean; it was marred, however, by the long and destructive Peloponnesian war.

Towards the end of the war two short terms of oligarchic rule broke the continuity of democracy in Athens. They are useful in that they remind us of the fragility of democratic institutions, but at the same time, because they were short-lived they also bear witness to its resilience. The second of these, the rule of the so-called 'Thirty Tyrants' was particularly bloody and saw the execution of some 1,500 of those who opposed the regime. Democratic rule was restored to Athens by military force in 403 and steps were made in the new dispensation to prevent a repetition of oligarchic rule. Following these turbulent events an amnesty was declared for all but a few leaders of the oligarchy. This is important because it helps us to characterise the restored democracy as a period of reconciliation rather than merely a triumph for the democrats. In these circumstances the *polis* needed, above all, political institutions and governmental procedures that were strong and inclusive.

Fourth-century democracy visibly learned from the mistakes of the previous era, and three measures put into place following the restoration of 403 are important to our investigation of lot. First was the increasing use of the Courts in *graphe paranomon* and *eisangelia* cases.[54] Second was the introduction of the *nomothetai* or legislative body. Both measures, it seems, were aimed at curbing the power of the Assembly, especially its vulnerability to the exhortations of demagogues or charismatic leaders. Both also sought to preserve and refine democracy, to make it more rational, more sensitive to the needs of the polity as a whole: and, therefore, more genuinely political. These measures served the same function as the system of checks and balances in modern representative democracy but did so

[53] Rhodes (1992) p. 91.
[54] *Ibid*. p. 44.

without the separation of powers and through direct recourse to an organ of the people: the randomly-selected *dikastai*. The *nomothetai* was a particularly important political development since it was charged with creating a body of permanent legislation in distinction from Assembly decrees, which had only temporary significance.[55] It was a move away from the perceived chaos of Assembly politics, but it was, at the same time, thoroughly democratic.

We can isolate a number of overriding principles or trends from this summary. In the first instance it is clear that each stage of invention was built on the political stability of the previous order, and that when breakdown occurred, such as in the late fifth-century oligarchies, active remedies and adjustments were made. Second, while it would be a simplification to suggest that every measure was a direct response to the threat of arbitrary rule, this threat, in its various forms, was a constant pressure during the period. Third, nearly all these steps took place within a political (i.e., rule-governed and public) context. Fourth, while the changes operated for the increasing benefit of one section of the population, the *demos*, they did so in a way that was inclusive in a general sense. There is a real ethos of fairness to this story that runs alongside the defence of democracy: the question of how government should be conducted is addressed with the same vigour as the question of who should govern.

Alongside these general observations we should remember that there were constant external pressures on the Athenian State during this period and internal political cohesion was as important as military prowess. We should also see Athenian political maturity against the background of the cultural and economic revolution that took place there in the fifth-century. We should, however, be careful not to make too close a causal connection in this respect. Most of the most significant political changes took place either before the period of rapid economic growth and regional imperial hegemony, or after it.

Investigating lot in Athens

Case Study 1: the Kleisthenic reforms of 507 BCE

This case study of Kleisthenes' reforms deals with two instances or possible instances of the use of sortition. The first is the creation of the ten tribes by lot out of the regionally divided *deme* clusters or *trittyes*. For this we have direct textual evidence which can be cor-

[55] Stockton (1990) p. 52.

roborated by an intelligent reading of the archaeological evidence of the geographical distribution of the *trittyes*.[56] The second is the claim that when Kleisthenes established the *boule* of 500, selection was made, not by election, but by lot. While we know that this was the method of selection by the fifth century, the date of its introduction is not clear from either archaeological or textual evidence. I shall argue that the use of lot for this organ of government is consistent with the overall orientation of the Kleisthenic reforms.

First we should recognise the precarious nature of the situation faced by Kleisthenes. There were internal dangers in the shape of the residue of support for the Pisistratid regime and the supporters of Isagoras' faction within the aristocratic clubs. There was also the possibility that localised conflicts based on the settling of old scores could escalate out of control. Sparta constituted the immediate external threat, but the danger from other neighbouring states needed also to be taken into account. The *demos* had played a major role in the ousting of Isagoras and his Spartan support—they were now a political class that could not be ignored. But Athens at this stage was far from being a democracy, and any upsurge in class-conflict would have threatened the fragile stability. Given these circumstances we can surmise that the main thrust of the reforms was to forge a unified *polis*.

My first example of Kleisthenes' use of lot fits in the centre of this package of measures designed to address this problem. The *Constitution of Athens* gives us the following description: 'He divided Attica into thirty sections, using the demes as his basic unit; ten of the sections were in the city area, ten around the coast and ten inland. He called the sections trittyes, and placed three into each tribe by lot, one from each geographical area.'[57]

The overall effect of this division can best be understood by reference to the map of the deme structure of Attica created by J. S. Traill (Plate 3).[58] While most of the *demes* are in compact *trittyes* which seem to follow the logic of the geographical features, occasional groupings seem to deviate from this pattern. *Trittytes* 10, III and 4 are the most noticeable cases in this category. This can possibly be accounted for as a means of breaking up local loyalties in the

---

[56] Aristotle (1986 [*Ath. Pol.* XX. 4].

[57] Aristotle (1986) [*Ath. Pol.* XXI. 4].

[58] Traill (1975), for plate 3 see below, illustrated section between pp. 56–7.

creation of the *trittyes* themselves.[59] In respect to the grouping of the *trittytes*, some *trittytes* allocated to the same tribe end up adjacent to each other (2 and II from the Aigeis tribe; VIII and viii from the Hippothantis tribe) while some (X and 10 from Antochis; IV and 4 from Leontis) are geographically distinct. This would suggest that the *Constitution* is correct and a process of random distribution had indeed been used. A more rational means of decision-making might be expected to distribute the tribal *trittyes* at more equal distances from each other.

This process of random distribution does not obviously make use of the blind break beyond the fact that the blind break is an intrinsic part of the lottery form; nor is the random distribution of the *trittyes* to their respective tribes strictly necessary in respect to their administrative role or function. To understand this process more fully we have to consider the other two options facing Kleisthenes: either he should make the decision himself, or the *trittyes* themselves should choose.

Allowing the *trittyes* to choose for themselves would be tantamount to allowing voluntary factions to form, and would have condemned the newly-formed *trittyes* to interminable squabbling. Since the aim of the re-structuring of Attica was to create greater unity, this would not have been a viable option. Kleisthenes had already made the major decision concerning the grouping—that of dividing the coastal peoples from the hills-people and from the city dwellers—once this had been achieved the exact make up of the new tribes was far less important. The political logic of leaving the final distribution to lot seems, therefore, to have been a concession made by Kleisthenes, a deliberate stepping away from the decision.[60] Having made drastic, sweeping changes to the structure of Attica, Kleisthenes now forestalls any accusation of tyranny by leaving the final choice to the gods.[61] It is also a symbolic dedication of the new polis to the people. It is the next-best thing to a collective decision.

We can characterise this as a weak use of lot since it does not make full use of the arational blind break, and sortition seems here to be playing a largely rhetorical or surrogate role. On the other hand, in

---

[59] Ostwald (1988) p. 313 describes the *trittyes* as 'the most artificial and crucial element in the system'.

[60] Eckhoff (1989) p. 13 talks of self-initiated lotteries as 'making the distributor redundant'.

[61] Ostwald (1988) p. 317 suggests that it was politically safer to use lot, than to be seen to 'derive personal or political advantage from the arrangement'.

the astute judgement made by Kleisthenes to head off any factional dissent, he is, in fact, anticipating the dangers to the new polis should the *trittyes* form voluntary alliances. It therefore has a hidden strong use, that of using an arational solution to disrupt the planning of alliances. Because this is a one-off decision, however, this hidden strong use is less politically significant than the weaker rhetoric of the deferred decision.

Opinion is divided about whether sortition was the original method of selection for the *boule* of 500, but where reasons are given, these are revealing. P. J. Rhodes suggests that, following the example of the archonship which was elective at the time of Kleisthenes, election should not be ruled out as the method of selection for the new *boule* also.[62] Hansen follows this general line,[63] while Ober claims that Kleisthenes would have used election in order to retain control amongst the elite.[64]

On the other side of the argument Stockton [65] endorses the use of lot by Kleisthenes for the *boule* on the grounds that the creation of a 'random cross-section' of the population was in the interests of the rising hoplite class or *zeugitai*.[66] Ehrenberg recognises that lot should not be seen as an exclusively democratic measure, and endorses the use of lot by Kleisthenes as leading to further democratic developments. He also raises the possibility that a lottery at *boule* level might have been preceded by preference votes at *deme* meetings to determine the pool.[67]

Much of the confusion comes from identifying lot primarily as a mechanism of democratic government, and this is further compounded by the idea that the method for selecting the *boule* should follow that of the *archons*. For those inclined towards this view, the evidence of the *Athenian Constitution*, that Dracon set up the original *boule* of 400 in the pre-Solonic period using lot and strict rotation, has to be ignored.[68] The writers of the *Constitution*, according to this

---

[62] Rhodes (1972) p. 7. See also Rhodes (1981) p. 251.
[63] Hansen (1999) pp. 49–52.
[64] Ober (1989) p. 73; Ostwald (1988) pp. 319, 322; and Whitehead (1986) p. 207 suggest that the Kleisthenic *boule* was elected, but do not explicitly follow either line of reasoning.
[65] Stockton (1990) p. 26.
[66] Griffith (1966) p. 213 sides with a lottery, as do Day and Chambers (1962) pp. 119, 177–8.
[67] Ehrenberg (1968) p. 94.
[68] Aristotle (1986) p. 149 [*Ath. Pol.* IV. 3].

interpretation, purposely exaggerated the achievements of the archaic period in order to give them greater democratic credibility.[69]

Behind this, I suspect, is a view of lot as a levelling mechanism derived, in part, from the fact that the story of Athenian democracy has been largely told by aristocrats. In this manner lot has become portrayed as a means of defending existing democracy — a result of democracy rather than as a factor that contributed to its development. Rhodes' comment that lot was used when 'loyalty rather than skill' was required is typical of this line of thinking.[70]

Against these arguments I would suggest that by the time the fifth-century democrats took the final steps in creating the full citizen-lot polity, the potential of sortition was well known. This would have been because it had already been used for the selection of the *boule* since the time of Kleisthenes, and possibly since much earlier. My case is that lot would have been used in this period because it has the capacity to inhibit factional organisation. This coincides with the greatest need experienced by the emerging *polis* — that of preventing *stasis* or internal fragmentation.

The use of lot to inhibit the growth and operation of factions works in a number of ways — all of which make a positive virtue of its arational features: the blind break and the random, or independent outcome, and, to a lesser extent, the lack of a direct subject. Lot is unpredictable and this means that making plans with the prospect of achieving a desired or willed result is subject to diminishing returns. A faction that planned to place a significant number of its members in office would therefore find its designs inhibited by the use of sortition. In addition, if rotation were used with lot, no faction could build on any gains it may have made by chance. We can think of the blind break in the lottery process, therefore, as breaking the rational links of pre-planning and pre-organisation of resources that might otherwise be used by anyone seeking to assert their will within the political arena. With a lot-based system no one can systematically promote themselves or their followers. It therefore operates in such a way as to diffuse, or break up, concentrations of power.

---

[69] See Hansen (1999) pp. 49–52, especially p. 50; and Moore in Aristotle (1986) p. 221. Although Hansen is unhappy with the early (i.e., Kleisthenic or pre-Kleisthenic) use of lot, he does recognise (1999 p. 84) that the enemies of lot stressed the notion of arbitrary equality while ignoring its wider political benefits.

[70] Rhodes (1981) p. 513. Rhodes is commenting on *Ath.Pol.* XLIII 1.

A random process of choice is also direct and unmediated. Here it is entirely distinct from the process of choice by election, in which argument, endorsement, promise and influence can play a major part. In a lottery choice there can be no relations of dependency or obligation between the candidate and any other person (such as a patron) or any collective body (such as a political party). Thus lot contributes to the ethos that public office-holders should be disconnected or independent of any particular external influence, and should work purely for the general good of the polity. From the other side of the equation, a choice made by lot is a demonstrably impartial choice. Where office-holders are selected in this way, the *polis*, which 'calls' the citizen to office, is perceived to be a genuinely impartial political entity.

It would seem reasonable, therefore, to think of sortition primarily as a means of inhibiting factions, and secondarily as a means of creating equality of opportunity. Indeed it could be argued that, in any real political context, its ability to deliver equality of opportunity is actually a result of its ability to prevent those with power or influence from gaining any illegitimate extra advantage. Expressed this way, equality of opportunity is a consequence of the use of lot to prevent powerful individuals or groups from controlling the election procedure.

The potential of sortition to promote unity and political integrity in this manner coincides with the gravest danger facing the Athenian polis during its protracted period of political consolidation between the seventh and the fifth centuries. This threat is evident from Athens' chequered history of the tyrannies, coups and conspiracies. Additional evidence about how seriously it was treated can be found in Solon's famous anti-stasis law, which stipulated that during periods of civil division citizens should declare for one or other party,[71] and in Thucydides' account of the sedition at Corcyra.[72] Thucydides makes it clear in his reflections on these events that factions are the main enemy of political stability: 'For party associations are not based on any established law, nor do they seek the public good, they are formed in defiance of the law and from self

---

[71] Aristotle (1986) p. 153 [*Ath. Pol.* VIII. 5]; Forrest (1966) p. 175. This law seemed to be aimed at averting the dangers of opportunistic vacillation at times of crisis and uncertainty. It is aimed at making citizens decide for themselves rather than wait in order to back the winning faction.
[72] Thucydides (1972) pp. 237–45 [III. 70–85].

interest.'[73] Moreover the term *stasis* itself means both civil unrest and faction, which points to the very close connection between the two ideas within Athenian political consciousness.

It is also worth noting that the greatest threats to the polity came from factions that were predominantly aristocratic in character. The older aristocratic families had the resources to win power, were already organised themselves into *hetaireia*, were likely to put family before *polis*, and often had family connections with other city-states.[74] This made their factional activity particularly dangerous. To this extent the efforts to forge political unity in Athens between the seventh and the fifth centuries took a particularly democratic path.

This adds weight to the view that sortition for the *boule* was introduced either by Kleisthenes or even earlier, and that its potential for defending the *polis* against oligarchy was then understood and further developed by the democrats of the fifth century. The direct evidence in support of this reconstruction is the passage in the *Constitution* that places responsibility for using lot and rotation in the *boule* in the hands of Dracon, Solon's predecessor.[75]

The case for lot can also be made by looking at the possible consequences of elections. Not only would preference elections have given those with local influence the platform to extend their power, but elections would have divided the citizen populations within the demes, possibly along the lines of the *phratriai*, at a time when the Kleisthenic system as a whole was still in its infancy. Elections for the *boule* could also present the opportunity for candidates in adjacent *demes*, or in groups of *demes*, to declare for a combined factional slate. A vote can also, of course, amount to a public declaration of numerical support, and as such can also be a distinct statement of factional power.[76] All these possibilities would contradict the ethos of *deme* loyalty and identity, which Kleisthenes was seeking to develop.[77]

---

[73] See Thucydides (1881) p. 222 [III. 82]. This quotation is most pointed in Jowett's translation. See also Murray (1988) p. 21.

[74] Ober (1998) p. 228.

[75] Aristotle (1986) p. 149 [*Ath.Pol.*IV. 3].

[76] Sinclair (1988) p. 18.

[77] Ehrenberg's idea of combined lot and election appreciates the role of lot in the general thrust of the Kleisthenic reforms. I would argue, however that the link between *boule* and *deme* would have been better preserved by direct sortition. Ehrenberg (1968) p. 94.

How we understand elections, however, depends on who is entitled to vote in any given situation. In the circumstances of
Kleisthenes' ascendancy in partnership with the *demos*, elections by
the masses, even at *deme* level, might have resulted in the removal of
loyal aristocrats—good public servants—from office. While lot
would have operated against the power and influence of the older
ruling caste in the longer term, in the short term it could also have
been a means of retaining their participation. It would keep them in
the political fold, and guarantee them equality of opportunity in
exchange for compliance with the new system.

It is therefore easy to see lot as part of a package of measures,
which included rotation and ostracism, designed to create a smooth
transition to the new-look Attica free from factional de-stabilisation.
Because sortition lowered the threshold to office and weakened the
power bases of the local aristocratic groupings, we can easily see it
as part of a deal between Kleisthenes and the *demos*, but it was also
inclusive in a general political sense. The cost of inclusion was
adherence to the laws, procedures and structures of a new entity:
the citizen-led political community.[78]

Case study 2: The People's Courts

The idea that the body politic—the body in charge of the political
community— should be non-partisan or impartial is also evident
when we consider the use of lot to select the members of the People's
Court, or *dikasterion*. The name derives from the word *dikē* – often
translated as 'rightness' or 'straightness' and by implication 'fairness' or 'justice'.[79] The *dikasterion* can therefore be characterised as
an institution dedicated to finding the right way. This unique institution was the subject of a long period of development—from the
time of Solon right through to the third century BCE—and, as with
the *boule*, the use of lot to select its members in the archaic period is
the subject of some dispute.

Solon is often characterised as a mediator who sought to find a
peaceful settlement between the great landowners of Attica, the
Eupatrid class, and the small farmers of the region who were facing
the constant threat of enslavement for debt and ruin in the hands of

[78] For a contemporary discussion of the idea of a political community see
Plato's *Protagoras* dialogue (Plato, 1940, pp. 246–9 [320–23]). Protagoras
presents a narrative of the formation of the *polis*. Anyone 'incapable of
partaking in shame and justice,' he suggests, 'be put to death as a pest to the
city' (Plato, 1940, p. 248 [324]).

[79] Barker in Aristotle (1946) p. lxx.

a corrupt magistracy. His solution was to abolish debt-enslavement on the one hand, and to establish a new Court of Final Appeal to deal with the excesses of the magistracy on the other. The appeals were to be heard by the *heliaia*, which has been interpreted to mean the Assembly, but could equally well mean *an* assembly or large group of people expressly chosen for the purpose.[80] Whichever interpretation we choose to accept, Solon's intentions are clear: to establish a system of justice that was ultimately based in the community. One further detail, the measure to allow a third party to bring a case to the new court, confirms that Solon was taking affirmative action to deliver justice to the poorer farmers by allowing them to use members of the more educated classes to plead their cases. In the circumstances of the introduction of the Court impartiality must have been a major consideration. This would suggest that an appeal hearing would not have been held in front of a voluntarily-convened assembly — this could only have created greater friction and division. It is therefore highly likely that sortition would have been used to select who was to take part.

By the fifth century the People's Court had become the court of first instance and began to be used for major public-interest cases.[81] These were distinguished from private cases and were usually heard by larger numbers of *dikastai*. As we have seen the *dikasterion* was used as a forum for approving legislation after the restoration of democracy in 403 BCE. Thus between the sixth and fourth centuries the People's Court — a means by which judgement could be exercised by the community — was given powers to cover a successively wider range of matters. Although sovereignty resided in the Assembly in the second half of the fifth century, by the fourth the balance of power began to shift towards the Courts.[82]

In terms of our inquiry, we need first to focus on the relationship between the Courts and the Assembly. It is clear from the changes made after the restoration of democracy that the *dikasterion* was considered to be a more stable institution, capable of delivering a better quality of judgement than the partisan and emotive cut-and-thrust

[80] Judgement by the whole Assembly is favoured by Day and Chamber (1962) p. 87; Rhodes (1981) p. 160; and Andrewes (1982) p. 388. Ehrenberg, who generally shows a greater understanding of the complexity of sortition, supports the notion that the *Dikasterion* was likely to have been a lot-generated institution from the time of Solon. Ehrenberg (1968) p. 67. This view is supported by Aristotle in Aristotle (1946) p. 88 [*Pol*.II. xii. 3; 1274a].
[81] Day and Chambers (1962) p. 184.
[82] Hansen (1990) pp. 216, 242.

of the Assembly.[83] But while this can be interpreted as an anti-democratic measure—a reduction in the assembly's powers—this does not concur with the context of its introduction. It was the war-weary Assembly that voted for the oligarchy of 411, and the shift of governmental emphasis from the Assembly to the Courts came immediately after the restoration of democracy in 403. This move can be interpreted, therefore, as a move to protect a new, somewhat fragile democracy against demagogues either of an oligarchic, or extreme democratic, persuasion. Rather than sortition defending the sovereignty of the Assembly, this new role for the People's Courts can be understood as a lot-generated body defending democracy *from* the Assembly.[84] What is more, it was doing so by giving greater emphasis to the ideas of considered judgement, due process and impartiality. It was a move against confusion rather than against democracy and is a very good example of how the political process was consolidated and extended by giving new functions to old forms.

It is tempting to read the authority of the Courts as deriving solely from the idea that it was a popular organ: an organ of the people. The use of such large numbers, and the increase in numbers when cases of higher public interest were to be heard certainly suggest that the *dikasterion* was primarily an institution of community justice. The extent to which it owed its authority to the idea that it constituted the 'population in miniature' has, however, to be questioned.

R. K. Sinclair suggests that the use of lot in the selection of the *dikastai* enabled decisions to be taken by a 'random cross section' of the citizen population.[85] If 'cross section' is interpreted as 'sample', I would argue that this is not only the wrong way to think of the use of lot in this context, but also the wrong way to think about the operation of the *dikasterion*. It is, moreover, a view based on the later premises of sampling theory and representative government.

The interpretation that lot was used to create a sample of the general citizen population points to a weak use. This is because it seeks to establish a rational relationship—a relationship of ratio—between the organ of government and the citizen population. This idea is also contradicted by the fact that the *dikastai* were a special

---

[83] *Ibid.* p. 218.
[84] This is Headlam's general line, although he is more concerned about the use of lot to select magistrates.
[85] Sinclair (1988) p. 79.

grouping in two respects: they were a senior group of men over thirty; and they were special office-holders because they had sworn the *Heliastic Oath*. They were also volunteers, both in terms of their coming forward to join the pool and in their appearance at the Courts on the day of the trial. This would argue that lot was never intended as a means of selecting a 'population in miniature' in any sense beyond the general notion of community justice advanced by Solon. This does not mean that they were not *similar* to the general population — and they would be decidedly more so than a group of legal specialists or professional politicians. But the notion that the *dikastai* were selected by lot with the primary intention that they should be a representative sample has to be ruled out.

The purpose of sortition in the selection of the *dikastai* is, in fact, quite straightforward. It is, in the first instance, to prevent any party who might seek to influence the outcome of the judgement from exerting any pressure on the selection process. The level of the threat can be understood by looking at the measures taken to counter malpractice. Quadruple sortition was used to select the individual *dikastai*. This consisted of the choice by lot of the original pool of 6,000, the double choice by the *kleroterion* at the appropriate door of the Courts, and the lottery to decide on which court panel the successful candidates would be asked to sit.[86] At the same time the large numbers involved would put bribery well beyond the organisation and financial resources of any single person. This would suggest that beyond the prevention of corruption by individual defendants or interested parties the system was also designed to cope with challenges from organised factions. This is reinforced by the fact that the Courts handled both private and public cases, the *graphe paranomon* and the approval of legislation. Corruption could have serious political ramifications. To the broad premise of inclusive community justice, therefore, must be added the idea that *dikē* was to be maintained by protecting the purity of the Courts and, by extension, the purity of the whole political process. The image that defines the use of lot in this context is of the Courts guarded by lottery machines at their gates. By these means the inner, political sphere, with its rule-governed public procedures, was protected from the outside world of factional conspiracy and private intrigue.

We can, perhaps, get another view of how the authority of the *dikastai* relates to their process of selection by considering one of the

---

[86] This was double sortition because *dikastai* tickets were first placed in a chest before being drawn out and placed on the *kleroterion*.

general principles behind the operation of Athenian justice. S.C. Todd defines Athenian justice as 'procedural' in the sense that, rather than following either statute law or common law precedent, verdicts were acceptable and authoritative if the procedure by which they were arrived at had been adhered to.[87] The *dikasterion* is a prime example of this and the complex four-part scheme of sortition by which *dikastai* were selected should not be regarded as ancillary or preliminary to the distribution of justice, but as an integrated part of the whole process of establishing *dikē*. The main quality of the lottery process in operation here is impartiality—a key requirement if confidence is to be maintained in any institution of public decision-making. Furthermore this confidence was significantly enhanced by the fact that the lottery process for selecting *dikastes* was open and public. Indeed, in order to maintain its authority it had to follow its complex procedures to the letter, and be seen to do so.

There is a further aspect of the use of lot in the selection of the *dikastai* that needs consideration. This is the value that is brought to the decision-making not by the lottery *process*, but by its *product*: the randomly-selected *dikastes*. In Book III of the *Politics*, Aristotle expresses the idea that the mass of the people have the intrinsic ability to produce sound judgements: 'Some appreciate one part, some another, and all together appreciate all.'[88] This principle, which is an extension of the maxim that two heads are better than one, only operates, however, if all the heads—in this case the *dikastai* – make judgements independently of one another. That this principle formed part of the rationale for the large numbers used in the *dikasterion* can be deduced from two aspects of the Court procedure: the *dikastai* were to vote by secret ballot, and they were to do so without deliberation. The *Heliastic Oath*, moreover, specifies that the *dikastes* should use his own judgement, especially where no law existed as a guide. The oath has been reconstructed as follows:

> I will cast my vote in consonance with the laws and with the decrees passed by the Assembly and by the Council, but, if there is no law, in consonance with my sense of what is most just, without favour or enmity. I will vote only on the matters raised in the charge, and I will listen impartially to accusers and defenders alike.[89]

---

[87] Todd (1993) p. 65.
[88] Aristotle (1946) p. 123 [*Pol*. III. cxi 3].
[89] Hansen (1999) p. 182.

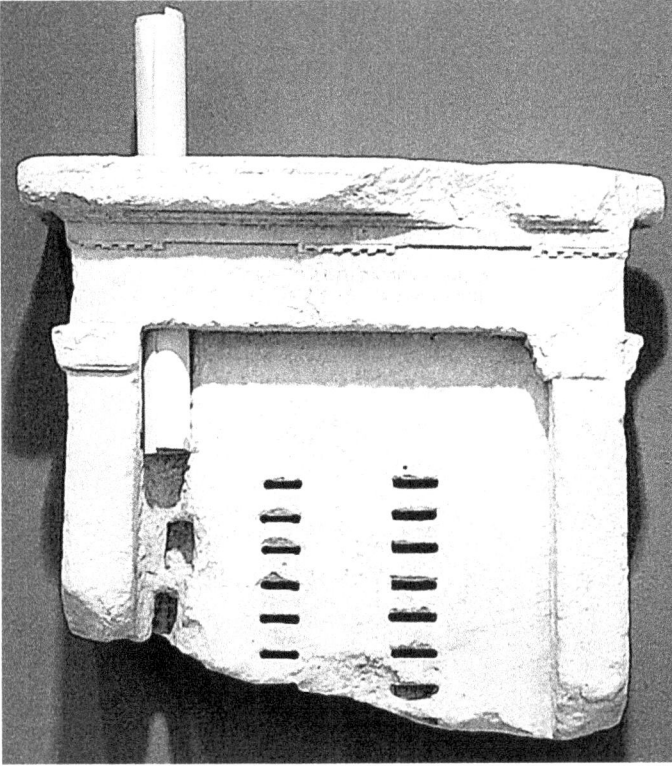

Plate 1: Hellenistic *kleroterion* (lottery machine), c. 200 BCE
Athens, Epigraphical Museum

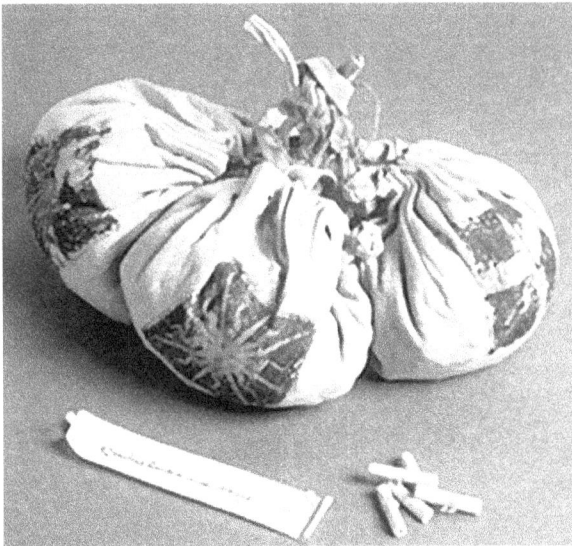

Plate 2: Leather *borse* containing names in a draw for the
Priorate of Florence in 1431. Archivio di Stato, Florence

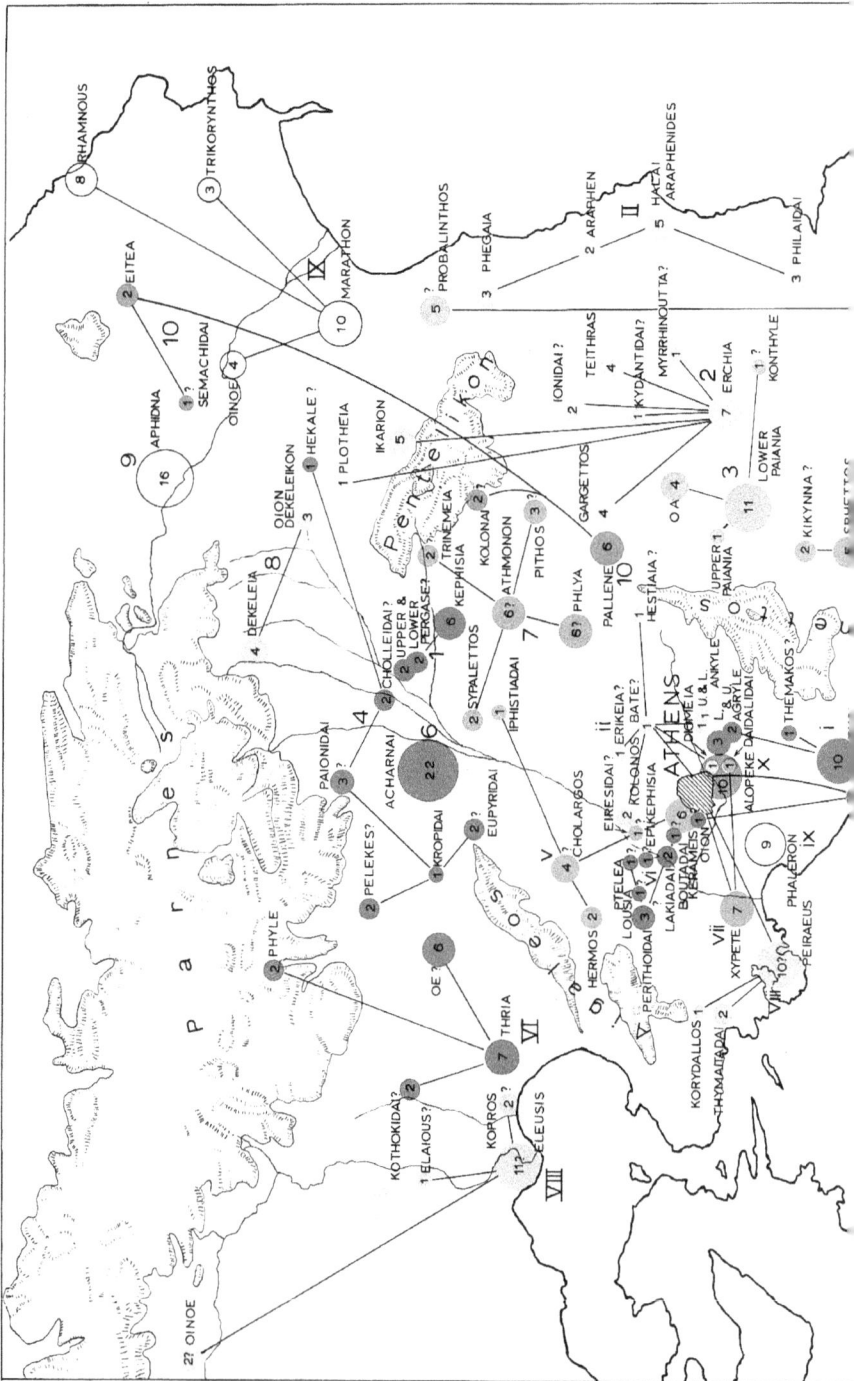

Plate 3: Attica Political Organisation. Reprinted from J.S. Traill, *Hesp*

ATTICA

POLITICAL ORGANIZATION

CITY TRITTYES i, ii, iii,.... x
COAST TRITTYES I, II, III,.... X
INLAND TRITTYES 1, 2, 3,... 10

Bouleutic quotas are shown within the circles.
Demes of the same trittys are joined by lines.

O? NAME = Approximate location; few remains.
O NAME? = Deme-site; name uncertain.

For the corresponding modern locations see text.

Scale : ca. 0   5 km

ATHENS

Scale : ca. 0   500 m.

N↑

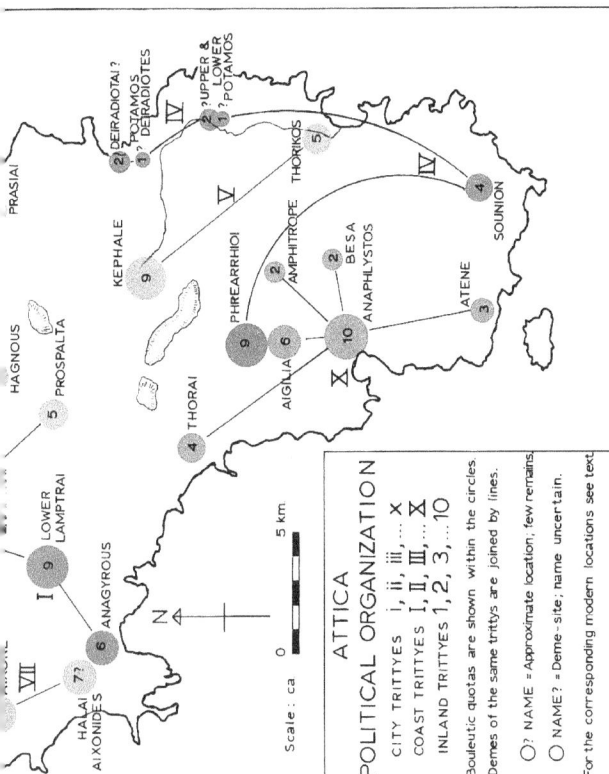

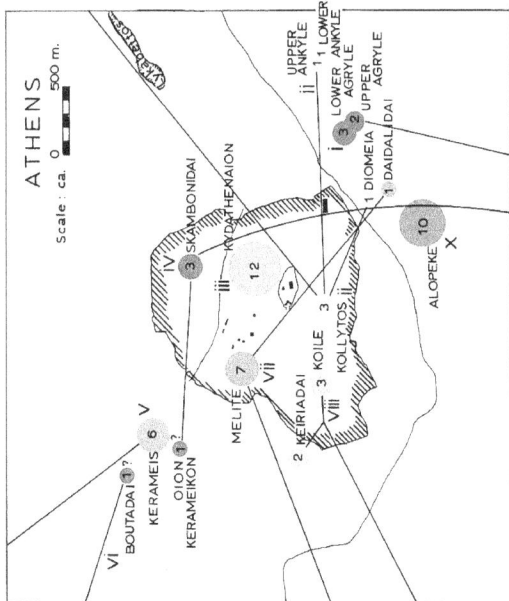

NOTE: The location of the following demes is not known and no attempt has been made to place them on the map.

JST 1972

Erechtheis	Aigeis	Pandionis	Leontis	Akamantis	Oineis	Kekropis	Hippothontis	Aiantis	Antiochis
② KEDOI I	① OTRYNE II	② KYTHEROS 1?	③ KETTOS IV?	② EITEA 5?	① TYRMEIDAI Vi?	① EPIEIKIDAI 7?	② HAMAXANTEIA Viii?	○ None	① EROIADAI 10?
⑩ PAMBOTADAI I?			② LEUKONOION iv?	③ POROS V?	① HIPPOTOMADAI Vi?		① ACHERDOUS VIII?		① KRIOA 10?
① PHEGOUS 1?			② AITHALIDAI 4?				① AURIDAI VIII?		
④ SYBRIDAI 1?			② HYBADAI 4?				② AZENIA VIII?		
			② KOLONAI 4?				③ ANAKAIA 8?		
							① EROIADAI 8?		

PRASIAI
DEIRADIOTAI ?
POTAMOS DEIRADIOTES
UPPER & LOWER POTAMOS
THORIKOS
KEPHALE
AMPHITROPE
SOUNION
BESA ANAPHLYSTOS
PHREARRHIOI
AIGILIA
ATENE
HAGNOUS
PROSPALTA
THORAI
LOWER LAMPTRAI
ANAGYROUS
HALAI AIXONIDES

SKAMBONIDAI
KYDATHENAION
LOWER ANKYLE
UPPER ANKYLE
LOWER AGRYLE
UPPER AGRYLE
DIOMEIA
DAIDALIDAI
ALOPEKE
MELITE
KEIRIADAI
KOILE
KOLLYTOS
BOUTADAI
KERAMEIS
OION KERAMEIKON

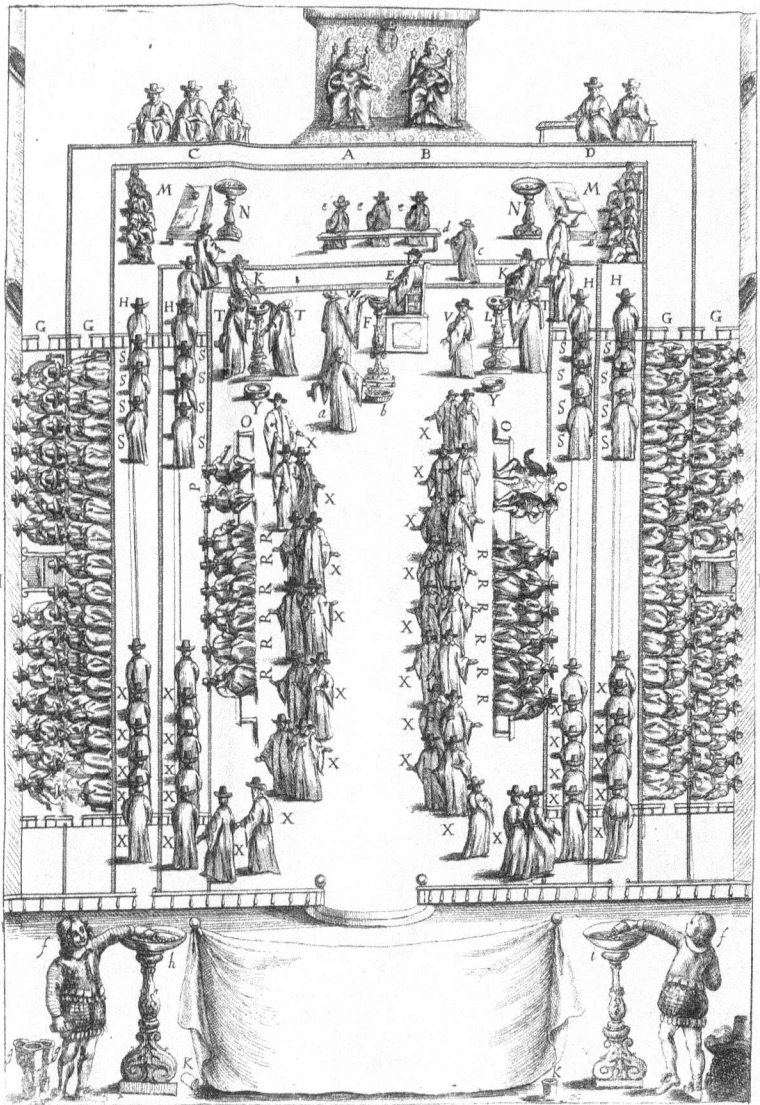

Illustration of the Venetian balloting system from a pamphlet
entitled *The use and manner of the Ballot* attributed to James
Harrington and published in 1660 (Bodleian Library, University
of Oxford, Wood 626 (13) Engraving of Balloting System).

ATHENIAN CITIZENS

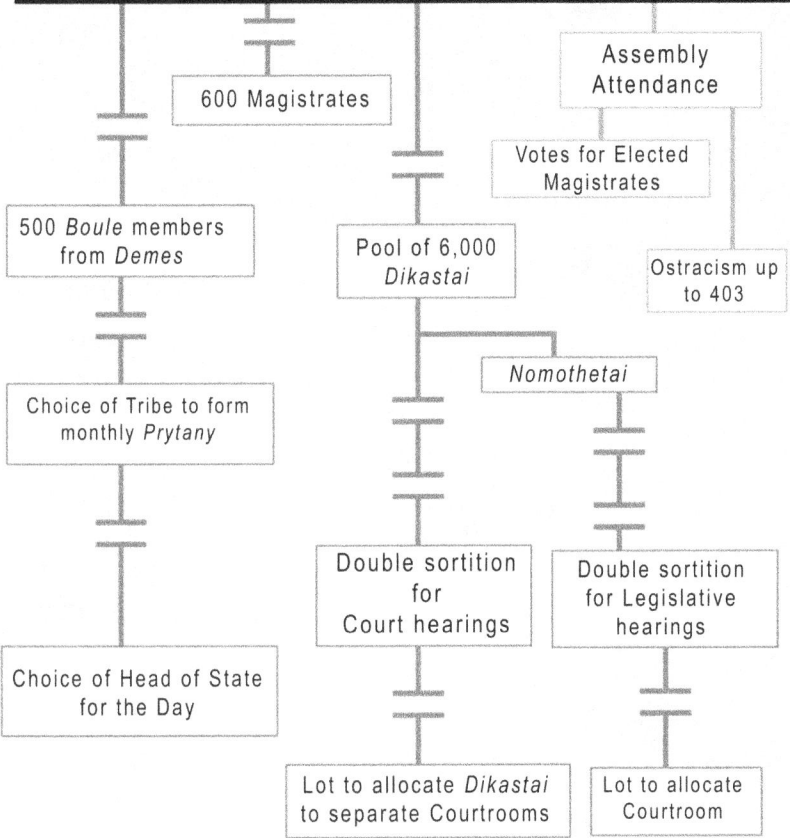

600 Magistrates

Assembly
Attendance

Votes for Elected
Magistrates

500 *Boule* members
from *Demes*

Pool of 6,000
Dikastai

Ostracism up
to 403

Choice of Tribe to form
monthly *Prytany*

Nomothetai

Double sortition
for
Court hearings

Double sortition
for Legislative
hearings

Choice of Head of State
for the Day

Lot to allocate *Dikastai*
to separate Courtrooms

Lot to allocate
Courtroom

*Denotes selection
made by lottery*

Ho boulomenos: the right of every
citizen to bring cases of *graphe
paranomon* or *eisangelia*
(denunciation) to the Courts.

Diagram illustrating the role of Athenian citizens in the
government of the *polis* and the extent that sortition was
used in their selection.

Nominating Body:

SIGNORIA *chooses* 28+ citizen nominators

CAPTAIN of PARTI GUELF *chooses* 28+ citizen nominators

FIVE of MERCANZIA *chooses* 28+ citizen nominators

NOMINATIONS FOR EACH SESTO

Voting Body:

7 Signoria

5 of Mercanzia

16 Gonfalonieri

2 Consuls from each of the 12 major Guilds

30 citizens appointed by the Signoria (5 from each Sesto)

VOTE BY SECRET BALLOT

Results only known to the Accoppiatori

Two-monthly draw of one name per Sesto

OFFICE HOLDER

Divieto excludes same family members

Main Bag for each Sesto

Remissi Bag used when there are no suitable candidates

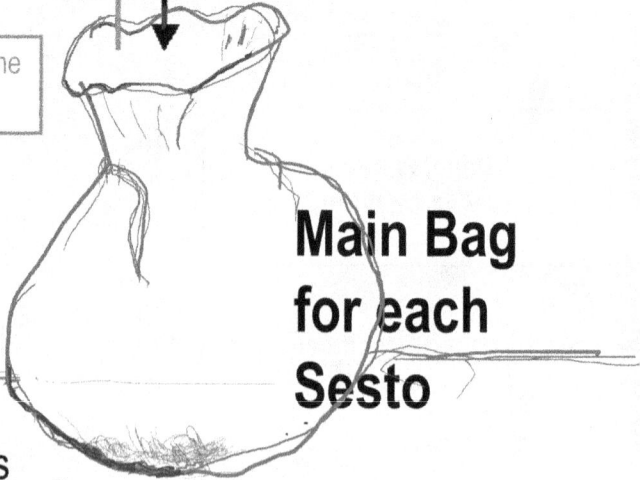

Diagram showing in simplified form how the Florentine *Scrutiny* and *Tratte* was used to select members of the *Signoria*.

CONSIGLIO GRANDE

Families of those nominated do not vote

Benches called up to the urns by lot.

60 members

36 members to form 4 Committees of 9

one nominator selected by lot from each cttee

Committee votes on nomination which must secure 6 or more votes

Committee members take no part in the secret ballot

Nominations voted on by a secret ballot of the whole Council

= a decision taken by lottery

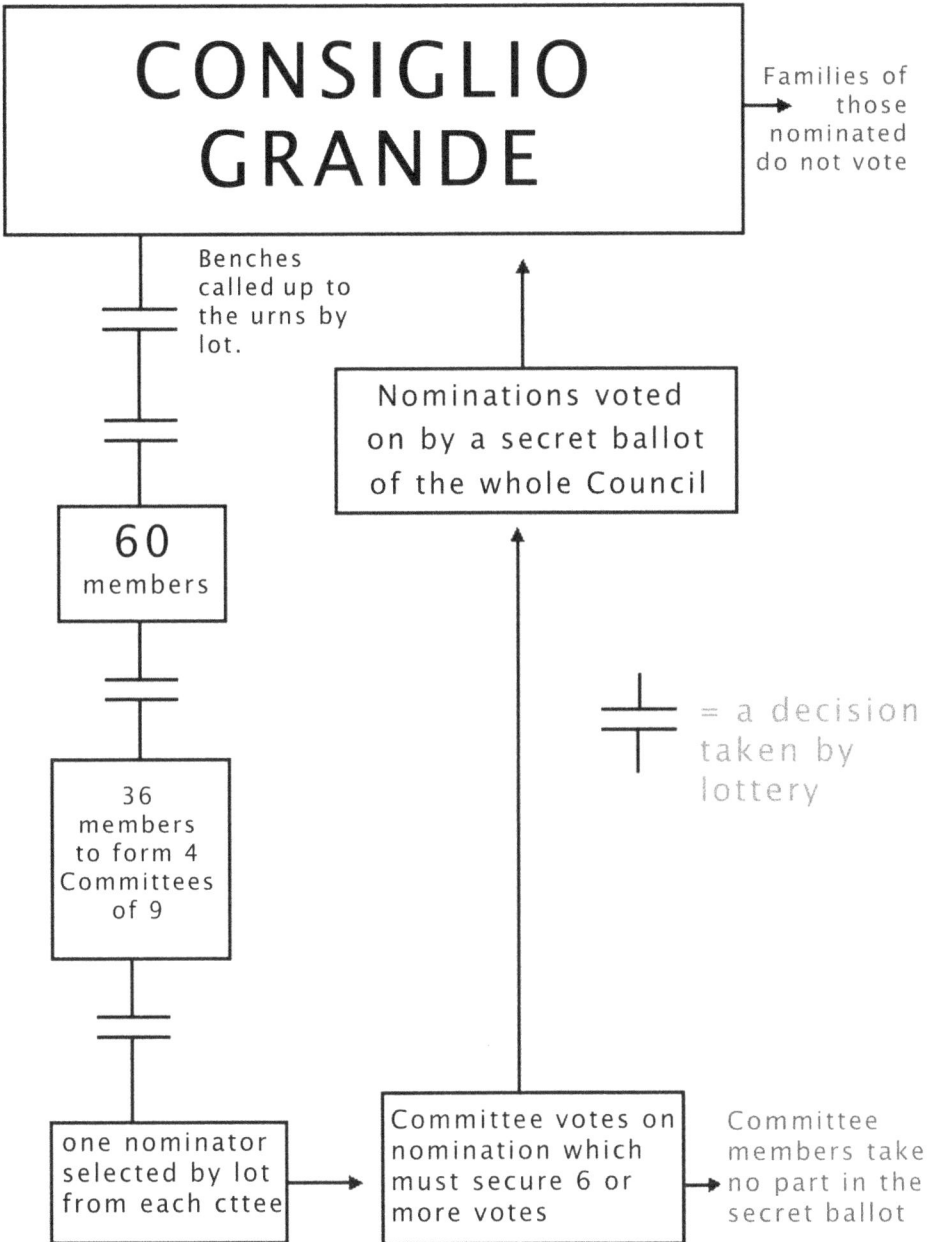

The Venetian system for nominating and electing public officers.
(See pp. 99–105)

Provosts can ask for issues to be considered by the 32, the Senate or the Consiglio by appeal.

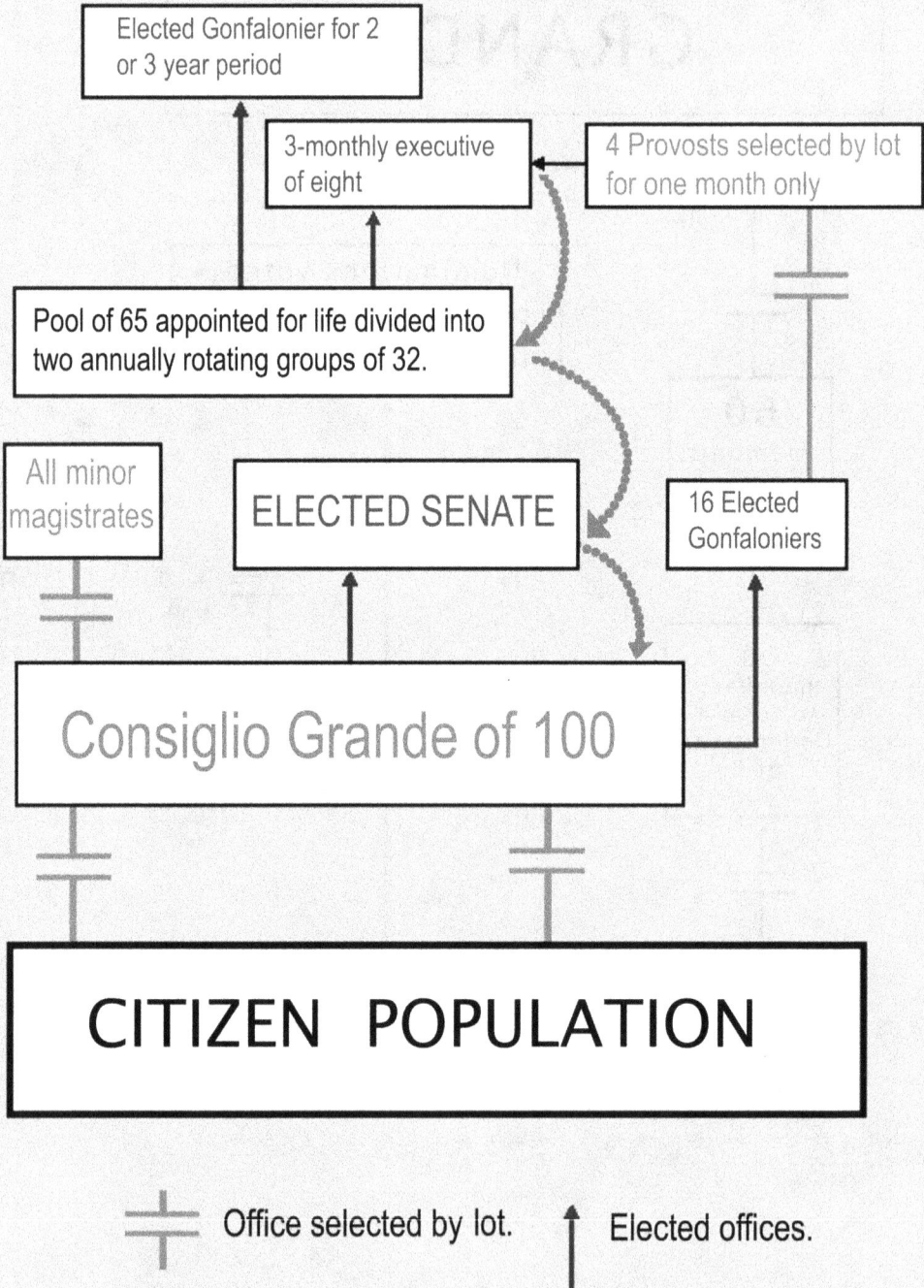

Elected Gonfalonier for 2 or 3 year period

3-monthly executive of eight

4 Provosts selected by lot for one month only

Pool of 65 appointed for life divided into two annually rotating groups of 32.

All minor magistrates

ELECTED SENATE

16 Elected Gonfaloniers

Consiglio Grande of 100

CITIZEN POPULATION

Office selected by lot.   Elected offices.

Diagram showing the structure and balance of Machiavelli's proposed Constitution of Florence from his *Discourse on the Re-modelling of the Government of Florence* of 1520. (See pp.117–123)

In this sense, therefore, we can read the large numbers used in the *dikasterion* as a means by which a higher or better quality of decision-making could be achieved. This embodies the idea that the best approximation to the truth in any given situation is obtained by a complex process of corroborative judgement in which many individual perspectives are brought to bear on the same matter. Because each *dikastes* is randomly selected, each is independent from every other. Their role is strictly *not* to act in concord or unison, but to think and act independently. The Athenian *dikastes* is perhaps the closest embodiment we can find in the political sphere of Chaitin's notion of randomness as complex independence. The decision of each *dikastes* is complex because the randomness of his selection — his disconnection from the others — is preserved throughout the proceedings. It is also complex because, like a randomly-selected number whose value cannot be assumed, predicted or programmed as part of any set or sequence, the single *dikastes* was to act and think independently, and was to make up his mind without referring to, or aligning with, anyone else.

Case study 3: The magistrates

At first sight the case of the selection of magistrates by lot in Ancient Athens seems more complex and contradictory than the case of the *dikastes* or that of the members of the *boule*. Magistracies were specialist administrative posts, and lot would seem an inappropriate means of selection. On closer analysis, however, it fits closely with the pattern established by our consideration of the Kleisthenic reforms: that the primary rationale for the use of sortition was political consolidation. Lot would bring more people into the political process, would present that process as impartial, or non-partisan, and would defend political institutions against factional corruption.

The confusion is caused, in part, by the fact that the measure to transfer the selection of magistrates to a process of pure sortition has become portrayed as a direct attack on the power-base of the aristocratic political caste. This then elicited the defence from the aristocrats that government should be the exclusive domain of those with specialist skills. This sentiment is conveyed in Xenophon's account of the charges against Socrates. Socrates is accused of 'saying how foolish it was to elect the magistrates of a state by beans, when nobody would be willing to take a pilot elected by beans, or an architect, or a flute-player, or a person in any other profession.'[90] It is also to be found in the satirical ramblings of the 'Old Oligarch';[91] and it is deeply implicit in Aristotle's distaste for 'arithmetical equality' — although the case against lot *per se* is not developed in the *Politics*.[92] Aristotle's position on lot is not easy to decipher, however. He seems to use the antipathy between election and lot as a means of exploring the classification of regimes in which lot is securely linked to democracy and election to aristocracy or oligarchy.[93] In Book Four of the *Politics*, therefore, he cites a wide range of mixed forms of lot and election by way of defining his ideal mixed polity.[94] While he mentions that lot was used to prevent electoral intrigue at Heraea, this role does not come into his discussion of sortition.[95] This omission even applies to his consideration of the *dikasterion* in Book Two.[96] From these sources we can see how easy it was for sortition to become identified with a democratic process of arbitrary equalisation and seen as an attack on the notion of merit in government. This, significantly, has had the effect of obscuring its stronger, more practical role in political consolidation.

There are two factors that make a considerable difference to the way that we understand the use of lot to select magistrates in ancient Athens. The first is that from the archaic period until the late fifth century a combination of sortition and election had been used for their selection. The second is that the date for the selection of all magistrates by lot, 403 BCE, places it at the point when democracy was restored after the bloody rule of the Thirty Tyrants.

Hansen gives an account of the gradual incorporation of sortition into the procedures used for selecting magistrates.[97] The account is based on known sources, principally the *Athenian Constitution*. Lot was apparently first used under Dracon but only for the selection of minor magistrates. Solon then introduced a system by which all magistrates, with the exception of the *archons*, were selected by lot from pre-elected pools. In the reforms of Themistokles in 487/6 the nine *archons*, who had previously been elected also became the sub-

[90] Xenophon (1940) p. 7 [*Mem.* I. 29].
[91] This is normally credited to the anonymous 'pseudo-Xenophon'. See Pseudo-Xenophon (1992).
[92] See Aristotle (1946) pp. 258–9 [*Pol.* VI ii 2 and 5] on this specific issue.
[93] *Ibid.* p. 61 [*Pol.* II. vi 19; IV. xiv 10].
[94] *Ibid.* pp. 197–9 [*Pol.* IV. xv 14-22].
[95] *Ibid.* p. 210 [*Pol.* V. iii 9].
[96] *Ibid.* p. 88 [*Pol.* II. xii 3].
[97] Hansen (1999) pp. 49–52.

ject of this process of mixed selection. Pools of ten candidates were elected by each tribe and the nine *archons* and their secretary were then selected by lot from the combined pool of one hundred. Only members of the top two economic classes were eligible for this office. From 403, however, all magistrates (with the exception of those directly elected by the Assembly) were selected by sortition alone. The *archons* were selected by a double sortition by substituting sortition for the election of the pools at tribal level and, in a significant move, the eligibility for this office was extended to the hoplite class.

Hansen is unhappy about the rationale for this sequence, because, he explains, lot is supposed to be '*par excellence* the democratic way of doing things,' and therefore he sees it as unlikely to have been used prior to the advent of democracy in the mid fifth century.[98] Such a sequence would, however, be perfectly compatible with the use of lot to ensure impartiality in the appointment of government office-holders. Furthermore the use of election (which would presumably be based on merit) combined with sortition right up until 403, shows that the question of specific skills and experience was an important consideration. Most magistracies were open to members of the top three classes, but we can surmise that they were invariably held by those with education, experience, free time and local standing. Election would have tended to consolidate the hold of this ruling caste on the magisterial posts, making it difficult for newcomers to gain access to office. The fact that this scheme of mixed selection continued throughout the Periklean age of fifth-century democracy, however, indicates that this was a workable arrangement for aristocrat and democrat alike.

The date at which this method of selection was changed to pure sortition is significant because it shows that it was part of the package of reforms which followed the overthrow of the thirty tyrants. Not only had this short-lived oligarchy been excessively cruel, but it also arose from conspiracy within the administration. In these circumstances we can see the main task of sortition as preventing any repetition of recent events. This, however, is too simplistic a reading of the situation.

While sortition always retained the potential to defend the *polis* by preventing powerful cliques from arising in the administration, when direct sortition was introduced for the magistrates, the changes on the ground might not have been very noticeable. Spe-

---

[98] *Ibid.* p. 50.

cialisation in office was already catered for by means of the directly elected magistrates, and many of the minor offices were regarded more as public chores than high status posts. Thus these posts would have been unlikely to attract large numbers of new volunteers. The drop in the population of Athens after the ravages of war and plague would only have added to this difficulty.

We know that while the immediate followers of the tyrants were executed, an amnesty was instigated to bring the middle ground over into the new regime.[99] We also know that the *dokimasia* was used during this period in the extraordinary but valuable role of preventing those with oligarchic sympathies from holding public office.[100] In these conditions it would have been important to maintain the law-governed integrity of the *polis*, and to do this it would have been necessary to retain experienced magistrates. Lot could therefore have been used *both* to bring more democrats into office, *and* to keep members of the older elites engaged in public life. In both cases the lack of conscious choice inherent in sortition would have served the interests of unity. The *dokimasia*, in front of the Courts, would have guarded the new regime against appointments which might have been considered a genuine threat to the new regime.

From this we can see how Headlam's claim that the use of lot to select magistrates was primarily aimed at preventing alternative power-blocs from forming is correct in a general sense.[101] It takes no account, however, of the ability of lot to moderate the excesses, or possible excesses, of the democrats themselves, or of its capacity to facilitate reconciliation. The ability of sortition to counteract a possible democratic backlash in 403 is a direct consequence of its non-human qualities, which, unlike election, insulate the process against the volatility of the masses.

In support of Headlam's suggestion that there is a certain levelling achieved by the use of sortition I would argue that the one area where this was most keenly felt, is the case of the *archons*.[102] The selection of *archons* by double sortition and the opening up of that office to the *hoplite* class was an important feature of the 403 reforms. Much more than the introduction of lot for the selection of other magistrates, this seems to have been a direct attack on the

[99] Stockton (1990) p. 161.
[100] Adelege (1983).
[101] Headlam (1933) p. 31.
[102] *Ibid.* pp. 152, 171,180.

aristocratic ruling caste and on the status of the ancient office of *archons* — which was essentially that of an elected monarchy. The *areopagos* was made up of ex-*archons*, and although Ephialtes had stripped it of its major powers back in 462, it still existed and performed a number of judicial functions. The office of *archon* and the *areopagos*, as a functioning organ of government, could still have been considered potential dangers to the newly restored democracy.

Moreover, the office itself was one of considerable prestige, status and responsibility; it had been traditionally associated with ability and leadership. The extension of access to this office and the introduction of sortition can therefore be interpreted as nothing other than a move to demote the office itself — or ultimately abolish it by letting it wither on the vine. The introduction of sortition for this office could have been seen in some quarters as a calculated rhetorical insult to the older élite.

To understand the measure fully we need to discern which part of the measure is doing the work — or, from an aristocratic view, doing the damage. In the selection of office-holders there are actually two sets of decisions in operation: the first defines those eligible for office; the second determines what method of selection is to be used to further distinguish between those meeting the first criteria. In the case of the *archons* the decision to extend the eligibility for office should be separated from the decision to use lot to effect the final selection. The former is the measure that actually attacked the ancient office of *archon*, the latter merely the means of making sure that those eligible actually had a chance to serve.

If the aim was to demote or disband the office — and once those of indifferent ability were given equal access, the office would be effectively changed beyond recognition — then there remains a mystery as to exactly why lot was used. The abolition of the office does not, in itself, require an arational process, and the creation of a completely new office, such as a board of Tribunes, or 'Guardians of the Constitution', might have served the purpose more efficiently. To use lot in this way seems gratuitous. The introduction of lot for this office might have been intended as rhetorical statement about the egalitarian intentions of the new regime, but this, again, could be achieved by different, rational, means. We can therefore characterise the application of lot for the express purpose of demoting the status of the *archons* office as a weak, or inappropriate use of the lottery tool.[103]

If, indeed, the democrats *had* used lot for this express purpose, it would have handed a propaganda weapon to the later generation of aggrieved aristocrats by endorsing their portrayal of lot as a blunt instrument for democratic levelling. This confusion of the criteria for the pool and the requirements for the office with the action of the lottery itself, in fact, dominated the subsequent debate on the value of sortition. In the process the more sophisticated potential of sortition to promote unity, impartiality and political stability became obscured.[104]

Conclusion:
political consolidation, lot, and the demos

The extent that lot was used in ancient Athens is unique in the history of politics. It also stands somewhere near the beginning of that history, which only emphasises its importance as a polity-type or paradigm.[105] In this snapshot view of the major institutions of Athens at the end of the fifth century we saw a series of complex organs of government which functioned according to precise rules and procedures and which together constituted an interlocking matrix of authoritative governmental operations. There were checks and balances between different organs of government, strict systems of accountability, and arrangements to ensure that personal influence was constrained. Patterns of power in general were diverse and shifting, rather than concentrated within one distinct locus or in the hands of the few. Politics, the art of the *polis*, was, above all, a public process involving a high level of citizen participation at all levels. It is also important that we understand Athens as a highly rational geo-political military unit, with a distinct administrative and political infrastructure in the *demes* and tribes.[106]

---

[103] Of course there might be some factor which we do not know about which prompted this decision. There is however, another instance of lot used in this way. This was the selection of the secretary of the *boule* which was transferred from election to lot in the 360s, which had the effect of demoting the status of the office. This could have been a response to corruption or factional pressure within the *boule;* it is less obviously rhetorical than the case of the *archons.*

[104] See Hansen (1999) p. 84.

[105] Roberts (1994); Grote (1907); Fisher (1938); Mill (1978); Nilsen (2004) p. 22.

[106] See Murray (1990).

This configuration emerged in a sequence of development or consolidation lasting 150 to 200 years. Throughout this process, the main concern was to preserve political and military unity. One of the major features of this process of consolidation was the gradual rise of the *demos*, or common people of Athens, as an independent political force. This involved, first, an enhanced role for the *hoplite* or *zeugitae* class, and then, later, the incorporation of the *thetes* or urban poor into the running of the *polis*. We can identify three innovative periods of *polis*-building, the first two occurring under the archonships of Solon and Kleisthenes respectively, and the last coming after the restoration of democracy in 403 BCE. Each marked a strengthening of the public organs of government, the institution of public office, and the role of the independent citizen in respect to these. Each step also signified an increased commitment to defend the political process against factional intrigue and potential fragmentation. Throughout this whole period of development and consolidation it is clear that the Athenians were well aware of what could be achieved by the use of lot: its political potential.

Given this view of the Athenian polity, I have sought to reconstruct the motives for the various applications of sortition. This was done by examining the context of each major area of its use with reference to the range of qualities and the potential of the lottery process. My findings in general support the early (i.e., pre fifth century) use of lot for the selection of the *boule*. This reading is based on the idea that the greatest threat to the embryonic *polis* came from *stasis*, or factional civil war, and that the unpredictability and impartiality of sortition made the lottery tool one of the most effective available means of countering that threat. Here a strong use of lot provides a solution to the major problem. This view of lot as a means of consolidating and protecting the political process is distinct from the idea that it is a levelling mechanism exclusively connected with democracy. If its use pre-dates the transfer of sovereignty to the *demos* in 462 (as the sources suggest) then this concurs with our reading of it as a general political measure that contributed to the rise of democracy rather than a measure instituted by democracy merely to serve its own ends.

Kleisthenes used lot in the creation of his new tribal structure. This was a weak, rhetorical use. Nonetheless it shows the potential of sortition to prevent divisions and promote the idea that the polity was a neutral body in respect to partisan divisions: that it belonged to all. A central component in the Kleisthenic reforms was the redefined citizen body. I argue that the use of lot for the selection of members of the *boule* is entirely commensurate with the tenor of these reforms because it has the potential to promote a direct and unmediated relationship between citizen and polity.

The *dikasterion*, or People's Court, was a unique institution that involved mass participation in matters of justice and public interest. The authority of the Courts derived from the number of *dikastai* that sat in each session, but they were also authoritative because they consisted of a special group of randomly-selected citizens charged with making independent judgements. The use of lot was to help ensure their impartiality and their insulation from corruption. Here the blind break operates to prevent wilful interference in the selection process. In an important act of consolidation in the late fifth century, the *nomothetai*, a legislative body organised along the lines of the Courts, was established. This is significant because it indicates a greater reliance on lot-based institutions.

My investigation of the selection of magistrates by lot shows how greater reliance on sortition after 403 BCE could have contributed to the process of reconciliation following the restoration of democracy. As a mechanical means of decision-making, lot would be less subject than direct elections to the temporary volatility of the citizen body in the immediate aftermath of political conflict. The selection of *archons* by lot, on the other hand, seems to be a weak and inappropriate use of lot if the aim was solely to strip this office of its traditional powers.

* * *

How, then, can I sum up the political potential of lot as exemplified by this period of ground-breaking political development in Athens? The focus is invariably drawn back to the historical point where the greatest changes were initiated — that of the Kleisthenic reforms. At this point the *demos* was given, and took, its place as the new force in Athenian politics. The idea that Kleisthenes' new structure and new notion of citizenship *channelled* this new force into the political process is a particularly useful way of thinking about what took place.

This channelling, this infusion of the *demos* with the art of the *polis*, is the point at which political consolidation and nascent democracy became part of the same agenda and were, for all intents and purposes, indivisible. In this process the three most significant characteristics of the Athenian lot-polity — mass citizen participation, the highly organised due process of decision-making, and the impartiality or non-partisanship of the institutions of govern-ment—have their common roots. Sortition was a tool versatile enough to be used to promote all three. Lot was the means by which the participation of the *demos* in government was assured in condi-tions of stability and unity. It was one of a package of measures for defending the rule-governed political process against major and minor corruption, and because it acted impartially it gave authority to the offices and institutions of the new *polis.*

As a fully developed lot-polity the Athenian *polis* is a unique example in European political history. Its fate was to be ignored because what it seemed to stand for—chaotic rule by the poor—was not what was wanted by the political thinkers of later eras. It was, as we have seen, highly rational and organised. When, in the eighteenth and nineteenth centuries, its democratic achievements were recognised, a major means by which they were sustained and defended — the use of lot — was, in the main, ignored. One reason for this must surely be the aristocratic persuasion of the surviving polit-ical literature. It is also probable that lot was in such widespread and successful use that no one thought it worthy of critical examina-tion or positive appraisal.

In terms of its more immediate legacy, the same conditions apply. The use of lot constitutes part of a practical-political, rather than a written political tradition and such traditions are easily disrupted or lost. There is, therefore, a distinct break between Athenian sortition and its later use in medieval Europe. The commune build-ers of the twelfth and thirteenth centuries found their way to lot, not because of what was done in Ancient Athens, but because it solved some of the problems they were engaged upon. This will be the sub-ject of the next chapter.

Bibliographical notes

The primary source materials I used most in the research for this chapter were Aristotle's *Politics* and *The Constitution of Athens* (the *Ath. Pol.*), and the *Histories* of Herodotus. For the *Politics* I used the 1946 translation by Ernest Barker. Barker's introduction was partic-ularly useful in clarifying the political language of Ancient Athens. For the *Ath. Pol.* I used J. M. Moore's 1975 translation and notes, with additional input from Rhodes' commentary and from Day and Chambers (1962). For the Herodotus I used de Selincourt's transla-tion of 1954 but with occasional cross-referencing from Waterfield.

Although not featured in the text, this chapter was informed by Plato's *Laws* and his *Protagoras* dialogue, Aristotle's *Nicomachean Ethics*, Thucydides' *History of the Peloponnesian War*, Pseudo-Xenophon's *The Old Oligarch* and Xenophon's *Memorabilia of Socrates*.

The most valuable secondary source for this chapter was undoubtedly Headlam's *Election by Lot at Athens* (1st edition 1891). Although I challenge his predominantly pro-democratic reading of the use of lot, it remains the only work devoted to the subject. Another important early contribution to the subject is Staveley's 1972 *Greek and Roman Voting and Elections*. These subject-specific works were supplemented by a number of shorter papers and longer studies on discrete areas of the Athenian polity. In the latter category major contributions such as J. S. Traill's 1975 *The Political Organisation of Attica*; Whitehead's study of the demes; the work of Rhodes on the Boule; and the works of MacDowell and Todd on Athenian law should not go unmentioned. In the former category are the important archaeological papers by Dow and Kroll on lottery machines and allotment plaques; Adelege on the *dokimasia*; Lewis, Ostwald and Ober (1990) on Kleisthenes; Hansen (1990) on the Courts and Yunis on the *graphe paranomon*.

Of the general works on Athenian Democracy, Hansen's 1991 (2nd edition 1999) *Athenian Democracy in the age of Demosthenes* provided my first port of call on most matters, but this was supplemented by a number other studies. Of particular value were Forrest (1966), Sinclair (1988) and Stockton (1990). I found Ehrenberg's 1968 *From Solon to Socrates* to be thoughtful and steady, and Hignett's early account a valuable foil to more conservative views of Athenian democracy.

I was fortunate to attend a series of lectures by Oswyn Murray on the social and economic life of Ancient Athens and share his view of the significance of Kleisthenes expressed in 'Cities of Reason'.

Chapter Three

The 'Brevia' and the 'Scrutiny'

Two lottery schemes from Late-Medieval and Renaissance Italy

In this chapter we enter the very different political landscape of the communes of late medieval and early renaissance Italy. Compared to the relative stability of Ancient Athens, with its long-lasting laws and structures, this period is characterised by rapid regime change, situations of dual power and factional turmoil. Out of this flux, numerous experimental governmental variants began to emerge, based on practical experience mixed with the remnants of classical legal theory. These then coalesced into a smaller number of longer-lasting models of workable communal government. Within this context, lot is used in a variety of different institutions and procedures—often in response to difficult and changing circumstances.

The *brevia* was a form of lot-generated indirect election in which a small group of electors were selected by lot. It became the main form of election in the northern Italian communes during the twelfth and thirteenth centuries and was used by the *popolo* regimes during the thirteenth century, sometimes in the form of selecting nominators, rather than electors, by lot. This latter arrangement was adopted by Venice and used successfully there until the late eighteenth century. The *scrutiny*—correctly called the *scrutiny* and the *tratte*—is found in the fourteenth century. By this time there were fewer republican governments in the area, and the dominant governmental form was the powerful individual ruler or *signore*. The *scrutiny* is mainly found in the relatively few cities that did *not* follow this line. Significantly, it was used in Florence for over one hundred years between 1328 and 1434. Similar schemes were practised in Orvieto, Siena, Pistoia,

Perugia and Lucca.[1] The *scrutiny* is the inversion of the *brevia* and consists of regular random drawings from a pre-elected pool. It was usually used for high-ranking magistrates in a strict, but usually very short, rotational cycle.

While we can learn much by contrasting the two models in terms of their effectiveness as lottery-based schemes, we can learn more about the political potential of sortition if we also understand the respective contexts in which each operated. In particular it helps us if we try to classify the type of government that each sets out to serve. This revolves around two main questions: who was involved, and what were their political objectives. In this respect the *brevia* presents us with a far clearer picture than does the later *scrutiny*. This is because the communal regimes in which it was used correspond in many ways to a straightforward ideal of an open, inclusive government committed to the rule of law and espousing a notion of the common good. Moreover, the problems encountered on the road to political consolidation in this new political landscape broadly resemble those encountered by the Athenian *polis*. These can be summed up as the need to forge a single unified political structure and the need to establish authoritative institutions and procedures with which to govern. The use of sortition to guarantee impartiality and freedom from electoral corruption fits easily and logically into this framework.

These aims are not absent from the series of regimes that together constitute the First Florentine Republic of the fourteenth and early fifteenth centuries. Our understanding of how the lottery-based scheme of the *scrutiny* operated within this context is, however, complicated by a number of factors. To begin with it was not designed as a lottery scheme *per se*. Secondly, it is inherently complex as a scheme and involved several rounds of election by different appointed and co-opted groupings the make up of which became the subject of incessant wrangling and frequent revision. Thirdly, it is far less of a public process than the *brevia*. The draw, for example, was not carried out in public, and the identity of those elected to go into the draw remained hidden from all but a small

---

[1] For Ovieto see Waley (1952) p. 147; for Siena see Bousky (1981) p. 60; for Pistoia see Herlihy (1967) p. 222; for Perugia see Blanshei (1976) p. 58; for Lucca see Meek (1978) p. 8. and (1980) p. 25. Siena and Lucca employed a different variant of the Florentine model. In this chapter I concentrate on the Florentine version of the scheme.

group of secretaries.[2] Fourthly the scheme itself was not formulated in order to develop a strong relationship between the governing and the governed in the wider political community; rather it served the purpose of making government possible within a relatively tight-knit ruling elite.

This chapter, therefore follows two separate stories: a broad account of the role of the *brevia* in the consolidation of communal government, and a narrative of how the *scrutiny* was instigated and operated in Florence during the fourteenth and early fifteenth centuries. I end with a comparison between the *brevia* and the *scrutiny* in which I assess what they bring to their respective political communities.

The *brevia* in its political context

To understand the *brevia* in its political context we need to look first at the process of commune-building that took place right across Europe in the late mediaeval period, then at the major problem of factionalism that beset the early communes in northern Italy.[3] Before looking at some of the lottery-based schemes of the period I introduce the reader to the *popolo*: the northern Italian regime type that was the natural home of the *brevia*.

Commune-building in the twelfth and thirteenth centuries

The revitalising of city life in feudal Europe between the eleventh and thirteenth centuries is of considerable political importance. Its driving force was a scale of mercantile and organised artisan activity not witnessed since the collapse of the Roman Empire. This meant that new legal and government institutions had to be forged to facilitate this activity. This was, above all a period of great political consolidation, and the leading agency in that consolidation was a new emerging mercantile class.

As this new social and economic class sought new laws to enable, for example, the alienation of property and the loosening of the ties

---

[2] The Italian word, *squizzione*, which furnishes us with the English term 'scrutiny', literally means 'secrecy' and applies to the first stage of the process — the secret ballot to produce the main pool.

[3] It is worth noting that delegates to the Curia and Cortes of Castille and Leon were chosen by lot from their municipalities in the late fourteenth century. (O'Callaghan, 1975, p. 586). There are possibly other areas outside of Italy where lot was regularly used. We should also be wary of viewing sortition as an exclusively republican phenomenon since it is found in other municipal and communal environments during this period.

of serfdom, they inevitably came into conflict with the older feudal and ecclesiastical elites. The protracted animosity between the feudal nobility — mainly based in the countryside — and the developing burgher class of the towns is a constant theme during this period and took many forms. In northern Europe the independent towns, for the most part, co-existed with the older nobility, and enjoyed the stability afforded by the strong monarchies. In northern Italy, however, direct control by the legal sovereigns of Pope and Empire was weak and the towns became, *de facto*, autonomous or self-governing. But this also meant that they became more vulnerable to hostile alliances of neighbouring states or the ambitions of feudal strongmen. Questions of internal order and organisation, therefore, became critical and we can characterise the process of consequent political consolidation as one of 'invention under duress'. It was a search for stable and settled forms of government often in conditions of volatility and instability.

Without doubt the primary consideration of the new towns was defence, and one of the first great communal acts was the building of the city walls. Defence, however, also meant the defence of the new social order. We can think of the cities in their early days as liberated zones in which new conditions and new political relationships were established. Because there was no serfdom in the new urban settlements they became known as 'free' towns. They were also law-governed communities in which peace prevailed. This again was recognised in the rhetoric of the new towns which emphasised the importance of the 'pax villae' along with the 'lex villae'.[4]

One of the key moments of political consolidation in these communities was the swearing of an oath of allegiance by all its inhabitants. These oaths would normally commit the inhabitants to obey the town's laws and respect the sovereignty of its magistrates.[5] This act of solidarity and obligation was primarily aimed at ensuring the integrity of the new legal and political entity. But it also reveals how the major movers, the mercantile elite, relied on the co-operation of the body of citizens. In general this fostered a spirit of inclusiveness and a certain level of formal political equality. *Cives*, or town-dwellers, were equal before the law, offices were rotated amongst the able citizens, endorsement for actions and appointments was regularly

[4]   Pirenne (1925) pp. 208–9.
[5]   See Tabacco (1989) p. 184. There is also evidence (Previte-Orton, 1926, p. 221) of boycotts against those who refused to be part of this 'sworn association'.

sought from the assembly, and the *cives* would be expected to contribute by upholding the law and voting for officers.

In the first instance the government of the new community was
undertaken by a group of 'law-worthy' men often known as the *boni*
homines, who formed a regularly instituted executive body. Their
collective title indicates that these were to be men picked primarily
on account of their virtue — not on account of their title or birth.
However, they would normally have been chosen from the higher
echelons of mercantile society where their 'worthiness' could be
assessed in material terms. Invariably they were men of sufficient
education and standing to speak on behalf of their communities, but
their title suggests that they were to be seen as the legal equals of the
rest of their community.

As internal judicial power began to transfer to the *boni homines*
from the previous feudal or ecclesiastical authorities the embryonic
governmental grouping also began to speak for the town in their
external negotiations with other political bodies. This was a gradual
process and often involved periods of combined authority when the
new communal laws and the older ecclesiastical laws would operate side by side. At this later stage we begin to see the main officers
of these new political communities referred to as *Consuls*, following
classical precedent. Consuls were appointed for a fixed period and
the social class from which they were drawn was often specified. A
quota of non-noble consuls was often considered to be important as
a means of promoting unity. Although nominated or selected by
smaller groups, the *boni homines* and consuls had to be endorsed by
the town assembly, an institution which had political status but
invariably no remit to initiate measures or discuss issues.[6]

The complexities of municipal politics, however, soon meant that
this simple form of endorsed leadership was augmented by a larger
deliberative body or council. Some of these were very large, involving more than 600 members, and sometimes another smaller and
more select council would also be constituted.[7] These large councils
with their smaller more select committees seem to mark an attempt
to fuse the idea of consent present in the earlier assembly format
with a concept of efficient collective decision-making which necessarily involved fewer voices.

---

[6]   Waley (1988) pp. 32–6; Previte Orton (1926) p. 232
[7]   Waley (1988) p. 37 also cites the 1254 grand Council of Verona as having
      1,285 and Modena as having 1600 in 1306.

Internal strife and the need for impartiality

The problem of internal strife in Italian cities during this period should not be underestimated. In the twelfth and thirteenth centuries these mainly took the form of family vendettas and feuds which often amounted to continuous open warfare and posed huge public order problems.[8] The major families had vast retinues and private armies and their internal political organisations even included enforceable penal codes. Blood-feuds and vendettas were commonplace and it was deemed dishonourable for any party to appeal to the communal authorities for justice. Another way that factional rivalry manifested itself was in the form of the *consortieri*, or tower society.[9] These were sworn associations of families and their supporters who would erect tall towers within the city area. The towers were not only visible status symbols but were also used for fighting against rival *consortieri*.

These problems were exacerbated by the tendency in Italy for the descendants of feudal knights to stay in the cities rather than the countryside, and to pay scant attention to the system of laws that were being established there. In 1281 we have the first evidence of the use of the term 'magnate' to describe such people. It refers to a citizen who was legally required to post security for their good behaviour.[10] Local factionalism was also intensified by the region-wide conflict between cities of a Guelf or Papal persuasion and those who supported the Ghiberline or Imperial faction. In practice, however, internal splits tended to follow pre-existing fault lines.

A unique regional remedy for the problem of factional unrest was the office of *podesta*. The *podesta* was a temporary head of state brought in from another city. This type of office probably grew out of the use of external mediators to solve factional disputes. In the early part of the thirteenth century, before the universal adoption of this form of nominal head of government, magistrates from another town or a senior member of the church could be called upon in times of deadlock for the sole purpose of choosing chief magistrates.[11]

The *podesta* would usually be employed by the commune under contract and would swear to abide by its laws and serve its general

[8] Davidsohn (1896) p. 368 uses the term *Kriegswesen* — urban warfare.
[9] Tabacco (1989) p. 224; Waley (1988) pp. 122–31.
[10] Becker (1967) p. 5. See also Lansing (1991); Waley (1988) pp. 118–31.
[11] Wolfson (1899) pp. 7–8.

interests.[12] He would be accountable to the communal authorities
and could be removed if he violated his terms of employment. Great
care was taken in the choice of *podesta* and lot was often used alongside voting at council or consular levels to make sure that the
appointment was not seen as orchestrated by a faction or clique.[13]
It seems, however, that confidence in the *podesta* was not always
easy to maintain, and even when lot was used to choose between a
final pool of candidates, suspicions of collusion remained. There
are also instances of more than one *podesta* being employed, each
appointed by a different body or section of the citizenry.[14] The phenomenon of the *podesta* is important to our study because it shows
how serious the problem of factional discord had become, and
demonstrates the importance of the search for impartial sources of
authority as a means of countering it.[15]

The popolo

Despite such measures, continual crises of authority occurred in the
vast majority of Italian communes. The perceived need to defend
such inclusive political institutions that existed against the threat of
arbitrary rule by a single ruler, and the need to enforce the public
peace against warring families, prompted the emergence of the
form of popular political society known as the *popolo*. These were
mass organisations with their own membership, officers, statutes,
laws and militias. The *popolo* usually took the role of an alternative
form of government, exercising jurisdiction amongst their membership and in areas of the city where they had established hegemony.[16]
A *popolo* might form a governing alliance with a communal government, or merely co-exist with it in a situation of dual power.
J.C. Koenig states that 'The final goal of the *popolo* was perforce to
take control of the commune and to reconstitute it. As part of this
offensive, the people … sought to have its laws recognised as
communal laws.'[17]

   Although a *popolo* would be led by members of the mercantile and
banking fraternity, it would not be coterminous with that social

---

[12] Waley (1988) pp. 40–5; Kohl and Andrews-Smith (1995) p. 165.
[13] Koenig (1977) p. 607.
[14] *Ibid.* p. 607; 531, Pelavinco had two; 217, Brescia had three in 1260.
[15] See Manin (1997) p. 52.
[16] In Vicenza, for example, citizens were required to take two oaths, one to the
      popolo and the other to the Commune. Koenig (1977) p. 55. See also pp. 221–2
      for Milan; pp. 255–34 for Brescia.
[17] *Ibid.* p. 242.

group, and would have widespread support from lesser merchants, tradespeople and skilled artisans. As such the *popolo* can be described as the voice of the commoners, in contrast to that of the older nobility.[18] In general the *popolo* movements supported equal application of the law, wide participation in electoral practices and a strong working relationship between government and guilds. The *Capitano del Popolo* was usually responsible for internal order and the safety of all citizens and had command of the civil militia.[19] In cities where the *popolo* had taken power, the supreme governing body was usually of twelve or so members, with an office rotation of between two and six months.[20] These were known as the *Anziani* or elders. While we would be broadly correct in thinking of the *popolo* as a form of early political party, they did not act in a pluralist electoral environment.[21] In the context of factional ravages, lawless *milites*, and the constant threat of despotism, *popolo* societies saw themselves as the only party capable of delivering civic peace and inclusive non-partisan government.[22]

As a general observation, the cities in this region were divided between those under *popolo* governments, and those under the control of a single *signore* or a tightly-knit family dynasty. The popular regimes were, on the whole, committed to open, participatory government, often using guild structures to facilitate this. [23] They were constantly on the defensive, however, and frequently lost power

---

[18] *Ibid*. p. 18. Note also that during this period unskilled workers would tend to side with the nobility, especially in the countryside. See Bucker (1968) pp. 255, 326; Heywood (1910) p. 34.

[19] The first *Popolo* government in Florence in 1250 organised an internal militia force to this end. See Villani (1908) pp. 189–92; Davidsohn (1896) p. 368.

[20] Waley (1988) p. 135.

[21] Often quotas were agreed between commune and *popolo* to fill public offices This effected a form of pluralism which was really a compromise or stand-off situation. See Koenig (1977) pp. 40, 72; Waley (1988) p. 136.

[22] The official documents from the *popolo* governments are replete with the rhetoric of non-partisanship. See Koenig (1977) pp. 250–1, 256, 584, 619; and Waley (1988) p. 132. The claim by Bartolus of Sassoferrato that the only legitimate party is one that seeks to secure the general good is clearly referring to the *popolo*. See Bartolus of Sassoferrato (1997) p. 6. The comment by J.K. Hyde that the '… triumph of the *popolo* … marked everywhere a revolution of the first magnitude in the life of the Italian cities' needs to be taken seriously. Hyde (1973) p. 115. While Hyde sees this as 'democratic' in a modern sense, it should also be seen as revolutionary in a republican sense – in terms of how it advanced the development of public institutions of government.

[23] On the importance of the Guilds see Becker (2002) p. 54.

soon after they had acquired it. Often the upper members of a town's mercantile elite would opt for a *signore* as a respite from this general level of insecurity. This invariably meant that the former members of the *popolo* would then form an unofficial opposition to the status quo.

Because they are the natural home of the *brevia* and other forms of selection by lottery, these *popolo* regimes and movements are important to our understanding of how and why lot was used. They present us with a very particular model of inclusive political development, one that championed the general good and in so doing took a strong line against factional activity and arbitrary tyrannical rule. We can think of them as forming the practical exemplar out of which the ideas of the northern Italian jurists and early republican thinkers developed.[24] Their high level of citizen involvement, links with the guilds and their complete absence of anything resembling an official political party distinguishes them instantly from modern representative forms of government. While not usually referred to as 'republican', their championing of open inclusive government makes them more republican in spirit than many later regimes that bear that name.

The brevia as a form of indirect election

We can think of the mechanisms for popular election during this period as developing through several stages. Each new mechanism is either an improvement on its predecessor or a response to its problems as they became apparent. The use of the open assembly to endorse the selection of consuls was probably the first stage; this was followed by indirect elections of consuls and other officers by a small group of appointed electors. A development of this was the *brevia*, in which the electors were chosen by lot. The final form was a combination of lot and election in which nominators were chosen by lot and elections for those nominees held by secret ballot.

The universal adoption of indirect election in the late twelfth and early thirteenth century in northern Italy indicates that there were problems with the running of direct elections in the town assemblies. We can guess that they were open to corruption or intimidation or that they constantly threatened to descend into chaos. On the other hand the inclusive ethos of the early commune would have been undermined if officials had merely been appointed by existing

---

[24] See Skinner (1978).

or outgoing office-holders. Indirect election, therefore, represented a compromise — but a useful one.[25]

An indirect election in the form of an electoral college enabled deliberation on the suitability of candidates to take place, and the choice of electors on a quota basis from different quarters of the town or city prevented parochial cliques from dominating the public bodies. Electors were also asked to swear that they would act as independent individuals and not enter into contracts with other parties concerning their choice of candidates. The practice of isolating electors in a conclave until they reached their decision also emerged at this time.[26] Initially very small groups of electors were used. Wolfson notes that during the late twelfth century Genoa used six consistently, and Parma and Pisa three. Later, with the introduction of lot and the secret ballot, numbers advance to twenty, thirty or even forty.[27] There is no indication in Wolfson's account that the office of elector was anything other than a compulsory duty required of those selected. The special role of the elector with its weighty responsibilities would have been discredited if those chosen could have simply declined to take part.

The use of lot in indirect elections was a natural extension of these earlier practices and for at least half of the thirteenth century the *brevia* seems to have been the sole means for filling government offices.[28] It was essentially a public means of guaranteeing that electors were not chosen because of their known affiliations, but it also remade the link between those making the electoral choices and the general body of citizens or guild members from which they were drawn. Elaborate procedures were devised to demonstrate that the

---

[25] Wolfson (1988) p. 9. To explain the process Wolfson cites the example of Vicenza where the *podesta* and council chose five men from each quarter of the city every year to act as an electoral college for the Council of 400, for which 100 were chosen from each quarter of the city. A smaller council of 40 was chosen by similar means with two electors from each quarter constituting the college.

[26] Note the similarity to a modern jury, and to papal elections.

[27] As many as 550 were used in Lucca in 1308. Meek (1978) pp. 188–9. Blanshei (1976) p. 58, notes that in Perugia the number increases from ten to thirty between 1279 and 1285.

[28] Wolfson (1899) p. 11. How early in the process of commune-building lot was used for the selection of officers is not totally clear. Pirenne suggests that it was there at the beginning, but Wolfson's suggestion that it was introduced to the northern Italian communes in the late twelfth or early thirteenth century to inhibit the influence of armed retainers at open assembly votes seems a more likely interpretation.

process was free from manipulation. According to the statutes of Bologna of 1245–50, lots were drawn from a cap by a small boy in front of the assembled guildsmen to select electors for the city's special councillors.[29] In Parma much the same process took place, but two caps were used instead of one and those selected had to leave the room once their name had been called. The Parma statutes also make it plain that the purpose of lot was to avoid damaging rivalries (*ad evitandum contentiones* …).[30] The relationship of the use of lot to the 'displacement' of choice characteristic of indirect elections is illustrated by the example of Ivrea, where those first chosen by lot were then required to pass on that lot to a second person who would then act as elector.[31] In Brescia black and white lots were used and two Dominican and two Minorite friars acted as tellers.[32] In all instances it is clear that the drawing of lots was an open public event designed to be witnessed, either by the citizen body in assembly or by members of a more select group such as councillors or guild members. As a general rule, before taking their vote, the electors would be required to take oaths to the effect that the choice they made was their own and that they had not taken bribes. Often it was stipulated that no office-holders should be present while voting took place. In line with the ethos of public transparency and impartiality evidenced by these measures, the statutes invariably demanded that the election be held immediately after the electors had been chosen and sworn in.[33] This is an important aspect of the process. In the *brevia* chance and deliberation were regarded as two distinct parts of the same process of selection, which had a clear beginning, middle and end.

We can presume from Wolfson's research on twelfth- and thirteenth-century statutes that all posts that were deemed contestable would have been filled by means of the *brevia*. This would include membership of the councils (except the very large councils whose membership was hereditary), consuls, the *podesta*, and other officers such as diplomatic representatives.[34] It is not always clear from some of the descriptions, however, whether the pool from which these electors were drawn consisted of the general citizen body or

---

[29] *Ibid.*
[30] Quoted in Wolfson (1899) p. 12.
[31] *Ibid.* p. 10.
[32] *Ibid.* p. 12.
[33] *Ibid.*
[34] Hyde (1973) p. 115. See Finlay (1980) p. 41, on how the Venetian Assembly became a hereditary council in 1297

members of a particular group such as councillors or guild members. If a number of electors were drawn from a particular quarter of their city, for instance, just who would have been considered eligible and who would have been excluded? The concept of citizenship in the commune was not as precisely developed as in the ancient Greek *polis*. Eligibility to the pool from which electors were drawn was probably limited to those who paid taxes, belonged to a recognised guild or owned property.[35] It is unlikely that the poorest members of the community would have taken part since they would have been considered vulnerable to corruption. Servants were also regarded as unreliable because they were not independent of their masters. There is, however, some evidence that members of the artisan class served on high executive bodies such as consulates, *priorates* or *anziani*.[36] Citizen participation in government and administration increased dramatically during this period, especially on a part-time, paid basis.[37]

The example of the election of twelve *anziani* for the *popolo* government of Vicenza in 1264 shows us some of the complexities of communal elections during the thirteenth century. Eight *Anziani* were elected from the guilds and four from the townspeople, one from each quarter. The guild members were selected by the master of each of the eight guilds submitting four names of good and true men from his guild. From this pool of thirty-two, eight *Anziani*, one from each guild, were to be chosen. The division was to be made '*cum busolis ad ballotas.*'[38] This early reference to Venetian style *bussoli* or balloting urns indicates that this vote would have been by secret ballot.

The remaining four *Anziani* were to be elected from the four quarters of the town. This involved the selection of two electors from each quarter, made by lot by the sitting Council. These electors would nominate four candidates, each from their respective quarters. These would then go forward for a final vote. This follows the common form of the *brevia* where lot was used to choose nominators. There are indications that ballot boxes of some sort were used in Vicenza during this period, and it is possible that the final votes would have taken place in the quarter assemblies with ballot boxes used to prevent intimidation or other forms of corruption.

[35] Waley (1988) p. 65.
[36] Heywood (1910) p. 28.
[37] Najemy (1982) p. 6; Hyde (1973) p. 107; Waley (1988) pp. 64–8.
[38] Wolfson (1899) p. 19.

The *popolo* government in Vicenza followed twenty-three years of rule by the *signore* Ezzelino III. One of its aims, one presumes, would have been to prevent the rise of another *signore*. To this effect the constitution is clearly designed to create a balance between different portions of the civic population in the composition of the *Anziani* group, and between different methods of choice: personal recommendation from the elected guild masters, sortition, and the popular vote. The preponderance of guild members (we should note that probably only the higher guilds were involved) was presumably to limit the influence of local nobility in the town, and thus to err on the side of corporate stability.

In this short account of the *brevia* in its context I have given some indication of the struggle to establish the rule of law, public political process and impartial norms of government that took place during the commune building period. In pursuit of this last ideal, necessity seems to have been the mother of invention. While the measures that were tried were not always successful, their accumulated effect, coupled with the inventive zeal with which they were applied, meant that the communes ultimately prevailed as workable political entities. Within this context, election of lot was used in a variety of forms and contexts, and was part of a general movement of ideas and practices which sought to establish politics: the art of the city, as an essentially public process. Its specific role was to protect the electoral process from corruption — from whatever quarter. I will be looking more closely at how the *brevia* operated in the final part of the chapter.

The Florentine *scrutiny* and its political context

We now turn to a very different lottery scheme, the *scrutiny* and *tratte* system that developed in Florence in the early fourteenth century and was the major form of selection there for over one hundred years. To understand how it operated we have to look at how it was initiated and the problems it purported to address. We also have to have a clear idea about what sort of regime was developing in Florence during this time and how the *scrutiny* served its ends. The key date for our purposes is 1328, when the scheme itself was drawn up and instigated. Our story has to begin earlier, however, so that we can consider the struggles that led up to the new constitution and look at a number of similar proposals and short-lived procedures that were made during the latter part of the thirteenth century and the early years of the fourteenth. We also need to see how the scheme fared during the remainder of the First Florentine Republic and how it was adapted to meet changing pressures and circumstances. This section of the chapter therefore consists of a description of the 1328 procedure sandwiched between two historical narratives. The first of these takes us up to the point of the scheme's introduction and includes a brief contextual discussion on the nature of Florentine government and its ruling class. The second covers some of the key points of the years from 1328 to 1443. I end this with a brief description of how the Medici came to power, and how they adapted the process to suit their own ends.

Florentine government up to 1328

Florence in the twelfth and thirteenth century followed a line of political development typical of most cities in the region. The Commune was founded in 1138. It had a 200-strong Council and an assembly or *parlamento* of all citizens. It suffered a period of extreme civil disorder in the late 1170s caused by a deep and bitter feud between two major families, the Uberti and the Donati. The first *podesta* was installed in 1202 and the split between Guelf and Ghibelline factions took place in the city in 1216. As with most Italian communes of the thirteenth century, Florence had a period in which it was ruled by a popular government. This was known as the *Primo Popolo* and it held power from 1250 to 1260. Under this administration a popular militia was established to maintain the rule of law. Significantly the *popolo* refused to take sides in the long-running dispute between the Pope and Empire. In 1260 the Ghibellines, with Sienese support, overthrew the *Primo Popolo* and established a pro-imperial order.[39] The next twenty-two years were marked by a succession of governments. These included, a brief popular government, a period under the papal protectorate of the Duke of Anjou, and finally a government sponsored by the papacy which consisted of a highly contrived executive of 14[40] based on a system of monthly rotation.[41] This ended in 1282.

In 1292 a popular guild-based regime was responsible for passing the 'Ordinances of Justice'.[42] This was a measure that denied all

[39] See Stephens (1983) p. 46, for popular governments overthrown by foreign intervention. Stephens (1983) p. 5, regards foreign policy as a major determining factor in the development of the Florentine polity.
[40] Eight Guelfs plus six Ghibellines.
[41] Najemy (1982) p. 18.
[42] Najemy (1982) p. 45. Plus Kohl and Andrews-Smith (1995) p. 139.

magnates the right to hold office and it is important because it finally enabled the new mercantile elite to remove the factious and lawless remnants of the feudal aristocracy from the Florentine body politic. Under the government of 1292 the peace of the city was to be enforced by a new office, the *Gonfalonier of Justice*, who was the chief officer of a thousand-man security force.

By the late 1290s opposition to the Ordinances came into the open, however, with battle lines drawn between the White Guelfs, who supported the Ordinances, and Black Guelfs, who opposed them. The rivalry was bitter and destructive and the final victory of the Black Guelfs in 1301 was achieved through their alliance with the French prince Charles de Valois. By the time of his entrance into Florence, however, guild power had seriously ebbed away leaving the White Guelfs — the popular party — seriously exposed. The victory of the Black Guelfs is a significant turning point in the internal politics of Florence. Although the Ordinances were not repealed it indicates that the ruling elite based on the higher mercantile and banking families had made a working arrangement with the magnates to oppose any return to popular republicanism.[43] It also alerts us to one of the most important factors in the story of the First Florentine Republic, the nature of the *popolani* and their rise to prominence.

The popolani

The political environment of Florence between 1260 and the fall of the First Republic to the Medici in 1434 is dominated by the rise of the *popolani*. This term refers to men of non-noble descent who owed their high civic status to their success as merchants or bankers. Although the ascendancy of this class came as a result of their leadership of the *popolo* movement of the mid twelfth century — which favoured broad, participatory government — by the fourteenth century this class faced in two directions. On the one hand they aligned with the older nobility, often by marriage, in what Becker perceptively calls a 'quasi-fused patriciate'.[44] On the other they vigorously opposed the lawlessness of many magnate families, and for this reason sought the co-operation of the middle strata of Florentine society to help establish law-governed norms of government and public behaviour. Within the ranks of the *popolani* there was also a discernible tension between loyalty to the family — the basic unit of organi-

---

[43] The magnates were not allowed back into power, however.
[44] Becker (2002) p. 100.

sation of the mercantile elite—and loyalty to the wider political entity of the commune or city state. This accounts for many of the particular features of Florentine governmental institutions.

Florentine political life therefore operated between two sets of polarities. The general interest, exemplified in the governmental institutions and procedures, stood in opposition to the sectional interest of the major *popolani* families. At the same time those outside the select ruling group, many supporters of the ideals of the earlier *popolo*, constantly sought to take a greater share in the workings of the body politic. Thus we see in Florence during this period a vacillation between what we can describe as popular regimes, in which participation in public office reaches down into the middle guilds, and governments of a more oligarchic complexion in which the patriciate closed ranks. The governmental centre of gravity, however, remained throughout with the high *popolani*, and can be closely identified with the *Mercanzia*, a group consisting of the consuls of the top five mercantile and banking guilds.

Mention also has to be made of a unique and important arrangement known as the *Monte* that operated in Florence during the latter part of this period. Essentially this consisted of loans made to the city by private individuals at a high rate of interest. Introduced in 1345 to overcome shortfalls in tax-generated public finances, the *Monte* 'dominated the formation of public policy' in the city.[45] It is significant to our inquiry into the use of sortition because it gave the most powerful families, and those aspiring to that status, an economic stake in the collective fortunes of the city. In these conditions public office in Florence was regarded as a means of social advancement rather than an onerous duty. Selection for the *Signoria*, the highest executive body, and becoming a contributor to the *Monte* were both recognisable steps in the progress of the upwardly mobile.

The frequent changes in the criteria for political participation meant that there was no clear sense of a citizen's entitlement, however. Unlike the Athenian category of citizenship, which was a vertical division including both rich and poor, nearly all political participation in Florence was organised in terms of the horizontal guild categories.[46] This left many excluded, and it was a recognised

---

[45] Becker (1968) p. 158. Becker devotes a full chapter to the operations of the *Monte* (pp. 151–200).

[46] This was a general characteristic of the communes and city republics of this period.

part of the political culture that the poor and manual workers, such as workers in the weaving trade, would regularly take to the streets to demand redress for their grievances. Popular governments were introduced in 1343 and 1378 as a result of such direct action.

Florentine governmental institutions

The institutions and procedures of the Florentine commune should be seen as reflections of these struggles. There was, however, no Kleisthenes, no great rational plan to sweep out the old and replace it with the new. There was no citizen solution. Such was the balance between different entrenched interest groups that it was easier to retain outmoded institutions and practices and strip them of their power by stealth than to risk drastic change. The result was an unwieldy, 'portmanteau' organic form of government, often of intense complexity, that grew here and shrank there in response to the interests and aspirations of the groupings within the body politic.

The primary need was for compromise and power-sharing, and the major organ by which this was achieved was the rotating executive council or *Signoria*. In 1282 a new executive magistracy of six *priors* (one from each *sesto* or sixth part of the city) was established. Its personnel were to be changed every two months. Together with the *Gonfalonier of Justice* they became known as the *Signoria*.[47] This grouping was the highest concentration of power in the polity. They alone were responsible for initiating legislation, but also had responsibility for the formulation of policy, the appointment of many offices and elective bodies, intervention in jurisdiction and the implementation of foreign policy.[48] The basic constitutional framework of the two-monthly *priorate* proved to be a lasting formula and remained relatively unaltered for over 200 years. Closely linked to the *Signoria* were the two advisory councils, the sixteen *Gonfalonieri* of the Companies who were selected from the different sectors of the civic militia, and the twelve *Buoni Uomini*. We should also be aware of the Florentine habit of holding wide consultative debates or *pratiche*. These would usually be called by the *Signoria*,

---

[47] A slightly later addition of 1293. By the mid fourteenth century the number of *Priors* was increased to eight.

[48] Brucker (1962) pp. 64–5; Najemy (1982) pp. 27–9.

who would also decide who would take part.[49] The *Signoria* also had the remit to appoint other bodies or special commissions. Thus most Florentine politics followed the 'descending' principle, whereby the less powerful governmental groupings were chosen by the more powerful.

The origins of the scrutiny

We have evidence that sortition was understood as an option for selecting officers in the popular Florentine regimes prior to 1328. Debates on the form of government in 1292 reveal that a proposal was made by the poet Guido Orlandi for the twelve guild consuls to nominate three candidates from each *sesto* for the *Signoria*, and that the final choice should be made from these by lot.[50] This indicates that a constitution similar to that of the Vicenza *popolo* was being considered, with lot used as a means of breaking the monopoly of power that would otherwise devolve onto the voting committees. Lot was also known as a means of resolving conflicts. According to Villani, the chronicler, a certain Cardinal Mathew Acquasparta, a papal legate, was sent to make peace during the struggle between the White and Black Guelfs. The Cardinal advocated a system of straight sortition where the names of those worthy to serve from each party were put into bags to be drawn every two months. The White Guelfs, who were then in power, refused the offer, fearing that it would be to their disadvantage.[51]

If we look at an early version of the scheme that emerged in 1291 it becomes clear that the *scrutiny* process comes from different roots from these other uses of sortition. While little is known of how the *priors* were elected during the previous decade, it is likely that a combination of the Consuls from the major guilds, the outgoing *priorate* and a number of *arroti* (members co-opted by the *priorate*) would have taken part. The new scheme, a process known as *imborsazione*, consisted of the election of enough *priors* for a whole year at one sitting, and the subsequent placing of their names in a series of six bags. Six names would then be drawn out every two months, one from each bag, just before the offices became vacant. It is also possible that at this early stage both the names of each batch

---

[49] Najemy (1982) pp. 30–2. Note also that the Florentine constitution also made use of advisory deliberative bodies, the *Pratiche* and two major legislative councils. All of these were appointed. See Rubinstein (1968) p. 454.

[50] Najemy (1982) p. 37.

[51] *Ibid.* p. 64.

of six *priors and* the date of their period of office would have been *imborsed* together. This would, in effect, have hidden the names of future office holders from the public gaze, and so prevented corruption, intimidation or even potential assassination.[52] No surviving documentation refers to the *imborsazione* of 1291 as lot or sortition, so at this stage it seems simply to have been a measure to ensure continuity in the electoral process. The arrangement was short-lived, however, and was rejected by the popular movement in 1292 in a great debate on the subject of elections to the *priorate* called by the *Capitano dell Popolo*.[53]

Another indication that the *scrutiny* bears little resemblance to the way lot was used in earlier *popolo* regimes can be seen in its relationship to the *balia*, or extraordinary commissions. *Balia* were appointed, usually by the incumbent *Signoria*, for a fixed term only and were usually used to oversee emergency legislation or respond to a particular constitutional crisis.[54] Between 1301 and 1328 *balia* were regularly called at intervals of between fourteen and twenty months to elect all the officers of the *Signoria* for that period. The names of those elected were then the subject of an *imborsazione*, in the same manner as the system of 1291, with their period of office stipulated in advance. This had all the ingredients of the later system, but there was no random or unpredictable element concerning the personnel in each *Signoria*. It is also possible that the result of the *balia*'s vote might even have been kept from the candidates themselves.[55] This aspect of secrecy was to become a key feature of the sortive process for the election of magistrates after 1328. Significantly it enabled the process to be manipulated behind the scenes while the public ritual of impartiality was maintained.

This close connection of the *balia* to the *scrutiny* should be noted, for it indicates that the device of placing pre-decided names in a bag to be drawn at intervals is really only a means of implementing a

---

[52] This reading of the protection of would be office-holders tallies with the convention whereby the *Priorate* plus the *Gonfalonier* of Justice had to take up residence in the *Palazzo della Signoria* throughout their term of office.

[53] Najemy (1982) p. 32.

[54] Note that the *balia* were accountable neither to the Communal Courts nor the Legislative Councils. Their members were also not subject to the customary financial scrutiny. See Becker (1967) p. 24.

[55] A document presented to the Legislative Councils in October 1321 dealing with the absence from the city of a *Gonfalonier* of Justice elect reveals that while the name of this individual was obviously known to the current *Signoria*, it was carefully kept from the wider meeting. Najemy (1982) p. 85.

decision taken by a group of special appointees. It is the *balia* that does the work; the *imborsazione* merely distributes the results. At its origins, therefore, the *scrutiny* bears little resemblance to a genuine lottery, and certainly makes no positive use of the blind-break. It is really only a form of secret list. As we look at the 1328 scheme we can see how much it owes to these, essentially oligarchic, origins.

The scrutiny scheme of 1328

The electoral reforms of 1328 are of considerable importance[56] because they established the procedural arrangements for the election of magistrates, which were to last for the next 150 years.[57] This is not to say that there were no amendments to the scheme during this period, but while there was intense and furious debate as to exactly who would take part in the procedure, the basic procedure itself remained surprisingly unchanged and was the subject of almost devotional respect from all sides. Its main purpose, that of preventing dangerous splits in the governing class, is confirmed by the chronicler Villani who states that Florentines began to 'deliberate on how they might provide the city with leadership and government in a way that would gain general approval and eliminate factions among the citizens.'[58] When the committee of thirteen entrusted with the task of developing the system presented the new system to a general *parlamento*,[59] they spoke of creating a consensus of 'good and law-abiding citizens' worthy of holding office, and of preventing 'those persons whose life renders them unworthy from zealously seeking the governance and rule of the city.'[60]

The major characteristics of the system are fairly straightforward, but problems and complexities began to proliferate once the system was up and running. The scheme involved five main stages. Nomination was followed by the *scrutiny*, or secret ballot. The names were then placed in the bags. The withdrawal of the names would

---

[56] Najemy (1982) pp. 99–125.
[57] The Medici retained the *imborsazione* but controlled the earlier selection of the names that went into the bags, restoring the original system on occasions. The second Florentine Republic introduced the Grand Council of 3,000 members in 1494, but retained the system for the *Signoria*.
[58] Najemy (1982) p. 99, quotes Villani, Cronica 3:103.
[59] Described by Najemy as a 'small and privileged group', only one individual had less than four years experience of serving on the *Signoria*. It would be difficult, however, for the scheme to have gained credibility with any less august body in control. Najemy (1982) p. 101.
[60] *Ibid.*

take place at the intervals decided by whatever office needed to be filled, and during this the final part of the process, the *divieto*, would take place. The *divieto* was the process by which members of the same family were temporarily excluded from office.[61]

Nomination was in the hands of three committees under the respective control of the *Signoria*, the Captain of the *Parte Guelfa*, and the five governing councillors of the *Mercanzia*.[62] Each was ordered to co-opt no less than 28 *popolani* citizens to form the nominating body. No limit was set on the number of nominations allowed from each committee. The voting members consisted of the *Signoria*, the *Gonfalonieri* of the Companies, the five of the *Mercanzia,* two consuls from each of the twelve major guilds and five members of the Guelf *popolani* from each *sesto* to be appointed by the *Signoria.* Originally the process of *scrutiny* took place every three years, but this ideal regularity became disrupted and intervals extended from two to five years.

Candidates would have to achieve a two-thirds majority to have their names placed in the bags. Of the eighty-two voting members, only twelve, the consuls of the lower six of the twelve guilds, could have come from the lower-middle or upper-artisan classes. Power was very much in the hands of the *Signoria* who made the appointments, but it is worth noting that only one member of any family was allowed on the scrutiny committee at any one time. Furthermore the guild members were to be picked by lot by the *Priors* and *Gonfalonier*, thus preventing the guild leadership and the internal democracy of the guilds from playing any significant role.[63] The scrutiny was a straightforward secret ballot using black or white beans as tokens of approval or disapproval. The results, however, remained a secret, which was (supposedly) known only to the officials or *accoppiatori* entrusted to the counting of the votes and the placing of the name tickets into the bags.

Once the name tickets were in the bags they were locked in a chest that was then placed in another locked chest and deposited in the church of S.Croce. The keys were entrusted to a Franciscan friar from S.Croce and a Dominican from S.Maria Novella, on the other side of town.[64] On the designated date the extraction was held in the

---

[61] These names for the parts of the procedure are given in Latin in Najemy (1982) p. 103.

[62] *Ibid.*

[63] *Ibid.*

[64] Finer (1999) p. 968.

presence of the incumbent *Signoria* and its colleges, the guild consuls, and the three main foreign officials: the *Podesta, Capitano della Popolo* and the Captain of the *Parte Guelfa*. During this process the *divieto* took place and those who were disqualified had to be replaced by further candidates drawn from the bags. It was at this stage that the names of some of those in the bag would become more widely known.

The exclusions from office proved to be problematic. In some cases, such as death, prosecution for fraud, or exile, the name ticket was destroyed once it had been drawn. For other reasons, such as the *divieto*, or because the person drawn was temporarily absent from the city, the ticket was returned to the bag. The *divieto*, or exclusion for family members, was fixed in 1328 at one year for fathers, grandfathers, brothers and sons, and six months for all other relatives of a sitting or selected officer.[65] Return to office was forbidden for three years. It was clear, therefore, that there would be times when a high proportion of the names drawn from any bag would be subject to exclusions of one sort or another. The initial response to a situation when no viable name tickets could be drawn, was merely to relax the rules and choose the first name that came out of the bag. This arrangement, which clearly favoured the powerful families, was soon replaced. But the new scheme merely exacerbated the trend. 'Parallel bags' were set up into which the name tickets of previous office-holders were deposited. These were known as *remissi* and would be used if there were insufficient names in any of the main *borsi*.

The officers elected by this method were the six *Priors*, and the *Gonfalonier* of Justice, and the two advisory colleges (sixteen *Gonfalorieri* and twelve *Buoni Uomini*).

This would make a total of 138 offices per year. To ensure a balance between the different areas of the town, one bag for the *priorate* was allocated to each *sesto*, and likewise for the draw for the *Buoni Uomini*. Sixteen bags were used for the *Gonfalonieri*, for nominations for these posts would have to come from their respective areas of the city. The *Gonfalonier* himself was elected from each *sesto* in turn according to a pre-ordained order. The bags acted as a 'pool' of citizens deemed worthy to govern. The pool was replenished by a *scrutiny* at prescribed intervals, but the earlier bags were kept in use until they were empty. It was therefore possible that magistrates could be appointed from a *scrutiny* held up to ten years earlier. The

---

[65] Brucker (1962) pp. 67–8.

system was in no sense designed to be a reflection of public opinion, or a system of accountability, nor was it meant to encourage new blood into the political arena.[66]

Changes to the system after 1328

The first series of changes to the system came during the popular government of 1343.[67] The office of the twelve *Buoni Uomini* was re-established and the role of the guilds increased. All twenty-one guilds seem to have been involved and the scrutiny committee was enlarged to 206, to include fifty-two guild consuls. The threshold for scrutiny votes was reduced from the customary two-thirds to just over one half. The *accoppiatori* were then asked to arrange the successful candidates into groups of eight[68] and to ensure that there was a quota of at least three members of the minor guilds in each *priorate*.[69] A special *borsa di spieciolata* was also set up into which the name tickets of candidates with fewer scrutiny votes were assigned as reserves. The incoming popular government also annulled the old *borse* and so prevented the candidates from earlier scrutinies from reversing their gains.

It is clear from these measures, especially the interference in the *borsa* by the *accoppiatori* to ensure adequate quotas, that the *scrutiny and tratte* was not regarded in the same way as earlier forms of selection by lot. It seems, however, that once adjustments were made to the criteria for participation, the system as a whole offered a stable enough basic form to suit the needs of both the narrowly-defined *reggimento* of the mercantile elite and the wider base of the supporters of popular government. Those in favour of popular government obviously did not feel that it was necessary, or indeed possible, to

---

[66] Herlihy (1991) p. 205, describes the 1328 government as the narrowest since 1291. Quoting the chronicler Villani, he notes that in the 1343 scrutiny, the 206 members of the scrutiny committee voted on a pool of 3,346 nominations. Only one tenth of that number were finally approved.

[67] The means by which the popular government came to power are instructive. Following the populist tyranny of Walter of Brienne in 1342, the Bishop of Florence formed a committee of fourteen who drew up plans to give the magnates a quota of seats on the *Signoria*, an increased role in nomination and an automatic one-third of the places on the Scrutiny Council. Because these measures also excluded the guilds, confrontation was inevitable and a popular uprising soon forced the expulsion of the new magnate *priors* from the *Palazzo Vecchio*. See Najemy (1982) pp. 130–2.

[68] The *Priorate* had since been enlarged.

[69] This seems to have been a direct response to the earlier proposals for a quota of magnates.

alter the system as a whole, but sought merely to adjust it to suit their own ends.

Similar changes were wrought by the popular government of 1378, which came to power in the months preceding the famous *Ciompi* rebellion of the summer of that year. The *borse* was annulled for the first time since 1343, and a *scrutiny* was held based on the radical principle of equal participation from all three strata of guilds: *majores*, *minori* and *minuto*. This gave power to some of the lower artisan class for the first time. It was an extremely popular measure and resulted in a large number of nominations, many coming from the poorer sections of the guild community.[70] The *Ciompi*, however, overstepped the mark and attempted to seize power. This caused the regime to take rapid counter measures against the extremists and to moderate its proposals for fear of losing the constitutional gains they had made earlier.

How the system as a whole commanded the confidence of the population is illustrated by a sequence of events from this year. During the popular agitation of July 1378 there was a call for direct elections from some quarters of the popular forces. A special meeting on this same issue was later initiated among the wider guild membership, but it voted against any change in the mode of selection for the *Signoria*. It was felt that a 'dangerous precedent' should not be created.[71]

The popular government of 1378–82 achieved the highest level of citizen participation of all the early renaissance regimes. In the years that followed, however, these gains were gradually reversed and the system was tightened to ensure that no repetition was possible. The proportion of representation from the mercantile class was increased to the detriment of those from the lower ranks of the guilds. At the same time, however, new features were added to ensure that an inner circle always retained overall control. The main weapon in this respect was the *borsillino*.[72] This was a small bag to be used in parallel to the main *scrutiny* bags. It contained the names of trusted and experienced members of the ruling group. A special committee of *accoppiatori* was assigned the task of selection for the *borsellino* on the basis of a quota from each quarter of the city. By

---

[70] A total of almost 6,000 citizens were nominated for the 1378 government, twice the level of 1343. Najemy (1982) p. 234. The *Ciompi* were the textile workers who had no recognised guild status and thus no political voice.

[71] Najemy (1982) p. 257.

[72] *Ibid*. p. 276.

1387 the *Gonfalonier of Justice* and two *priors* were elected by this method in each two-monthly draw. The previous method of *imborsazione*, it was admitted, left 'too much to chance'.[73] It was under this dispensation that the humanist Leonardo Bruni described Florence as an Aristotelian mixed constitution. The short terms of office and the use of lot he characterised as 'democratic', while he regarded the fact that laws were made by a small body of citizens with no right of amendment as an aristocratic quality.[74] This is an indication, if one is needed, of how the rhetoric of the mixed constitution was often used to describe regimes of a hidden aristocratic or oligarchic complexion.

Although the electoral system with the new *borsillino* in place was virtually impregnable from below, it was vulnerable from above — but only if a concerted effort was made. Designed to consolidate the rule of a broad class, it could submit to the rule of a single faction but only if that faction was large and powerful enough and took a long-term view on gaining influence within the ruling group.

Such was the strategy behind the Medici family's rise to power in the early fifteenth century.[75] A nouveau-riche family by Florentine standards, but with a rapidly-expanding banking empire, it first consolidated control in its home sector of the city by offering financial opportunities and the prospect of social advance to its supporters. In true Florentine style the Medici organisation operated as a 'state within a state' with its own retainers and institutions, and used its influence to gain overwhelming majorities in all areas of the electoral procedure. In 1443 this, plus a certain amount of luck, gave them the control that they needed. By forgetting to annul the earlier *scrutiny* after he had sent Cosimo de Medici into exile, the main rival to the Medici, Rinaldo degli Albizzi, left the possibility open for a pro-Medicean *Signoria* to be drawn. Within a year this had taken place and Cosimo returned in triumph.

Once in power, Cosimo de Medici's tactics were to retain the republican constitution — and thus guarantee political advancement to his supporters — while retaining a tight grip on the hidden levers of influence.[76] The *scrutiny and tratte* system, however, was too unpredictable for these purposes. He therefore relied on other

---

[73] *Ibid.* p. 282.
[74] Rubinstein (1968) p. 447.
[75] See Rubinstein (1966) and Kent (1978).
[76] As a major player in European finance he was particularly well placed to do this on the diplomatic front.

means: the *balia*, choice of candidates for the higher magistracies by the *accoppiatori* (a practice known as *a mano*), and a system of smaller appointed councils in which he could guarantee a majority of his own supporters. The use of the *scrutiny*, however, was re-introduced periodically to assuage popular discontent.[77] Even when elections were held *a mano*, the ritual of *imborsazione* and *tratte* took place regularly, retaining a public face of institutional impartiality. In these conditions demands for the reinstatement of the pre 1434 arrangements were seen as positively democratic.[78] After the fall of the Medici in 1494, lot for the *Signoria* was re-introduced by the Second Florentine Republic. This time it would be in the context of a Grand Council based on the Venetian model.[79]

The *brevia* and the *scrutiny*: a critical comparison

Both the *brevia* and the *scrutiny* are schemes which combine lottery with voting, but they do so in different ways, in different circumstances and in order to achieve very different political objectives. They are both two-part processes, and the relationship between the two parts is important in the way we understand their qualities and characteristics. The *brevia* uses lot from a wide pool as a preliminary to a process of electoral choice. The *scrutiny*, on the other hand, uses lot to make the final choice as to who takes office when, but uses voting as a means of establishing a suitable pool from which the draw is to take place. Although it is a straightforward matter to characterise the *brevia* as a form of lot-assisted election, the *scrutiny* is not simply a form of election-assisted lot. This is because the two processes of selection by preference in the *scrutiny* — nomination and voting — dominate the process by determining whose names should go into the bags. Moreover, the choice made by lot does not include or exclude any of the pool from office, it merely decides who should be in which *Signoria*. Lot therefore distributes, rather than selects or rejects, office-holders.

As electoral schemes the two systems differ fundamentally. The *brevia* operates on the ascending principle, in the sense that those who are not in government select those who are to govern. The *scrutiny*, on the other hand, works on the descending principle where those in government, or appointed by those in government, select those they regard as suitable for office.

---

[77] Rubinstein (1968) p. 459.
[78] *Ibid.* p. 466.
[79] See Butters (1985) and Gilbert (1968).

We can also learn much from the respective histories of the two schemes. The *brevia* is one of a number of solutions used by communal and *popolo* governments designed to balance the idea of a wide, inclusive electorate with greater control over the procedure of election. The basic model for this was the vote, or acclamation of office, by a citizen assembly. The difficulty in holding open elections without intimidation or other forms of interference, however, meant that another form of selection, indirect elections with appointed electors, was then tried. This maintained control, but inhibited wide participation. It was also vulnerable to accusations of partisanship. One means of resolving the difficulty, therefore, was by the use of sortition to select the electors. By granting everyone in the pool a stake in the selection of electors, the *brevia* was a reflection of the inclusive ideals of the law-governed political community. It guaranteed the impartiality of the selection procedure itself. Not only was direct interference inhibited, but the process was simple, coherent and transparent. The later variant, the selection of nominators by lot followed by a secret ballot, re-introduced the wider electoral constituency, but retained a sortive element as a means of controlling partisan tactics.

The use of sortition in the *brevia* is fairly easy to understand because we have encountered similar uses in Athens. In all aspects it constitutes a strong application of lot because the arational qualities of the lottery process are used positively to achieve recognisable ends. The main purpose of sortition was to maintain the authority of the electoral process by protecting it from partisan interference. The process could then be understood as the impartial common property of all citizens.

The *scrutiny*, on the other hand, developed from a system of appointment by the Florentine special commissions or *balia*. Linked to the earlier introduction of the two monthly rotation scheme for the *Signoria*, a measure designed to prevent any one family holding absolute power, this scheme did not initially involve a random element. Its introduction was not based on any ethos of inclusive government except as far as that term applied to those in the tight ruling group. The history of the *scrutiny*, moreover, abounds with adjustment and changes. The constitution of the nominating and *scrutiny* committees were extended from time to time when popular regimes were in power, and contracted when more oligarchic regimes took over. Secretaries were asked to organise the names in the bags according to quotas, and additional bags and new procedures were regularly added, usually to counteract the unwanted effects of chance. This would argue that the arationality of the lottery principle was not always highly valued.

If we now look at the use of randomness, or arationality, in the *scrutiny*, a very different picture emerges from that of the *brevia*. The function of the lottery aspect of the procedure, possibly not fully understood until the 1328 version of the scheme, was to complement the rotational scheme for the *Signoria* by ensuring a mixed pattern of office holders. This would have had the express purpose of preventing any one family or alliance of families from developing a permanent power base within government. It was not designed to produce a permanent common bond between those in the pool, but a controlled compromise or stand-off between naturally competitive forces. The arational element in the mechanical random distribution of offices is thus compromised by the idea that some sort of proportionate or balanced mix is what is really required. For this reason, real randomness, like the occurrence of two members of the same family in one draw, was undesirable, and had to be counteracted by a special measure — the *divieto*.

It is, moreover, a weighted lottery because the basic units in the pool are not individual candidates, but members of families and members of allied families. Thus the success of the lottery is measured by the balance between groupings in the pool obtained in the draw and in aggregation over the rotation: a balance which is designed to ensure that no *grouping* will dominate. The aim was not to produce random individuals, but to obtain an unpredictable mix such as would keep all parties interested in maintaining the system. The fundamental organising principle of the First Florentine Republic, enshrined and institutionalised by the practice of the *scrutiny*, is therefore, that of a compromise between competing elites.

Another point of contrast between the two schemes is to be found in the public openness of the *brevia* which contrasts with the secretive nature of the *scrutiny*. The lottery draws for electors or nominators were great public events in which the general population played the role of witness to the fairness of the draw. This ethos of clarity and transparency is also carried through in the design of the procedure as a whole. Although the electors would go to a secure location to deliberate, this would have been a public, not a private, location, and their activity would take place under the auspices of the public office for which they were selected. The relatively short time-scale of the *brevia* also allowed it to be responsive to public concerns.

In the *scrutiny*, in almost complete contrast, no candidate knew whether he had been elected to the pool until his name was drawn from the bag. From the point of view of creating an unpredictable mix between potentially factious families, this was a necessary measure. Had the make up of the pool been general knowledge the more powerful families would have been able to form power blocs with other groupings to increase their possible influence on the final draws.

From the point of view of the hopeful candidate, however, the secrecy of the *scrutiny* system meant that he would be unaware whether or not his name was in the bag until the very moment it was drawn. This kept a whole swathe of lower *popolani* tied into the system in the hope that they might have been voted into the pool. Although it seems that the arational blind break is operating here, it is the fact that the make up of the pool is kept secret that makes the greatest contribution to this effect. The descending system of election would also have meant that ambitious citizens would actively seek favours from the more powerful families. More seriously, however, the inherent secrecy of the system meant that the extent of any ruling group and its political complexion remained hidden from the citizenry at large. The nature of the ruling class—its size and composition—was therefore not a 'thing of the public' in a true republican sense. It was, moreover, not a private secret, but the early equivalent of a state secret, known only to members of the embryonic state apparatus, the *accoppiatori*, and, of course, to anyone with sufficient influence over them. Nothing could be further from the way sortition defined the commonality of the political project in the case of the *brevia*.

Both the *brevia* and the *scrutiny* contributed to political consolidation in different ways and in different periods in the growth of politics of the region. The *brevia* in its elector and nominator forms belongs to a period of republican consolidation where the city polities needed to establish impartial forms of government and manageable, uncorrupted forms of election. It belonged, to quote Wolfson, to a period which valued, and hence sought, 'purity in elections'.[80] In its various forms the *brevia* was a central mechanism in the northern Italian *popolo* governments of the thirteenth century and is commensurable with their ethos of ascending power, equal-

----

[80] Wolfson (1899) p. 21.

ity before the law and popular sovereignty. Along with other measures such as the use of the *podesta* and the secret ballot it contributed to the political consolidation of the early period of commune building. The *brevia* is a strong form of the lottery principle in that it makes a positive virtue of the arational blind break to inhibit corruption and electoral intimidation. It values the random or independent outcome of the lottery by drawing from a wide citizen pool. In this way it strengthens the relationship between the citizen and the polity.

The *scrutiny* belongs to a later period and to a Florentine regime which was seeking a new form of mercantile hegemony by forging a tight, unified *reggimento*, or ruling class. In a period in which most cities in the region had handed government over to a single *signore*, Florence was developing a strong collective alternative. The *scrutiny* certainly helped to achieve this. The government form forged by the *scrutiny* was essentially a compromise between competing elites, distributed in office by a form of weighted lottery. At the same time the electoral element was designed to keep power out of the hands of the popular forces in the city. Shrouded in mystique and ritual, this particular sortive scheme borrowed the trappings of earlier republicanism, but kept the hidden levers of power in the ever tighter control of its cabal of ruling families. The relatively small pool and the fact that that pool was a result of preference election from an even narrower electorate, meant that the system was continuously vulnerable to corruption and control by patronage networks.

In the next chapter we shall see how the *brevia* becomes part of a rigid Venetian aristocracy, while the Florentines, under the Medici *stato* and in its direct aftermath, resurrect the *scrutiny* as an ideal of popular government.

Bibliographical notes

While the Florentine electoral system is well catered for in English secondary literature, the practical political systems of the earlier communes are under-researched. This applies particularly to the *popolo* regimes. Of the available works I have relied on an old, but excellent short paper by Wolfson, 'Forms of Voting in the Italian Communes', *American Historical Review*, Vol V, No.1 October 1899 pp.1-22). This is supplemented by a PhD thesis by Koenig which deals with the *popolo* regimes in great detail, but has very little to say about electoral systems.

My general view of the period was informed by two older studies, those of Pirenne and Previte-Orton, and by the invaluable 1988 *The Italian City State Republics* by Daniel Waley. Hyde's 1973 study, *Society and Politics in Medieval Italy*, was steady and perceptive and Tabacco's 1989 *The Struggle for Power in Medieval Italy* provided a useful overview.

Much of how the *brevia* operated had to be pieced together from studies of individual cities by different writers. Of note in this respect are Kohl (1990), Meek (1978 and 1986), Waley (1952), Blanshei (1976), Bousky (1981), and Herlihy (1958 and 1967).

If practical details were in short supply, there is no shortage of exploration into the political ideas of this period. The work of Canning, Skinner and Ullmann provided a solid background in this area.

For my investigation of the Florentine system my main anchor was Najemy's thorough *Corporatism and Consensus in Florentine Electoral Politics 1280-1400* of 1982. This was supplemented by Becker (1967), Brucker (1962), and the work of Rubinstein, Kent and Lansing. Early works by Sismondi (1907) and Villani (1908) contributed to the overall picture.

Chapter Four

Sortition and the Defence of the Second Florentine Republic

This chapter is the centrepiece of the study for a number of reasons. To begin with it contains the clearest and sharpest example of how lot was actually used to protect the public nature of the political process against the concentrated power of tyranny. We see this during a brief republican revival that took place in Medici-controlled Florence in 1465–6. We also see a reflection of this role of lot in the power struggle following the overthrow of the Medici regime in 1494 when the attacks of a newly invigorated aristocratic party forced the republicans to replace an earlier voting scheme with sortition. Unlike the example of Ancient Athens, where we saw lot employed largely in a preventative capacity, here we see lot in action against well-defined threats to the political community. These events, moreover, are well documented and unambiguous. This chapter is also at the centre of the study as a whole because it describes the historical point where the Florentine model of popular republicanism, with all its problems and complications, makes its last stand in the arena of European politics. With its final collapse in 1530 goes the last major polity to use sortition comprehensively in a way that we would regard as broadly democratic: i.e. where it offers the prospect of participation in open government to an increasing number of its citizens. As well as giving an account of lot in action, this chapter also tells a story about the changes in political thought that accompany the demise of this polity type in practice. For this reason we take an important excursion into the realm of the written word to look at a constitutional proposal by Machiavelli and several works by Guicciardini.

Machiavelli's proposal is very much in the republican tradition and advocates the use of sortition to serve the ends of inclusive, responsive government. Guicciardini on the other hand formulates a new form of government that is designed to cede a leading role to the re-vitalised aristocratic faction. This vision involves the greater use of the popular vote. It is also likely that *Del modo di Eleggere gli Uffici nel Consiglio Grande*, his fictitious dialogue on the use of lot loosely based on the debates of 1494–9, was designed to further this cause. He returns to the same theme in a much later work, his *History of Italy*. By examining these works alongside an historical account of the defence of the Second Florentine Republic we can get a real idea of how these theoretical positions relate to the combative political struggle for the republic and its values.

I start the chapter, however, with a description of the Venetian system of selecting political officers. This used sortition in the nominating process but then used a secret ballot of all members of the Grand Council for the final vote. Understanding this system is vital to the study. In the immediate context of the chapter we can gain a real insight into the debates of the Second Republic where a new Venetian style government was being introduced. This in its turn also helps us to take forward the discussion on the role of sortition in different polity types. Venice, for all its complex electoral systems, and despite its reputation as a model of Aristotelian mixed government, was essentially ruled by an aristocratic oligarchy. In terms of the wider picture of the use of sortition Venice is a major link between Italian and northern European republicanism: as republican ideas began to spread to northern Europe in the seventeenth century, it was Venice, rather than Florence that served as the major example.

The Venetian electoral system

For our purposes the most important date in Venetian constitutional history is 1297 when the consolidation of the *Consiglio Grande* took place. Possibly as a means of defining the citizen body in the face of immigration, the *Consiglio*, which had been in operation since 1172, was enlarged, and then closed.[1] We can understand this as a measure designed to control the previous electoral and assembly arrangements. There were to be no more elections to the *Consiglio*, and membership, which was now for life, was determined

---

[1]   Lane (1971).

by hereditary descent and regulated by the so-called *Libro d'Oro*. But while the *Consiglio* initially numbered around 1,200 and represented an increase in participation, it very soon created a closed group of citizens, differentiated from the vast majority of the residents of the city by their access to the body politic. Its members were entitled 'noble' whatever their social status. Although the *Consiglio Grande* was the official sovereign body, the power in Venice lay with the smaller, more select bodies: the Senate, the *Quarantia* (judiciary committee of 40), the ten and the *Collegio* of twenty-four. This latter body operated as a steering committee for the Senate and the titular head of state, the *Doge*.[2]

The structure of Venetian government has been represented by a pyramid.[3] This is broadly correct, but can be misleading since it gives no account of the differences in function and operation between the various organs of government. In particular the higher offices became increasingly ceremonial and, significantly, the *Consiglio Grande* had no deliberative or initiating role. This meant that the Senate was, *de facto* the driving force of the republic, and the senate, moreover, was dominated by the major families of the city.[4] Unlike Florence, which had denied political participation to a number of its leading aristocratic families via the Ordinances of Justice of 1292, in Venice the aristocracy had found a constitutional means of retaining and exercising power.

The potential for electoral violence and destabilising factionalism was present in Venice no less than in any other city state of the period, but the measures taken to combat these problems seem to have been more effective than elsewhere in the region. There is no doubt that the complex combinations of preference voting and sortition that characterised the election of magistrates contributed to the unity of the republic and the longevity of its constitution.

Nearly all magistrates were elected by the *Consiglio Grande* and consequently this task took up a sizeable proportion of its programme. In general terms, the election procedures derived from the *brevia*. In Venice, however, lot was only used to procure nominations; the final choice was made by a secret ballot of the whole coun-

---

[2] See Lane (1973) p. 90, for the idea that the Doge was 'hemmed around with advisory councils'.
[3] See Finer (1999) p. 994; Finlay (1980) pp. 39–43 for limitations on this model; similarly Lane (1973) pp. 96 and 429.
[4] Finlay (1980) p. 38.

cil.[5] The closing of the *Consiglio Grande* limited the electorate and this created much greater predictability and stability than in Florence where the make-up of the nominating and *scrutiny* committees was the subject of constant political friction. The Florentine system was, by the same token, more responsive to pressure from the lower guilds and artisan class and, in this respect, could be considered as having more democratic potential.

For ease of understanding the Venetian electoral system can be divided into three phases:

1. The choice of nominators by lot from the whole Council.
2. The nominating procedure undertaken by lot and choice by (usually) four committees of nine in smaller separate chambers.
3. The vote on the nominations by the whole Council.

For the first phase three urns were placed on a dais facing the councillors. The two outer urns each contained thirty golden balls plus a large number of silver balls of the same size and weight. The central urn contained sixty balls of which thirty-six were golden. The members were called up bench by bench, in an order decided by lot, and each drew one ball from either of the side urns. Those drawing golden balls would then draw from the central urn and this would produce thirty-six nominations from the sixty first-round winners. These would form the four nominating committees of nine members each.

In the second phase the members of each nominating committee would withdraw to a separate room and, in descending order of age, draw lots, labelled one to nine, which corresponded to specific posts on the list of vacant offices allocated to that committee. The drawer was then entitled to nominate a candidate for the appropriate vacancy and each nomination would then be voted on by the nine. Those gaining two-thirds or more of the votes would be put forward to the council for a full vote. If any nomination failed to gain the six votes required, the nominator in question would be asked to put forward another name until one was found that satisfied the requirements. Once the nominating committees had reported back to the Council they were dismissed and would take no part in the vote.

After the name of each candidate and his nominator were announced, the candidate's family would be asked to leave the

---

[5] Nominations for the Senate were obtained by means of a scrutiny vote by existing members of that body itself. Queller (1986) p. 59.

Council Chamber. For the vote itself urns called *bussuli* were carried around and the ballots, or small linen balls, were dropped into one of two compartments which signified either approval or disapproval of the candidate in question. Each voter would be required to show his ballot to his neighbour before voting. The office would go to the candidate who achieved the highest number of affirmative votes if that constituted a majority of the whole Council.[6]

In the last chapter we saw how the *brevia* and the *scrutiny* were means by which the consolidation of republican government was facilitated and greater impartial norms established for the selection of governmental officers. By the end of the fourteenth century the electoral systems of Venice and Florence were well embedded in the political habits of their respective cities — but they had also been manipulated to suit the needs of their ruling groups. In Florence this took the form of measures such as the use of the *borsillino*, and the constant changes to the make-up of the *scrutiny* and nominating committees. In Venice the constitution had remained comparatively unchanged, but its main feature, the division between the voting *Consiglio* and the deliberating Senate and upper committees, kept the lower echelons of the 'nobility' excluded from the real political community.

Donald E. Queller's discussion of the socio-political hierarchy of the lower Venetian aristocracy puts the complex ritual of the Venetian election procedure into a useful perspective. A major feature of Venetian society during the late medieval and early renaissance period was the large number of impoverished lower nobility who depended on paid governmental posts for their advancement.[7] This gave rise to extensive systems of lobbying both inside and outside the Council chamber — evident from the number of statutes forbidding such practices. These include specific reference to activities such as the exchange of lots in the nominating chamber and walking up and down behind the voting urns in order to canvas support. A system of fines and other penalties was also instigated.[8] It seems, however, that very few cases of electoral corruption, known as *imbroglio*, were the subject of prosecution. Queller suggests that a certain amount of low-level corruption of the system by ambitious individuals was tolerated, so long as the danger of factional

[6]   Full descriptions of this procedure can be found in many accounts; one of the best is Queller (1986) p. 55.
[7]   *Ibid.* pp. 29–49, 51.
[8]   *Ibid.* pp. 64–70.

take-over, arising from personal power-bases inside the Senate and upper governmental committees, could be avoided.[9]

If we are to draw any lessons from Queller's narrative and analysis, it would be to emphasise that measures such as sortition did not always eliminate electoral problems at all levels.[10] The extent of the *imbroglio* should lead us to view with some caution the Venetian ideal that 'the office should seek the man' for there were clearly many ways that office was actively sought, especially by the lower nobility. We should also be sceptical about claims that the sober judgement of individual merit was the sole, or main, criterion by which members of the Venetian Council voted. It is more likely that the outcome of elections rested on a complex pattern of interlocking favours and personal dependency.

The fact that the *reggimento* was hereditary and accession to the *Consiglio Grande* strictly limited, meant that there was very little new blood in the body politic. The political affiliations of all council members would probably have been well known. In these circumstance groups loyal to the various Venetian families that made up the ruling elite inevitably dominated the lottery pools. We should therefore understand the lottery elements in the process as weighted lotteries, and thus prone to corruption by high levels of personal patronage and dependency. The system as a whole operated on the basis that there would be a limited level of unpredictability between known elements or groupings, and this would tie potentially antagonistic families into the system in the knowledge that no faction could easily gain absolute power.

A central feature of the system as a whole, and a central factor in our understanding of the polity types of this period, is the division between the high level of qualitative political engagement enjoyed by the members of the deliberating governmental bodies and the paucity of genuine participation experienced by the members of the *Consiglio*. Indeed it has been argued that the degeneration of the voting procedure into issues of minor bureaucratic ambition was the direct result of the 'long absence of the tradition of public political discourse' from the Venetian polity and the subsequent de-politicisation of the ordinary members of the *Consiglio Grande*.[11]

---

[9]   *Ibid.* p. 75.
[10] *Ibid.* p. 18; Lane (1971) p. 121.
[11] From Bouwsma, *Venice and the defence of Republican Liberty*, quoted in Robey and Law (1975) p. 6.

We should not, therefore, think of the lottery for nominators as helping to assuage this division. There were, in fact, two distinct pools in operation — one for nominators and another for candidates. Where these overlapped was in the scramble for low-level offices. In the elections for members of the Senate and other high offices, however, candidature was *de facto* limited to those of high birth and education who had sufficient influence or reputation to be nominated.

This entrenched division of political labour marks the greatest distinction between the Venetian and Florentine polities. In the latter city the *popolo* movement remained strong and exerted a consistent level of influence within the body politic — even though it held power relatively rarely. While the ideal of *La Serenissima*, the infinitely stable Adriatic republic, entered the rhetoric of Florentine ruling circles as a paradigm of mixed government, the reality of aristocratic rule was well known to those within the popular republican tradition. As early as 1320 Henri of Rimini, states that: 'Amongst all republics of Christian peoples in our time, the republic of the Venetian race is seen to approach that of a mixed regime.'[12] We also find this view expressed in the sixteenth century. Giannotti regarded Venice as having achieved: 'At worst parity with Rome as an exemplar of the ideal mixed constitution of classical antiquity.'[13] Guicciardini's Paulo Antonio Soderini in the *History of Italy*, describes Venice as having a 'popular government' because so many citizens are involved in the *Consiglio Grande*:[14] and Contarino suggests that the 'Grand Council represents in this commonwealth the form of a popular state.'[15]

In contrast to this view, Machiavelli recognises that in Venice the 'Guardianship of liberty has been put in the hands of the nobles just as in Rome it was in the hands of the people.'[16] But a proposition put forward by Francisco Vettori expresses the tradition of Florentine popular republicanism far more directly: 'Is it not tyranny when 3,000 persons hold sway over 100,000 persons and none of the common people can hope to become patricians?'[17]

---

[12] Robey and Law (1975) p. 54. 'Inter omnes politas que nostris temporibus in populo Christiano fuerunt politia gentis Venetorum ad hoc regimen mixum videtur appropinquare.'

[13] Queller (1986) p. 9.

[14] Guicciardini (1984) p. 79.

[15] Contarino (1969) p. 18.

[16] Machiavelli (1998) pp. 115–16 (*Discorsi* I, 3,5).

[17] Finlay (1980) p. 36. From *Sommario della historia d'Italia*, pp. 145–6.

These perceptions of the Venetian republic constitute an important link in the story of the defence of Florentine republicanism that takes up the majority of this chapter. They show us how the Aristotelian concept of the mixed polity was used to mask aristocratic rule, and they show us the line that could have been taken by the newly returned Florentine aristocracy of 1494 as they argued for a Venetian settlement in Florence. First, however, we return to Florence in 1465 to see how sortition was understood and employed by those seeking political liberty and a popular republican constitution.

Lot in action

1: The Florentine republicans of 1465-6

The remarkable achievement of the rule of the Medici between 1434 and 1494 was that Cosimo, Piero or Lorenzo never regularly held high office, but used a mixture of patronage and intimidation to manipulate the entire governmental apparatus from the background.[18] Part of their skill lay in their ability to maintain a veneer of public governance that was just substantial enough to hide the true arbitrary nature of their rule. To do this they regularly changed and adjusted the various organs of government, relying on appointment and closely controlled elections to place their men in key positions.[19] They also made regular use of the *balia*, or extraordinary commission, to appoint the pool for the *Signoria*. The names were then chosen *a mano* (by hand) by the *accoppiatori* every two months.[20] Another tactic used to maintain a semblance of authority was the *parlamento*. This was a stage-managed version of the mediaeval assembly in which the *Piazza della Signoria*, invariably lined with Medici troops, would be filled with members of the general citizenry. A major question, such as the commissioning of a *balia*, would then be put to the multitude for their approval or disapproval. Another of the ways in which the Medici incorporated the institutions of republicanism into their rule was their occasional re-introduction of the lottery *tratte* for the *Signoria* when they felt that they needed greater public support and had calculated that it was safe for them to do so.

It was in opposition to this form of 'constitutional dictatorship' that a republican grouping emerged in the 1460s under the leader-

---

[18] Kent (1978), especially pp. 228–33.
[19] Rubinstein (1966) p. 133.
[20] *Ibid*. p. 80.

ship of Luca Pitti, Niccolo Soderini and Agnolo Acciaiuolo.[21] In September 1465 large majorities on the advisory councils and the *Cento*, or senate of one hundred, called for the restoration of sortition. The target was the Medici's system of patronage. As Niccolo Soderini explained: 'Not without cause did our ancestors ordain that high offices be filled by lot and not handed over.'[22] This was followed by a concession in which lot was introduced for several of the key committees which had previously been elected by the *Cento*.[23] A call then went out for a *scrutiny* to create a new pool for the *Signoria*. During a *pratica*, or debate between invited participants, on the subject, the idea of a Venetian-style constitution seems to have been raised. The tenor of the debate indicates that the participants associated lot with popular government and voting with aristocratic rule, which they saw as epitomised in the constitution of Venice.[24]

In May 1466 a law to extend the principle of sortition to all offices save a specified few was passed.[25] The republicans were emboldened and published a petition of 400 signatures of those who swore to defend republican government. This demanded that no illegal pressure should be brought to bear on private citizens, and that citizens should have the right to discuss and decide on public affairs. These demands not only indicate how the Medici had been operating, but they also show how the call for sortition in the 1460s was part of a broadly conceived republican platform which placed freedom of political expression high on its list of priorities.[26] A vivid first-hand description of this is provided in the letters of one Marco Parenti, who was connected to the Strozzi family. Many of the proper names in these letters were omitted and code numbers inserted in their place, an indication of the atmosphere of fear and suspicion that existed in Florence during these years.[27] Parenti writes:

> The matter of [closed electoral purses] is accepted by [Pitti, Dietsalvi and Acciaiuolo] so that the larger part of the

---

[21] Alamanno Rinuccini, the author of *De Liberate*, was also a supporter of this group. See Phillips (1987) p. 170.
[22] Rubinstein (1966) p. 144. This was from a debate held on 29 October 1465.
[23] *Ibid.* p. 145.
[24] See *Testi e Documents* (1961) p. 261.
[25] Rubinstein (1954) p. 326.
[26] Rubinstein (1966) p. 157. Rubinstein's judgement is that 'In no other document of the Medici period is the constitutionalist programme formulated so incisively and so comprehensively.'
[27] See Phillips (1987) p. 139. The coded words are indicated by square brackets.

[principali] go along with them and are in good cheer. [Piero de Medici] with some of the [principali] at the last moment made a great show of wishing [closed purses] but secretly it is thought that they lamented it. But they could not resist it. Now, after the fact they made a show of great unity.[28]

Parenti's description tells us much about the balance of power within Florentine Society during this period. The Medici, held power, but only by maintaining alliances amongst the other powerful families in the city. To do this they simultaneously maintained a veneer of open political process while they retained power by largely conspiratorial methods.

The return to lot for the *Signoria*, however, was a direct challenge to Medici power, and the Medici countered with the line that lot would create uncertainty and contribute to civil disorder. The *scrutiny* system then produced two strategically significant pro-Medici *Signorias*, which enabled Piero de Medici to call a *parlamento* in September 1466. This endorsed the formation of a *balia* to appoint the pool for subsequent draws — once again securing Medici control over the commanding political heights of the city.[29]

A postscript to this brief *risorgimento* is supplied by Alamanno Rinuccini's dialogue *De Liberate* of 1479. A conservative republican, Rinuccini is one of the few fifteenth-century writers to show an interest in Ancient Athens, and his attitude to lot was probably inspired by that model. One of the fictitious participants in Rinuccini's dialogue, Alitheus (the truthful) advocates lot in preference to a system in which:

> ... all positions that bestow some dignity on a man and yield some profit are filled, not by lot, but by appointment. The result is that no good men, no men noted for prudence and ability are chosen, but satellites of the powerful or servants of their desires or pleasures.[30]

The argument here is an inversion of Socrates' claim that lot denies office to the capable. In a corrupt government, neither appointment nor election could be trusted as a means of producing office-holders of integrity or ability.

This story of the republican opposition in the 1460s is important because it shows a group of republicans advocating a lot-based

---

[28] *Ibid.* p. 148.
[29] Rubinstein (1966) p. 161–8. There were accusations that the bags had been tampered with. Rubinstein, however, sees this as an example of the problems caused by the use of sortition (1966, p. 160).
[30] Rinnucini (1978) p. 206.

agenda as a remedy for the culture of private patronage and organised terror that was sustaining the Medici regime. It is a rare
well-documented example of lot advocated as a corrective rather
than a preventative measure: in this case against a sitting tyrant.
What is more, the republican agenda was not based exclusively on
the restoration of the older *scrutiny* and *tratte* system. Lot was advocated because election and appointment had proved unsatisfactory
as a means of distributing power. It is a good example of lot used in
a political context where its arationality is a desirable quality; more
importantly it goes straight to the key interface in the Medici system: the point where citizens were selected for public office. Lot is
impervious to the actions of the individual will and unpredictable
in its outcomes, thus it instantly curtails the ability for one individual or group of individuals to control others by the exercising power
over the distribution of public offices. There was simply no other
mechanism in the working repertoire of the Florentines that could
be applied so quickly and effectively against private patronage.

In terms of its overall political context, the use of lot also formed
an integral part of a more general republican platform that was
self-consciously attempting to re-establish the political freedoms of
the citizenry. It is the nearest that we get in the Renaissance to an
Athenian understanding of lot as the mainstay of the polity in direct
opposition to the threat of tyranny and the tyrannical *stato*. I would
argue, moreover, that this application of lot should form the vantage point from which we should view the events and debates over
lot in the Second Republic.

2: The debates and events of 1494–9

In the events of 1494–9 we have another story of the use of lot to
defend Florentine popular republicanism—this time against a
newly-formed aristocratic grouping. The Second Republic first
opted for a voting system on the Venetian model, but, as the popular
movement came under attack, resorted to lot in order to defend
their gains. In this story it is important that we understand who is
taking which position and why—not least because Guicciardini's
History of Italy (written 1537–40) puts a rather different slant on the
lottery debate. The resulting contrast between 'lot in action' and 'lot
in history' gives us an instructive insight into how attitudes towards
sortition were beginning to change, and with them ideas about the
form and priorities of republican government.

It would be true to say that the 1494 Florentine settlement was new territory for most political actors, and that this is reflected in a level of general uncertainty that followed the end of Medici rule.[31] But as in most such situations, whoever took the political initiative and had a sufficiently strong following to maintain stability would have control. In this case the initiative came from an unexpected quarter: the Dominican friar Savonarola. During the closing years of the Medici regime Savonarola had delivered a series of sermons attacking the corruption and depravity of that government. This public platform gave him a huge level of support. When the French entered Florence in 1494 and the Medici fell, government was placed, initially, under the control of 20 powerful *accoppiatori*, some of whom were known to have been supporters of the Medici. In the meantime, blueprints for a new constitution were actively sought.

Savonarola called for a wide input from the Florentine citizenry in the project, but the consultation seems to have been hijacked by the major magistrates.[32] Four schemes emerged. One came from Dominico Bonsi, a member of the 20-strong ruling *accoppiatori*, and one from Piero Capponi favouring an aristocratic select council.[33] The other schemes were submitted anonymously. Both featured a combination of sortition for minor magistrates while major magistrates were to be elected — their nominators having first been chosen by lot. The more comprehensive of the two schemes, was thought to have been the work of a grouping known as the 'Ten of Liberty and Peace' which included Paulo Antonio Soderini and other republican leaders from major Florentine families. This advocated a Venetian-style *Consiglio Grande*. In its considerable preamble much of the blame for Florence's unstable polity is put on the combination of sortition used amongst a narrow ruling group to select high officers, and the use of more indiscriminate sortition for lower officers. The former was prone to corruption, the latter encouraged incompetence.[34] The answer was to combine election on the Venetian model, for the higher officials, with sortition for all minor magistrates.[35] References in the draft to the idea that this constitution was divinely

[31] Guicciardini's character of Bernado in *Dialogue on the Government of Florence* expresses his reaction to the new form of government in the phrase 'I don't know what to baptise it'. Guicciardini (1994) p. 14.
[32] Weinstein (1970) p. 255.
[33] *Ibid.* p. 257. Bonsi favoured a Venetian-style Grand Council but suggested that high office be restricted to council members.
[34] *Ibid.* p. 258.
[35] *Ibid.* p. 260.

ordained mark this scheme as designed to appeal to the followers of Savonarola.[36]

The final scheme, however, moderated many of these more popular measures. The new *Consiglio* ended up as similar in size to its Venetian counterpart – around 3500 citizens.[37] Members had to be of legitimate birth, over twenty-nine, free from debt and had to have had an ancestor in the last three generations who had held office as one of the top three magisterial posts.[38] These political heirs were known as the *beneficiati*. This arrangement inevitably meant that there would be a proportion of Medici supporters within the Council, but it also gave a renewed political voice to those whose families had not held power since the First Republic. Every three years forty-five citizens from the *Arti Maggiori* and fifteen from the *Arti Minori* or minor guilds could be voted onto the *Consiglio*.[39] Twenty-eight citizens were drawn by lot from the *Consiglio* to act as nominators for this purpose.[40]

One of the greatest differences between the Venetian and the Florentine systems was that Florence retained its traditional office of the *Signoria* with its two-monthly rotational scheme. Correspondingly the new *Ottando*, which was the equivalent to the Venetian Senate, was far less powerful than its Venetian counterpart. On the other hand, the voting scheme for the *Signoria*, which became law on 23 December 1494, drew heavily on Venice. Sixty citizens were selected by lot from the *Consiglio* to act as nominators. Each could nominate one citizen. All candidates had to be over 50 years old, but did not have to be members of the *Consiglio*. The sixty candidates were voted on, together, in a secret ballot, and the six with the most votes were then endorsed by a majority in a second ballot. The provision that non-members of the *Consiglio* could be elected favoured the *ottimati*, or aristocrats. There were, however, two statutory places for members of the fourteen minor guilds on each *Signoria*.

[36] *Ibid.* p. 259.
[37] Pesman-Cooper (1985) p. 75.
[38] This applied both to those who had taken their magisterial seats and to those whose names had been drawn from the bags but had failed to take up their posts. *Ibid.* p. 74.
[39] *Ibid.* p. 78.
[40] How much this new system actually extended participation is the subject of debate. Weinstein (1970) p. 265, suggests that an 'impressive' new level of participation was achieved, but Pesman-Cooper (1985) p. 79, claims that access to office was in fact no greater than during the last years of the Medici regime. See also Gilbert (1965) p. 60. It is worth noting that Machiavelli did not qualify as a member of the Consiglio under the new arrangements.

As with its Venetian counterpart, the new Florentine Council had no deliberative function, but the continued existence of the Florentine *pratica*, and other traditional forums of deliberation, meant that most members of the *Consiglio* would have had the opportunity to take part in political debate. In a significant departure from the draft schemes, many of the minor officers were to be elected rather than selected by lot. This brought the new arrangement significantly closer to the Venetian model.

On the surface the discussions on the new constitution focussed on the difference between *governo largho*, broad government, and *governo stretto* or narrow government. This was merely a discussion on the level of citizen participation within a general republican framework. There were, however, other, more dangerous forces in the field which threatened the new, precarious republic. It is useful to see how these conscious political forces line up.[41] By far the largest political grouping were the supporters of Savonarola, known as the *piagnoni* or weepers.[42] These were mainly drawn from the lower merchants and upper artisans, a stratum normally delineated by membership of the *Arti Minori* or lesser guilds. This grouping gave Savonarola's theocratic vision its political momentum. But there was also strong support for the new republican settlement from the *popolani*, the upper mercantile group who had been the bedrock of the First Republic and who had survived the Medici years, usually by a process of compromise. This class constituted the *reggimento* or ruling group in the new settlement — defined by *Consiglio* membership.

In strong, sometimes violent, opposition to the *piagnoni* was a small but vocal grouping known as the *arrabbiati*, or 'enraged'. This was a heterogeneous grouping which included some republicans who distrusted Savonarola's charismatic leadership, but was mainly formed of young *ottimati*, who agitated and conspired in order to break the hold of the *piagnoni* on the *Consiglio Grande*.

The *ottimati*, or aristocrats, were divided between those who had supported the Medici and those who had opposed them. The pro-Medicean group were known as the *palleschi* and later as the *bigi*. This group kept their heads down during the early years of the republic. On the other hand, with the fall of the Medici other members of the older aristocratic, land-owning, families saw their opportunity to make a bid for power — their ranks swelled by returning

---

[41] Roth (1968) pp. 60–2.
[42] They were also known as the *Frateschi*.

exiles. Many members of the *ottimati* were descendants of the magnates, and as such had been denied a role in Florentine politics since
the early fourteenth century. We should therefore think of the
ottimati, not solely as a socio-economic class, but as a new political
group in Florence united behind a distinct political platform. The
Rucellai family provided a focal point and a forum for this group in
their famous debates in the Orti Orticellari.[43] They were renowned
for their support for a Venetian settlement for Florence. In practice,
however, there was considerable opportunism both within the
ottimati and amongst the higher *popolani*, as many leading actors
hedged their bets and waited to see how the new regime would settle down. There were constant fears that a pro-Medici alliance could
emerge.

While it is possible to differentiate how the forces in Florentine
political society lined up behind each viewpoint, it would be
wrong to think of them as political parties in the modern sense of
the word. Parties, known as *intelligenze*, were regarded as detri-
mental to the republic and were therefore illegal.[44] Political associations were therefore very loose, and were often based on ties of
friendship or kinship, or around specific issues. Covert factionalism and political opportunism were rife, and common cause
was often made between strange bedfellows. Paulo Parenti, the
historical writer, talks of the factions of this period as 'intelligenze
in spirito'.[45]

The law of the 23 December 1494 that set up the *Consiglio Grande*
created a broad alliance of temporary agreement between *ottimati*
and *piagnoni*. The *ottimati* were worried about Savonarola's mass
following and by some of his more democratic measures, such as the
introduction of a progressive property tax. They supported the
Consiglio Grande and their long-term strategy was to engineer a
Venetian style electoral system, which could guarantee their
supremacy. At the same time, they were frustrated by the *piagnoni*
majority on the *Consiglio* and adopted wrecking tactics to subvert
the popular movement.

As Gilbert has pointed out, the Venetian-style settlement
assumed a more democratic role in the immediate post-Medici
years.[46] A fixed *reggimento* meant security in office for many whose

---

[43] See Gilbert (1977).
[44] Weinstein (1970) p. 273.
[45] *Ibid.* p. 277; Butters (1985) p. 26.
[46] Gilbert (1968) p. 478.

advancement was no longer dependent on the fickleness of the nomination and scrutiny committees or the Medici patronage system.

The voting scheme also allayed fears that a Medici might engineer a return, either through the use of the old bags, or by a conspiracy organised by the twenty *accoppiatori*. Moreover, in the new dispensation open debate in the *pratiche* was encouraged. There is no doubt that, at least initially, the system as a whole, and the voting scheme in particular, favoured the *piagnoni*.

Another important factor in this settlement was that Savonarola himself was opposed to lot and favoured preference voting. His basic political orientation followed Aquinas in the belief that the Kingdom of Heaven, ruled by the undivided will and power of God, should be reflected in earthly institutions. Thus he favoured a monarchy but recognised that other forms of government, such as civic republics, might be instrumental in preventing a monarch from becoming a tyrant. He was also a Dominican, and the comprehensive use of voting in that order might have influenced his view of what was best for Florence.[47] Above all, he believed in the importance of the individual's moral judgement in political matters, and this is probably the principal reason he opposed sortition. A voting decision is a matter solely for the individual and God — before whom we will all ultimately be judged. This combination of views led him to the position, expressed in his *Treatise on the Constitution and Government of the City of Florence*, that the people's sense of moral obligation should be moulded by religious rather than political institutions. The implication is that it is the people's duty to vote, but not to govern.[48] In this way, and with a true Thomist synthesis, Savonarola is an advocate of the equality of citizens, popular sovereignty and aristocratic rule at the same time. Furthermore, since the main enemy was tyranny and its main example the corrupt Medici regime, Savonarola had an easy target:

> It is necessary, therefore, to institute a system which lets only the whole people distribute offices and honours. One citizen, then, will not need to look up to another. Every man can consider himself the equal of any other.[49]

---

[47] See Barker (1913). It should be recognised, however, that holding elections in city republic is a far more daunting and variable project than in the controlled and disciplined environment of a monastic order.

[48] Savonarola (1978) pp. 251–2.

[49] *Ibid.* p. 251.

Savonarola's role of the people as the guardians of good monarchy or aristocracy is expressed in a multi-layered phrase: 'The Council must, however, preserve always the right to distribute offices and benefices. Everyone must pass through the gates of judgement. This, as I have said, will eliminate the source of all tyranny.'[50]

Not only did the candidates have to pass the judgement of the citizens, but the citizens have a certain responsibility in making that judgement. The metaphor of the 'gates of judgement' would not have been lost on his Christian readership whose belief was that their ultimate salvation was dependent on their temporal actions and choices. There is little space in this moral framework for sortition, which would have been seen as an abdication of moral responsibility.

Although the voting system gave the *piagnoni* a comfortable majority on the *Consiglio*, Francesco Valori, the leading secular member of the group, favoured electoral reform on the grounds that the system could damage the interests of the *piagnoni* in the longer term.[51] In Parenti's words. '... il modo della lectione non ad altro fine trovato era, che per rendere lo stato alla nobilta.' This can be translated as '... the method of election was found to have no other outcome than to return power to the nobility ... but the use of the word *stato* indicates that this would have been regarded as a condition of arbitrary power, rather than political rule.[52]

Valori's call for reform proved to be a significant, and tragic, foresight. Once the revolutionary enthusiasm of the immediate post-Medici years had worn off, attendance in the *Consiglio Maggiore* began to wane. The *Consiglio* had turned out to be larger than first envisaged, and had to be split into three groups to make meetings possible in the newly constructed chamber in the *Palazzo della Signoria*. Meetings were often inquorate and by 1497 the political initiative was beginning to swing in favour of the *ottimati*.[53] There had also been irregularities. An *ottimati intelligenzia* was discovered in 1496 advocating a slate of anti-*piagnoni* candidates. Guicciardini in his *Corsa Fiorentina* talks of *ottimati* attempts to sabo-

---

[50] *Ibid.* p. 253.
[51] Polizzotto (1994) p. 45.
[52] Rubinstein (1954) p. 324. Also see Viroli (1992), Rubinstein (1971) and Russell Price's translator's notes for Guicciardini (1997).
[53] Villani (1908) p. 526.

tage the voting procedures during this period.[54] The *ottimati* were also waging a complex tactical battle. By voting for a populist solution on the question of judicial appeal they had tried to create splits in the *piagnoni* ranks. In the tense summer of 1497 a plot to reinstate the Medici was uncovered and the perpetrators executed on the orders of Valori.[55]

The events that shaped the debate — as they did the history of the Second Republic itself — came when Savonarola was first excommunicated by the Pope in June 1497, and then arrested and executed by the Florentines in 1498. Furthermore, a mob, probably organised by the *arrabbiati*, murdered Valori on the night of Savonarola's arrest. The movement was therefore left without leaders. Electoral reform now seemed inevitable.

New laws had already been passed in November 1495, May 1497 and July 1498, each restoring further elements of sortition to the constitution to the detriment of the electoral process.[56] Francesco Valori's call for reform was finally heeded and the *scrutiny* for the *Signoria* was finally restored on 31 May 1499.

The revised *scrutiny* for the *Signoria* was a three-part process. First nominators were drawn from the Council members by lot. Their nominations were then voted on by the Council as a whole, and those with an absolute majority had their names *imboursed* and would be drawn at two monthly intervals as required.[57] The new system differed from the scrutiny of the First Republic in a number of respects. There were no appointed nominating or scrutiny committees; instead nominators were chosen by lot (ensuring a broad, or at least unpredictable, spread of candidates) and the vote then taken by the full Council. Selection was therefore based on the ascending rather than the descending principle. It is also possible that the process was far more public than the *scrutiny* process of the First Republic, and those whose names ended up in the final bags might have known that they had received the majority of votes cast.[58] One of the critical differences between the new system and the voting scheme which preceded it was that only members of the *Consiglio Grande* could be nominated for the scrutiny. The effect of

[54] Guicciardini (1964) pp. 60–1.
[55] Weinstein (1970) pp. 281–2.
[56] *Ibid.* p. 325.
[57] Butters (1985) p. 34.
[58] It seems unlikely that the results of the *Consiglio* vote would have been concealed. Butters seems to suggest that the new arrangement was far more open than the traditional scrutiny.

this was to narrow the ruling group and prevent the newly-returned *ottimati* from securing places on the *Signoria*.

How then can we account for the decision to revert back to lot? Butters gives three reasons.[59] Middle-ranking families wanted a wider distribution of offices, voting favoured those who could muster support, and the lot was easier to administer than frequent elections. Guicciardini talks of a compromise that was reached almost by accident after the *ottimati* had tried to discredit the voting system.[60] A third version of events is presented by Rubinstein's claim that the December law that brought in the elective system was regarded as a temporary measure.[61] There is some truth to each of these interpretations, but they all tend to play down the intensity of the political struggle that was taking place. The execution of Savonarola and the threatened break-up of the popular movement is too large a factor to ignore.

Guicciardini while underestimating the significance of the measure, is right to identify lot with compromise. The return to sortition represents a slight retreat for popular republicans faced with the threat of a permanent *ottimati* majority or a Medici comeback. It is, however, a tactical, consolidating, retreat which offers those *ottimati* on the *Consiglio* a stake in the higher offices, while denying the prospect of overall control to the *ottimati* as a whole. At the same time, the measure to limit candidature to members of the Council that was brought in with the reforms effectively closed the door on further *ottimati* gains. This seems the most likely strategic reason for the measure. It retained the *reggimento* as a participatory body, kept the *scrutiny* vote in the hands of the *Consiglio*, and prevented electoral manipulation from favouring those with power and influence.

The strong Florentine republican affinity with sortition makes it likely that this move was always on the cards once the constitution had established itself and the old Medici bags had been destroyed. In this sense Rubinstein is correct. The return to lot was certainly aided by the self-interest of the *popolani* who wished to retain access to higher office; it was also far more efficient than regular voting, particularly given the difficulties in calling full Council meetings. The overall outcome in preserving the undivided *reggimento* and preventing *ottimati* hegemony suggests, however, that the decision was taken for more important strategic reasons: it was nothing less

---

[59] Butters (1985) p. 35.
[60] Guicciardini (1964) pp. 60–1.
[61] Rubinstein (1954) p. 322.

than the defence of the republic and the values of Florentine popular government.

As a postscript to the reintroduction of lot as a means of defending the republican cause against impending *ottimati* power, an incident in Prato from this period emphasises how sortition was seen as a means of moderating the threat of electoral instability, whatever its origins. In the light of a new popular party that had emerged, during the election for the *podesta*, a group of concerned citizens demanded the re-instatement of lot, 'to escape from the judgement of the people' (*ed uscire dello arbitrio del popolo*).[62] This perception is a useful reminder that sortition was seen to act against the excesses of democracy just as much as those of aristocratic factions.

The modernisation of the Florentine constitution

1: Machiavelli's contribution

At this stage we need to look at a different, but nonetheless important aspect of the debate over the Florentine constitution. This is the idea there was much in the older arrangements of the First Republic that was outmoded, inefficient, and in desperate need of reform — and this applied particularly to the means of selecting office-holders. The major problems were the power invested in the office of the *Signoria* itself; the discontinuity created by the two-monthly rotation; and the absence of a direct role within the constitution for individuals with ability. Indeed, the very success of the *scrutiny* system in thwarting the political ambitions of powerful individuals can be seen as responsible for the rise in the extra-constitutional hegemony of the Medici. The length of time between *scrutinies* also meant that the system was unresponsive to political change.[63]

Machiavelli recognises not only the oligarchic origins of the *scrutiny* and *tratte*[64] but also the short term thinking behind the scheme:

---

[62] *Ibid.* p. 328.
[63] On the question of institutional efficiency the Medici years had been a mixed blessing. By creating small, controllable councils, the Medici vastly improved the efficiency of the republic, especially in foreign affairs. Many of the smaller groupings were elected by the *Cento* or council of 100, and this would have sent distinct signals to members of the Florentine ruling class that there were alternatives to lot. At the same time, however, the Medici retained power by keeping certain areas of the constitution deliberately vague so they could be easily manipulated.
[64] Machiavelli (1989) p. 101.

> These baggings were later called 'squittini'. Because the
> squittini were held every three or, at the most, five years, it
> appeared that they would relieve the city of the annoyance and
> remove the cause of tumults that arose at the creation of every
> magistrate because there were so many competitors. Since they
> did not know how to correct it, they took this way and did not
> understand the defects that were hidden under this small
> advantage.[65]

Although he does not elaborate on these 'defects' in the context of
the *History of Florence*, he does so in his *Discourse on the Remodelling of
the Government of Florence*, which takes the form of a proposal for a
new Florentine constitution made to Giovanni de Medici in 1520:

> Its defects were, among others, that it prepared the lists of those
> eligible to office far ahead of time; because of this, fraud was
> easy, and the choice could not be good, for since men change
> easily and turn from good to bad and, on the other hand, places
> were given to citizens much ahead of time, it could easily hap-
> pen that the choice was good and the drawing bad. Besides this,
> nothing was established to cause fear in great men, so that they
> would not cause factions, which are the ruin of government.[66]

Compared to those who extolled the merits of the first republic,
Machiavelli is under no illusions about its oligarchic essence; neither does he make a simplistic connection between the use of lot in
the *scrutiny* and the so-called liberties of the period.[67] What matters
more in his estimation is that the relationship between the institutions of government and the different sectors of the governed population is rational, stable and workable.

Machiavelli's actual proposals in this *Discourse*, however, are of
considerable interest for our inquiry into the use of lot. To satisfy the
political aspirations of all classes, he proposes a pool of sixty-five for
the *Signoria* appointed for life, a *Gonfalonier* elected from that group
for a two or three year term, a Senate of 200 and a Grand Council of
between 600 and 1000 members who would be chosen by lot from
the entire citizenry — a considerable widening of the 1494 arrangement.[68] The sixty-five were to be divided into two (once the
Gonfalonier had been elected) and each half would serve alternate
years in office. From each thirty-two, four groups of eight would
rotate every three months to form the active governing executive.

---

[65] Machiavelli (1988) p. 83 (Bk. II chap.28).

[66] Machiavelli (1989) p. 102.

[67] Compare Rinnuccini (1978) p. 206.

[68] *Ibid.* p. 111. 'The Hall must be re-opened and this allotment made to the
generality of the citizens'.

The Grand Council would select the members of all minor magistracies by lot from its own number. In addition, Machiavelli proposes a new feature: four Provosts, selected by lot from the sixteen elected *Gonfaloniers* for a period of one month only, would sit on the *Signoria* as non-active witnesses who had, nonetheless, the right of veto over all measures transacted by that body. Vetoed measures were to be referred, firstly to a meeting of the full thirty-two in the pool of *Signoria* members for that year, and subsequently, by appeal, to the Senate and thence to the Grand Council if this proved necessary. Provosts had to be present at all the appeals.[69]

This proposal constitutes one of the most finely drawn-up model constitutions of the period. It seeks to balance the interests of all classes, and understands how to exploit their particular capabilities. The need for permanence and experience is recognised, as is the need for accountability. What is more, it seeks to combine features of Roman and Athenian government and place them, feasibly, in a distinctly Florentine tradition. Three different forms of selection are proposed: appointment, election and sortition.

From our point of view the most interesting feature is the fact that he proposes that the Council should be selected by lot from the citizen body. The size of the pool immediately places this proposal on a par with Athenian democracy and distinguishes it from most medieval and early renaissance practices.[70] It is essentially a citizen solution rather than a *reggimento* solution because it creates a political community that is wider than the various temporary ruling groups that it produces. The use of lot is strong in that the blind break of the lottery ensures that the council is drawn directly without prejudice or favour from the citizen body. The wider pool also breaks the hold of the previous hereditary groupings, but it also ensures that the make up of the council is less predictable than if the draw was merely made from a small élite. This would have the effect of breaking up old habits of allegiance and dependence.

The office of Provost itself does not come from Athenian democracy, but is modelled on the Roman Plebian tribune. The Provosts' veto is the most powerful element in the constitution but is designed as a defensive measure against abuses of power and the tendency of the appointed few to pursue their own interests in office. It is a

---

[69] *Ibid.* pp. 111–12.
[70] This feature might also derive from the fact that Machiavelli himself was excluded form the 1494 Consiglio because he did not meet the criteria of being a descendent of a previous office holder.

means by which the sovereignty of the Grand Council can be maintained while allowing those most capable and experienced to manage the republic both in the long term and on a day-by-day basis. The use of lot for the selection of the Provosts is a reflection of the constitutional value of that office. A Provost is charged with acting as a guarantor against the misuse of power and therefore his selection should not be open to corruption or partisan interference. It is not clear, however, how much of a deliberative role was assigned to the Grand Council, and it seems that initiation of legislation was to remain firmly in the hands of the *Signoria* and Senate. In this respect, the fact that the Provosts were to be silent witnesses enhanced, rather than diminished, the division of political labour. On the other hand, the Provosts' veto resolutely calls the bluff of the aristocratic claim that the few necessarily act for the common good, and provides the Council with a potential deliberative role in considering measures vetoed by the Provosts.

In the history of the democratic use of sortition, Machiavelli's proposal marks a significant milestone and shows how the use of lot could be integrated into a broadly-based mixed polity. The situation in 1520 and the fact that he feels he has to appeal to the Medici means that this constitution is a compromise between aristocratic and popular republican features. Despite this, however, its bold design cuts through limitations of the constitutional proposals of the 1494–9 period, which were still largely modelled on the inefficient but time-honoured system of *scrutiny* and *tratte*.

2: Guicciardini's Logrogno Thesis

Guicciardini's first and most direct contribution to the modernisation argument comes in a paper entitled *Del Modo di Ordinare il Governo Popolare* which he wrote as a young ambassador to Spain in the town of Logrogno in 1512.[71] In this he proposes what is, in all essentials, a Venetian constitution for Florence; but, like Savonarola, he attempts to place it in the context of the Florentine traditions of popular government. He therefore appeals to those traditions.

The discourse consists of a series of practical proposals, which are advanced, or so it seems, to deal with an existing political context. On closer reading, however, we find that some of these proposals had already been part of the Florentine polity for a number of

---

[71] Guicciardini (1997).

years.[72] There is a sense, therefore, that we should see Guicciardini as using this as an opportunity to advance and develop political argument. As we shall see, the proposals replicate the platform of the Florentine *ottimati* that we explored earlier.

Critical of the rapid rotation of the *Signoria* and their appointment by lot, Guicciardini argues for a *Gonfalonier* for life supported and controlled by a council of around eighty who would be elected by vote by a slightly enlarged Grand Council. The Grand Council would be made up of life members, selected, as in the 1494 settlement, from ex-office-holders. He also proposes a Senate of 200 members.[73]

His emphasis throughout is that efficiency and liberty go hand in hand — and efficiency cannot be maintained unless the most capable people hold the highest offices. Thus he criticises the current system severely because it takes little account of individual talent and offers no rewards specifically based on the merit of the individual. It is irrational, he claims, for someone who gets 501 votes out of 1000 to have the same opportunity of office as one who obtains 800.[74] Justice and rationality are to be measured by merit, and merit is to be measured by voting. He goes further by suggesting that the use of lot will undermine the sovereignty of the Council: 'Moreover it is not compatible with popular government in which the great Council should be sovereign, not the lot, and public office-holders should derive their authority from it, not from luck.' [75] In Guicciardini's view, therefore, sovereignty, and authority are specifically linked to the process of electoral choice.[76]

Guicciardini does, however, suggest that all minor offices should be chosen by sortition, or a mixture between sortition and voting, and that a forty-strong appeals tribunal and a similar body for dealing with charges of magisterial misconduct be appointed in this way.[77] He also recognises the advantages of lot in inhibiting envy

---

[72] In particular the abolition of the *parlamento*, the creation of the *Gonfalonier* for life, and the introduction of the senate. This last measure was, however, adopted by the Florentine ottimati after the flight of Soderini in 1512 and was almost immediately abolished by the Medici.

[73] Guicciardini (1997) p. 218.

[74] *Ibid.* p. 210.

[75] *Ibid.* p. 210.

[76] This argument and its context reinforces the claim made by Manin that the idea of consent is behind the decline in the use of sortition. Manin (1997) p. 92.

[77] Guicciardini (1997) pp. 227–8.

and rivalry and in promoting participation.[78] He is not, therefore, wholly opposed to lot on principle, but focuses his arguments for appointment on the grounds of merit on the strategically significant offices of the *Signoria*.

The division of political labour between voters and governed that features in the Venetian arrangement and in Savonarola's arguments can also be found in Guicciardini. In a similar manner to Savonarola, he exaggerates the equality between citizens that voting will create.[79] The Grand Council is not to be a deliberative body because, he explains, this would create confusion. Its role would therefore be to vote for office-holders, and to approve legislation that had originated in the Senate. To help the council to reach a decision, however, these proposals would be published on the day before the vote.[80] For all his popular rhetoric, Guicciardini is advocating 'controlled assembly' politics on the Venetian model.

Where he differs from his immediate predecessors, however, is in his consistent emphasis on the principle of merit. Whereas Savonarola had endorsed preference voting on the basis of judgement — particularly judgement of the moral qualities of the political leadership — Guicciardini is responsible for elevating the notion of merit as a principle independent of wealth and power. His suggestion that the poor could rise to political prominence if they had ability would seem to fly in face of experience, but in terms of the argument this is a vital point because it allows the principle of merit to be promoted as 'pure', or impartial.[81] He is also keen to reintroduce the notion of personal ambition as a potential virtue. To seek office in order to promote the wellbeing of the republic is no bad thing.

This is an important step, for it successfully rebuffs an argument which had long been used to support the use of sortition. The word 'ambition' itself derives from the electoral context. The Latin word *ambio*, to go round, originally referred to the action of canvassing for votes. Another word, *ambitio (-onis)*, means 'a canvassing for office in a lawful manner' and has a second meaning of 'striving after honours' or a 'desire for office'.[82] Ambition therefore became associated with an immoderate desire for political power by the individual,

_____

[78] *Ibid.* p. 210.
[79] *Ibid.* p. 207.
[80] *Ibid.* p. 211.
[81] *Ibid.* pp. 205–6.
[82] *Cassells Latin Dictionary.*

and in the late medieval period approached the status of a deadly sin or vice, alongside pride and greed. Savonarola, as one would expect, makes this connection: '… men have within them pride, ambition and envy, and from this springs quarrels and intolerable wars.' [83]

Guicciardini, however, differentiates between honourable ambition for a worthy end, and its corrupt, self-seeking counterpart: 'Ambition is not to be condemned, nor should we revile the ambitious man's desire to attain glory by honourable and worthy means … Ambition is pernicious and detestable when its sole end is power.' [84] There is much virtuous classical 'gravitas' about this position, and although Guicciardini's sentiments differ from Savonarola's more theological approach,[85] both address the inner qualities of the individual and the importance of moral choice in the political arena.[86]

In the context of his time, therefore, Guicciardini breaks new ground by suggesting that voting is compatible with popular republicanism and that lot is outmoded. Machiavelli's proposal of some eight years later, however, shows that the inefficiencies of the old *scrutiny* and *tratte* can be addressed in a manner more commensurate with the genuine traditions of popular republican government, and that lot can work in a way that complements, rather than excludes, preference election.

Del Modo di Eleggere gli Uffici nel Consiglio Grande

Guicciardini's interest in the debate between voting and sortition does not end with the Logrogno discourse. He returns to explore the theme on at least two more occasions: in *Del modo di Eleggere gli Uffici nel Consiglio Grande* and in his later *History of Italy*. In both cases he uses paired fictitious speeches that present arguments for and

---

[83] Savonarola (1978) p. 232.

[84] Guicciardini (1965) p. 13. (Ricordi no. 32). See also Patrizzi (1594) p. 123.

[85] Pocock (1975) p. 133, notes that ambition is not a Christian virtue.

[86] Machiavelli's main contribution on the question of ambition comes in poetic form. In a vigorous Tercet on Ambition he describes the destructive power of personal ambition but suggests that it can be virtuous if joined to a 'valiant heart, and well-armed vigour.' The main theme, however, is that unbridled ambition must be contained and channelled under good laws and wise judgement. See Machiavelli (1989), pp. 734–9 (line 91). See also the closing lines of the poem:

'… And already she (ambition) has scattered so many sparks amongst those people swollen with envy that she will burn their towns and their farmsteads if grace and better judgement does not bring her to naught.'

against sortition.[87] Such speeches can be seen as belonging to a renaissance genre deriving from classical historians, particularly Livy. They were included within the historical descriptions simply to portray the type of arguments that might have been employed, animate the narrative and provide examples of rhetoric. Guicciardini uses this device extensively in his later historical works: in the unfinished *Cosa Fiorentina* and elsewhere in the *History of Italy*.[88]

Del modo di Eleggere ... is problematic for little is known of the circumstances of its creation, or the author's intentions. There are a number of options that are worth mentioning at this juncture. It could have been intended as part of an historical narrative, it could have been written as an example of the author's rhetorical skills, or as part of a wider discourse on the nature of government. It could have been written for discussion at an *ottimati* forum such as the Orti Orticellari, which Guicciardini regularly attended.[89] It is also possible that the piece was written entirely for the purpose of self-clarification with no particular readership or audience in mind. Despite these difficulties it is a remarkable discourse, and as we look in more detail at the presentation of the arguments, it is clear that Guicciardini is attempting a complex synthesis of classical thought and modern practical realities.

Guicciardini's first speaker

The first speaker in *Del modo di Eleggere* ... sets out what is essentially a case for the good management of the polity by the most capable, and the most capable are understood as those who gain the highest number of votes in the Grand Council. The way that the case is made, however, is rich in references to other areas of argument and thought. The speaker, who is clearly pushing an aristocratic agenda, starts by proclaiming his republican credentials. Those who decide on affairs of government and freedom in the republic must first: 'ensure that such freedoms are so instituted that each citizen may stand equal before the law, and no distinction is made between rich and poor';[90] and then follow the principle that the offices and salaries: 'be spread to all and in a way that makes it possible for all

---

[87] In *Del modo di Eleggere* ... the speakers are not named; in the *History of Italy*, however, Paolo Antonio Soderini is presented as a proponent of voting, while Guido Antonio Vespucci supports the use of lot. Guicciardini (1984) pp. 76–80. See below pp.132-3.

[88] Luciani (1950) p. 112.

[89] See Gilbert (1977).

[90] Guicciardini (1932) p. 176.

citizens to participate as much as possible' because: 'they are all children of the same mother.'[91]

This inclusive vision is, however, succinctly and absolutely qualified by the notion that increased participation will create increased danger for the republic, and bad management will herald 'disorder and ruin'.[92] The management of the republic stands or falls 'by the quality of its office-holders', and the affairs of government are likened to the running of a private business. Immediately we can see how Guicciardini's tactic of courting the ideals of popular government is echoed in the rhetorical devices of this speaker.

This reading is further endorsed by his depiction of the vote as a confirmation of popular sovereignty. Voting will not produce a *governo stretto* the speaker explains, because the decision is in the hands of the people: 'since it is you who distribute the offices to whomever and however you please.'[93] In this way, in two pages, the popular identification of majority voting with aristocratic rule arising from the electoral advantages of the educated classes is repudiated by arguments for efficiency and safety and an appeal to the sovereignty of the people.

The speaker recognises, however, that there are likely to be some teething problems with voting, and that not everyone will vote intelligently and without favouritism or prejudice. But he stresses that there are a few hundred who will 'scrutinise more diligently', and by choosing according to merit alone, will effectively hold the balance of power. The question of voting loyalty is thus touched upon, but the question of factions or parties is not raised. In fact neither of the two speeches mentions the capacity of lot to counter fractions.

In a similar manner the speaker rather weakly deflects the argument that voting will lead to the concentration of power in the hands of a few by suggesting that the votes taken so far prove this not to be the case. Furthermore, he explains, if the people wish to have diversity then they can vote for it.[94] The speaker recognises, however, that the people would be genuinely disadvantaged by the

---

[91] *Ibid.*
[92] *Ibid.*
[93] *Ibid.* p. 178.
[94] The encouragement of diversity among office-holders is, as we shall see, a major argument for the use of lot. It is developed as such by Guicciardini's second speaker.

loss of lot, and so he presents this as a sacrifice that is necessary for the public good.

This speech adopts a higher moral tone when Guicciardini attacks what he regards as the amorality of the lottery. Lot is not only dangerously unstable, but it also provides a bad example of justice for the young and impressionable: 'They suggest you stifle your love of virtue and industry, and erase all difference between good and bad ... damaging you and the good nature of your sons.'[95]

There can be no doubt from this that Guicciardini is using the paired speeches and the debate between lot and vote to explore the idea of proportionate justice. The arbitrary, essentially amoral, operations of sortition cannot easily be reconciled with the idea of justice as proportionate to moral goodness. At this point the argument moves from one about the practical issues of good management to become one of political and moral principle. Lot is presented as an abdication of political responsibility and thus a sign of moral degeneration. There is more than a hint of Savonarola's moral purity in this.

From here it is easy for Guicciardini's speaker to paint lot as contributing to the petty ambition of the Florentine middle classes — which constitutes a clever inversion of the notion that lot acts as a brake on excessive personal political ambition. Citing the examples of Venice, Sparta and Rome as support for the elective principle, he also suggests that lot is an indulgence, verging on the incontinent, and a danger to freedom:

> And if you give in to their imprudence and ambition they will come to you every day with new ideas and new disorders wishing to alter the order of things ... and in the end they will bring you to ruin because they do not care about the honour and gain of the republic, but only about their particular appetites and passions.[96]

In an argument well known to the humanists, and with more than a touch of rhetorical exaggeration, Guicciardini gets his speaker to suggest that lot is an excess and an indulgence that will destroy the very freedoms that its supporters wish to preserve:

> The ancients write, and it is true, that free governments only become disorderly as a result of excessive licence; and this can only mean that government is too broad and too many important matters are put in the hands of the multitude. From this fol-

---

[95] Guicciardini (1932) p. 183.
[96] *Ibid.* p. 184.

> lows confusion in the city, division amongst citizens and, in the
> end, either the loss of the dominion, or tyranny.[97]

The speaker therefore ends the piece by praising the virtues of
moderation and calling for a curb on such excesses. He suggests that
in this way the safety and prosperity of the city will be preserved.

Because we have already seen the Logrogno discourse we know
what to expect from Guicciardini's first speaker. Popular sovereignty is linked to the proposal for voting, voting is presented as a
means of ensuring good government, and the dangers of irresponsible participation in government are flagged up. It is an argument for
rule by the best that is slanted to appeal to the Florentine traditions
of popular government.

Guicciardini's second speaker

The second speaker, on the other hand, provides us with somewhat
of a surprise.[98] Although invented by an avowed supporter of aristocratic government, this persona is the nearest we have to a true
radical republican voice from the period. Unlike the first speaker,
whose class background is not mentioned, Guicciardini creates a
speaker from a specific background and tradition of thought. The
speaker explains that he is from the lower half of Florentine society,
Although there is some answering of the first speaker's points, this
speech sets the tone of the discussion above that of mutual
point-scoring or a mere exercise in rhetoric; his arguments are consistent, strong and structured. Many aspects of this speech also ele-
vate the debate above its proposed historical context. There are four
main themes which we can usefully examine: the implications of the
voting scheme on the unity of the citizen body, the practical impact
of class on the proposals for 'rule by the best', the idea of moderation or compromise, and the question of whether the citizens are
self-confident enough to participate in government.[99]

From the outset it is clear that Guicciardini's second speaker
believes that all citizens have a right to hold office, and that the proposal for elections will create a dangerously divided citizen body. In
answer to the self-evident truth that all citizens cannot hold office at

---

[97] *Ibid.*

[98] Discussion of this piece in Manin (1997) pp. 61–2, ignores the second speaker
      entirely. Pocock (1975) p. 134, does better but does not prepare us for the
      strength of argument of the speaker or his identity as a 'lost voice' of
      traditional Florentine republicanism.

[99] This theme is introduced at the beginning of the speech and returned to at the
      end. I will deal with it last.

one and the same time, the speaker suggests two alternatives. Either those excluded should 'not be considered citizens at all', or the exclusions should only be temporary. 'If advantages and honours were not open to all', he explains, 'we would have a part of the city in charge of power, and the other in a permanent state of servitude.'[100] The tendency for election to split the citizen body is presented in equally direct terms later in the speech:

> Therefore, I think it would be more honest to tolerate the small amount of disorder that this procedure might engender, rather than exclude us and our peers for ever, as if we were enemies or citizens of another city, or as if we were donkeys, whose task is always to carry wine and to drink nothing but water. We carry burdens much more than they do, because we are poorer and every weight has a much higher significance for us than for them: why should we not be entitled to have access to advantages as well?[101]

Access to office by lot is presented as being fair, just and natural, and the speaker conveys a sense that something that belongs to the citizenry at large is being taken away. The notion of equality before the law, evoked by the first speaker, is cited here by the second, but the use of lot to fill magisterial offices is presented almost as if it is the next clause of that provision:

> ... not only would the excluded be deprived of something that reasonably belongs to them, but also the very securities and equalities, granted by the fact of being all subject to the same laws and officers, and for the sake of which liberties were invented, would thus be altered and weakened.[102]

In this way the speaker is depicted not just as the mouthpiece for an argument, but as someone coming from a distinct tradition of thought. This is the tradition of the popular governments, who established communal law in the thirteenth century in the face of anarchic opposition from the magnates and nobility. This voice echoes the ideas of popular sovereignty of Bartolus, Marsilius and the other early jurists. As we proceed into the second speech we become more and more aware that Guicciardini is creating a complex synthesis of history, ideas and argument.

Perhaps the strongest impact of this speech, and certainly its most 'modern' feature, comes from the speaker's awareness of class

---

[100] Guicciardini (1932) p. 187.
[101] *Ibid.* p. 192. It seems as if Guicciardini has used an Athenian-style citizen lot scheme as his model.
[102] *Ibid.* p. 187.

struggle within the Florentine republic. This is especially noticeable because the first speaker has presented his vision of meritocracy and popular sovereignty by vote as if class was not a factor in electoral choice. This claim of class impartiality is challenged in one key passage in the second speaker's contribution. This starts relatively meekly:

> Those who oppose this provision say that, when officers are elected by majority vote, the offices are assigned to those who most deserve it, because it is reasonable to think so if the majority has the same opinion about them. I would share this view, if those who are entitled to vote, namely the members of the Council, were all of the same kind and of the same station.[103]

The first speaker has presented the body politic as a level playing field; the second speaker insists that it is not so. Turning the meritocratic argument on its head, he claims that once the rich hold office, they will accrue the credibility that will keep them there. In this they will be aided by the deference of the lower classes. Luck and sharp practice, rather than any specific virtue, have given the rich their electoral advantage, and they maintain their power by lobbies, slates and coalitions. What is more, they can maintain their hegemony by the consent of the voters:

> I talk about real liberty because they have only showed us liberty so far, without really granting it to us: on the one hand, they gave us the power to vote and they convinced us that we could all equally take part in all honours and advantages; on the other, they managed to set up things in such a way that they can still enjoy all advantages with our own consent, with no violence and no explicit oppression, and we are, therefore, still their servants in many respects. Therefore, we go to Council meetings with the same curiosity with which bears look for honey, and we do not realise that it is just useless effort and servitude, and that, if we make a balance at the end of each year, it always turns out that we have not gained anything really relevant.[104]

This is a truly remarkable passage in which Guicciardini, a member of the *ottimati* class who later plays a key role in the destruction of the Second Florentine Republic, reveals how his own class manoeuvres to give freedom with one hand and take it with the other.[105] He also suggests how the concept of consent, the centre-

---

[103] *Ibid.* p. 188.
[104] *Ibid.* p. 194.
[105] Roth (1968) p. 91, describes Guicciardini as a 'creature of the Medici.'

piece of later social contract theory, is used to disguise what is essentially the loss of the right to office.

Although Guicciardini draws on what he knows of the republican tradition for much of this speech, he also gives the speaker a chance to develop arguments and concepts that derive from classical sources. In contrast to more popular republican elements in the argument, the speaker also portrays lot as a middle way. He puts forward the following proposition. Given that the rich will not change their ways, the popular party are left with two options, either to use their majority to vote in a permanent government of the lower classes — which would cause dangerous divisions — or use sortition — which would give all an equal chance of holding office.[106] In this way Guicciardini presents lot as an alternative to the arbitrary rule of the poor and thus as a means of establishing a genuine *polity* in the Aristotelian sense of the term. He also makes it clear that the *scrutiny* element means that some level of judgement by merit is not entirely ruled out; the scheme is 'tempered' (*temerata*), convenient (*conveniente*) and broad but not disorganised or slovenly (*non disordinino ... larghezza non sbacata*).[107] Any problems that might arise from lot, such as choosing someone who is not competent, could be handled by the collegiate system of office-holding, and anyway, the speaker explains, such problems are preferable to those of deep social division.

The second speech started with an exhortation to the citizens of Florence to cease thinking and acting as servants and assert their rights as free citizens. This theme is taken up again at the end of the speech. In this advocacy of active citizenry Guicciardini suggests that greater political participation is obstructed not only by the vested interests of the rich, but also by the mediocrity and servile attitudes of the members of the speaker's own class. He asks them to be more conscious, more decisive and, above all, more responsible. By ending the speech in this way Guicciardini suggests that the problems of government are two-sided: opportunities have to be given, but opportunities also have to be taken. There is more than a hint here that the rank and file might be unwilling or unable to follow the advice of their eloquent spokesperson.

What becomes clear from this examination is that Guicciardini is not using this piece merely to display his rhetorical skills or simply to animate an historical narrative. Aspects of both are present, but

[106] Guicciardini (1932) p. 188.
[107] *Ibid.*

the overall thrust of the piece and its philosophical and practical richness indicate that it is more than a sum of these parts. One interpretation of the role of this work lies in Guicciardini's identity as a modern political thinker with a new agenda to pursue, but a thinker who, at the same time, shows a considerable awareness of ancient political thought. Both speeches are underpinned by classical language and concepts, and there are allusions to the work of classical writers, Cicero, Polybius, Thucydides and particularly Aristotle — who is the only ancient writer to deal with the issue of lot.[108]

Thus it is possible to view the work as a contemporary re-working of Aristotelian themes in Livian format — a piece of renaissance political art. In this way the debate between lot and voting can be seen as a debate between Rome and Athens, or Sparta and Athens, or the mirroring of a possible debate between Athenian democrats and aristocrats. Because there is no such debate in Aristotle, Guicciardini could have seen himself as bringing out an issue which is latent, but unresolved, in Aristotle's *Politics*.

There is, however, more of a practical edge to this work. Guicciardini's aristocrats had lost the debate of 1494–9, and their new vision for the republic was denied by the Medici in 1512 and the second phase of the Florentine republic of 1527–30.[109] On these grounds we can read the work as a particularly pointed means of exploring principles with an eye to future practice: a piece of *ottimati* self-criticism. Such a reading would go a long way towards explaining the strength and honesty with which Guicciardini approaches his opponents' arguments, and could explain why he gives his second speaker such an astute grasp of aristocratic tactics.

----

[108] The notion of liberty as the equality of all before the law is a Ciceronian tenet; the degeneration of democracy into tyranny is a well-known thesis from Polybius; there is a reference to the Pisan expedition, which can be read as a parallel to Thucydides' portrayal of the Syracusan expedition from Athens (see Butters,1985, especially pp. 83–112). The first speaker's interest in the morality of choice echoes Aristotle's exploration of the voluntary, rational choice and deliberation in the first two books of the *Nichomacean Ethics* (Aristotle, 2000, pp. 3–36). The second speaker's understanding of the polity seems to come directly from Aristotle's categorisation of constitutions in *Politics* Bk. IV ; comparisons between business management and the well-run republic reflect Aristotle's interest in *oeconomica*; and a central theme of the two speeches — the difficulty of differentiating between rule by the best and rule by the rich — is central to Aristotle's political discourse. See *Politics* Bk. II chap. 11 § 8–9. (Aristotle, 1946, p. 85.)

[109] See Butters (1985).

Of importance to this study, however, are the arguments that Guicciardini omits from this ostensibly two-sided account of the issue. Although the second speaker is given an intuitive under-standing of how the rich and powerful can use voting to their advantage, neither of his two speakers directly expresses the idea that lot was used to retain the public ownership of the process of selection. In this way, the strongest argument for the use of lot and the reason for its most consistent deployment—a reason especially pertinent to the defence of Florentine popular republicanism—is hidden. While Guicciardini's second speaker suggests that lot pro-tects the citizens from 'servitude', he nonetheless fails to define how lot defends the public political process against private or factional power.[110]

Guicciardini's re-writing of the debate

The mystery surrounding Guicciardini's portrayal of sortition is enhanced by the fact that he offers us three different accounts of the 1494–9 debates on sortition. In the *Cosa Fiorentina* as we have seen, the debate is down-played to the status of a simple compromise, made because agreement was proving difficult. In *Del modo di Eleggere ...* he exaggerates the importance of the debate, and widens its political scope—presenting it as a piece of rhetorical theatre. Nonetheless we know from other sources that the two sides of the argument presented by Guicciardini in this work are very close to the positions and traditions of thought of the parties taking part in the controversy of 1494–9. There is a cautious aristocratic modern-iser in the mould of the young Guicciardini himself, and an advo-cate of popular republicanism—an articulate artisan following Rinuccini's line that liberty and lot are dependent on each other. In his last word on the subject, the debate in his *History of Italy*, Guicciardini gives us yet another view of the controversy.

In the *History* the debate between sortition and voting is pre-sented in a pair of speeches set in the period after the fall of the Medici, but before the adoption of the new Florentine constitution. The dominant argument is between popular government and the aristocratic position of *governo stretto*, or narrow government, and within this context the debate between selection by lot and prefer-ence voting makes an appearance. The speaker for popular govern-ment is Paulo Antonio Soderini, a republican who proposes that

---

[110] In this respect even the more immediate role of lot in preventing electoral corruption is omitted from the speeches.

Florence adopts the Venetian model. Opposing him is Guido Antonio Vespucci, a leading member of the *ottimati*. Soderini declares his
preference for a Venetian-style settlement on the grounds that it
includes rotation in office and government by the best. Voting is a
means of combating factions because government officers will be
accountable to the electorate.[111] Vespucci, on the other hand, portrays voting as potential anarchy, and the multitude as lacking the
responsibility to hold power.[112] This will result, he says, in the 'tyranny of the people'.[113] Lot, he explains, is better than election by the
few, or by the many, and prevents appointment either by factions or
by the 'will of particular citizens' — arguments notable by their
absence from *Del Modo di Eleggere* …

Soderini was a known supporter of Savonarola and a champion of
a Venetian settlement. To this extent Guicciardini's account is based
on fact. In terms of the arguments that Soderini presents, however,
these come straight out of Guicciardini's own Logrogno thesis of
1512. Vespucci, however, presents sortition as a means by which the
aristocracy seek to maintain power by denying the vote to the people. This is a conservative argument for sortition that surfaced in the
early Second Republic but was certainly not a line held by the
ottimati.[114]

Guicciardini's presentation of the lot/voting controversy in the
History of Italy, therefore, is a deliberate inversion of the traditional
links between sortition and popular republicanism on the one hand
and between voting and the *ottimati* on the other. The effect is to
hide the combative role of lot in the defence of the Second Republic,
and to portray preference voting as the popular choice.

Conclusion

This chapter, and this story, is central to the study. We have seen
two battles for control of the process of selection of public officers,
one during the period of Medici rule, and one during the first few
years of the Second Florentine Republic. In the first case republicans
were attempting to break the hold on government exercised by a
rich and influential family that held power by maintaining complex
systems of patronage and intimidation. In the second a popular
movement was attempting to keep the republic out of the control of

---

[111] Guicciardini (1964) p. 78.
[112] *Ibid.* p. 81.
[113] *Ibid.*
[114] We have seen something of this line in the Prato incident. See above pp. 117.

a new aristocratic party whose platform was based on a Venetian style settlement for Florence. In both cases sortition played a central part in the political tactics of the republicans and in both cases that role was to keep the selection of public offices in public hands.

It is clear, moreover, that this use was well understood. Sortition had been part of Florentine republican practice since the *Primo Popolo* of the mid-thirteenth century, and possibly earlier. In both instances the application of lot was strong — it made positive use of the blind break — and lot was used in circumstance where the political stakes were high. It was obviously known that if control over the process of selection was lost, the type of political process which valued open discussion, citizen participation, and freedom from arbitrary rule was also in jeopardy. This possibility was defined by Guicciardini's second speaker as a potential state of servitude. Although *Del modo di Eleggere ...* is laced with invention and rhetoric, I have little doubt that this was how the popular republicans of Florence understood their situation. In this context sortition was a tactical mechanism, but we should also think of it as linked to matters of political principle.

In this chapter we also saw, for the first time, the interaction of political thought and practice in respect to sortition. Guicciardini, I would argue, is astute enough to realise the potential of lot to frustrate the *ottimati* cause. He is the only writer of this period to give it serious consideration, and at the same time the first writer to attempt to develop a platform for election in the context of the popular republic. What is also significant is that he seeks to hide the full potential of lot from successive generations by failing to state its republican content clearly and by removing it from the republican tradition to which it so obviously belonged. As well as writing for his time, Guicciardini's works seem to prefigure many aspects of modern government. Although the line between them is a little thin, liberal democracy — with its reliance on popular voting and its marked division between those who vote and those who govern — can be seen as a direct reflection of his ideas.

In contrast, Machiavelli's proposal for a mixed-polity constitution belongs securely in the older tradition and gives us a chance to see lot in the context of a planned scheme that draws both from contemporary Florence and from classical republican ideas. The two proposals for the use of lot in his 1520 constitution — the selection of members of the Grand Council and the selection of Provosts — are both examples of lot used for the same basic function. By ensuring that the citizen's entrance into the body politic is independent of partisan influence, and that no Provost can be strategically placed in office, they help to keep political power in public hands.

This chapter marks a parting of the ways in the development of the western polity, both in theory and practice. If Guicciardini's ideas anticipate liberal democracy and the professional managerial politician, the practical tradition that spawned Machiavelli's political acumen came to an end not long after he wrote his *Discourse*. The Florentine republican lot-polity was to fall to the combined forces of Pope and Empire in 1530. Chaotic and complex by Athenian standards, it nonetheless represented nearly three hundred years of practical experience in the political use of lot. The Venetian electoral system carried on relatively unchanged until 1797 and for some writers, such as James Harrington, Venetian, rather than Florentine, institutions, would provide the answer to the question of how the model republic should be structured.

In the next chapter I will be looking at how the sortive tradition finds its way from Venice to the New World via English republicanism and at how other political institutions, such as the randomly-selected jury and the secret ballot, develop from it. It is a story of how the problem-solving potential of sortition re-asserts itself in very new and very different political surroundings.

Bibliographical notes

I start with the works of Guicciardini. For the Logrogno thesis ('Del Modo di ordinare il Governo Popolare') I use the translation by R. Price in Kraye, J. ed. (1997) *Cambridge Translations of Renaissance Philosophical Texts* (Cambridge University Press); for the *History of Florence*, Grayson's 1964 translation abridged by Hall; and for the History of Italy the 1984 Princeton edition translated by S. Alexander, 'Del modo di eleggere … ' is found in *Dialogo e discorsi del Reggimento di Firenze*. A cura di R. Palmarocchi. Bari Laterza (published in 1932). I was assisted in the translation of this by T. Torresi and M. Ronzoni. For Machiavelli's work I used the Gilbert three volume set of 1989, plus the 1988 Princeton version of the Florentine *Histories*, and the Penguin 1998 *Discourses* translated by L. Walker. Rinnuccini's *De Liberate* and Savonarola's 'Treatise on the Constitution and Government of the City of Florence' can be found in a translation by R. N. Watkins in Watkins, R. N. ed. (1978) *Humanism and Liberty. Writings on Freedom from fifteenth-century Florence*, published by the University of S. Carolina Press. Transcripts of the debates on lot from 1465–6 can be found (in Latin) in 'Testi e Documenti' (1961) *Archivio Storico Italiano* 119.

My use of secondary material draws strongly from the works of two writers: Rubinstein and Gilbert. Gilbert's 1968 'The Venetian Constitution in Florentine Political Thought' was particularly valuable, as was his 1977 study of the *ottimati* circle that that developed around Bernado Rucellae. Rubinstein's 1954 'I primi anni del Consiglio Maggiore di Firenze (1494–99)', found in *Archivio Storico Italiano* n. 403, a cxii , 1954 II. p. 51, gives an account of the first years of the new republic. His 1966 *The Government of Florence under the Medici 1434–1494* is particularly good for its treatment of the republican movement of 1465–6. Other secondary works that need to be mentioned are Butters (1985), Finlay (1980), Stephens (1983) and the earlier account of the fall of the second phase of the Second Republic by Roth first published in 1936. For their attention to detail Queller's 1986 study of the Venetian nobility and Pesman-Cooper's paper on the Florentine *reggimento* were indispensable.

My background in the political ideas of this period was well served by Bock, Skinner and Viroli's 1990 *Machiavelli and Republicanism*, Viroli's *From Politics to Reasons of State*, and Pocock's *Machiavellian Moment*. None of these, however, specifically explores the use of lot.

Chapter Five

Sortition in England and America in the Seventeenth and Eighteenth Centuries

So far we have looked at sortition in political contexts where it was used extensively and where its potential was well known. This chapter deals with a far more piecemeal pattern of application. Lot was not part of the path of political development that emerged in northern Europe during the late Middle Ages. The levels of popular participation that we saw, for example, in the *popolo* polities of thirteenth-century Italy were unheard of further north. Here the dominant political form was that of the monarch holding sway over the feudal nation-state, rather than the small communal republic or city-state ruled, by and large, by its citizenry. As the ideas of renaissance republicanism filtered north, however, and as classical political literature became more widely available, some interest in sortition also came with it. By the beginning of the seventeenth century in England, therefore, scholars knew of the political use of lot, lot was used or advocated to solve particular problems, and had become an established practice in some local areas. But it was never a central part of the northern polity in the way that it had been in Athens, Venice or Florence.

This limited interest took on greater significance during the English revolution when writers and political thinkers were actively searching for new structures and procedures to match the new circumstances in which they found themselves. In this context we find a major republican work, Harrington's *Oceana*, self-consciously advocating a Venetian style constitution for Britain. While *Oceana* made no impact on the immediate course of English politics, interest in the idea of a constitution, or set of fundamental laws, found an outlet in the New World, particularly in the English proprietary colonies of North America. In the draft constitutions of these colonies we find that sortition was advocated, but only in the case of one particular measure, the randomly-selected jury, do we see the use of lot become part of regular political practice. This story forms the basic narrative structure of this chapter. The examples that I cite, however, fall into two main categories: those that show lot as part of general governmental thought or practice, and those where lot was advocated or used merely as a solution to a particular problem at hand. This distinction can help us to understand what the examples can show us about the political potential of lot. The examples in the latter category (I call these 'stand-alone' examples) are illustrations of good and bad schemes, strong and weak applications of lot, or appropriate and inappropriate uses of the lottery mechanism. On the other hand, those schemes where lot has a greater governmental or constitutional significance tell us about the wider political potential of sortition and what qualities it can bring to the overall orientation of the polities in question. They also enable us to locate the use of sortition more securely within the shifting pattern of political practices and ideas that was taking place during this period.

I start the chapter, therefore, with a discussion of three instances of sortition in the ideas and political practice of England in the early seventeenth century. I then turn to Harrington's *Oceana*, and from there to the proposed 'Harringtonian' constitutions of the proprietary colonies. This leads me to a consideration of the relationship between lot and the secret ballot. I then look at several individual instances of the use and advocacy of lot during the revolutionary period in America before examining the emergence of the randomly-selected jury in some detail. This was a truly transatlantic affair. The jury had been used in England since the early Norman period, but the first time that lot was officially adopted as a means of selection was in South Carolina in 1682. Britain adopted random selection in 1730 and most of the remaining colonies followed shortly afterwards. I discuss the political importance of the jury during this period and how it relates to the earlier republican use of lot.

Three examples from early seventeenth-century England

Great Yarmouth

According to Yarmouth historian C. J. Palmer, the mayor, bailiffs and the vestry of local officers (consisting of four Aldermen, three Common Councillors, the Chamberlain, two Churchwardens, two

Morangers, two Collectors of Fishing Doles, four Auditors and sixteen Tellers of Herrings) were chosen by a method known as the 'inquest'.[1] At a special open Grand Assembly, the names of the
Aldermen and Common Councillors were first called out and then
written on slips of paper. These were marked numerically and put
into four hats, which were placed in front of the mayor—six in each
hat and more in the last hat if more than twenty-four were eligible
for the draw. If fewer than twenty-four were available the number
was to be made up from the freemen present at the meeting.[2] An 'innocent' or 'person unlettered' — usually a boy from the crowd — was
then asked to draw three names from each hat, and these twelve
would act as electors for the officers. In true Italian style the electors
would be locked in the hall 'without meat, drink, fire or candle' and
forbidden to speak to anyone else until they had reached their decision. Nine votes were sufficient to elect any post-holder. During this
time they could only be asked whether or not they had reached
agreement.[3] The inquest itself was introduced in 1491 and was last
used in 1835 to elect the mayor. The practice was discontinued
under the terms of the Municipal Corporations Act of that year.[4]
Contemporary documents indicate that the scheme was introduced
as a response to electoral disputes. These are described as 'Vari-
ances and discordes' which resulted from the 'neglygent kepying of
the ordenaunces and reules.'[5]

Yarmouth during the late medieval period had developed a
strong independent corporate identity. It was the centre of the her-
ring industry and was heavily involved with the wool trade to the
continent. Moreover it had to fight for its commercial survival
against feudal landowners from its immediate north and south, and
for greater independence from the Cinque-ports, under whose jurisdiction it originally fell.[6] Its initial Charter was granted in 1208, and
its Borough Ordinances of 1272 unusually granted it the right to

[1]   See Palmer (1856) p. 55 and pp. 51–9 for a full account of the system. See also
      Manship (1954) p. 358. Palmer himself arranged for Manship's 1619 history
      to be published for the first time in 1854. Details of the inquest are to be found
      in Palmer's explanatory notes to this account, and they include a greater
      emphasis on the office of bailiff than in his history of 1856, together with
      slightly different details of the officers elected by this method.
[2]   Palmer (1856) pp. 55–6.
[3]   Palmer (1956) p. 59. Apparently this procedure was also used to select
      burgesses for parliament. *Ibid*. p. 197.
[4]   Manship (1854) p. 358.
[5]   *Ibid.*
[6]   *Ibid*. pp. 168–9 and 181–4.

elect its own reves.[7] Manship, writing in the early seventeenth century, describes Yarmouth as a 'commonwealth'.[8]

The most remarkable feature about the Great Yarmouth inquest is the number of years during which it was in operation. It clearly suited the needs of the community and provided responsible and stable local government. It is difficult to know, however, whether it is an isolated example on English soil and whether it had continental origins. The details of the enclave are uncannily similar to the procedures of modern trial by jury.[9] Because the officers involved were central to the regulation of the local economy, the use of an arational method of selection helped to prevent corruption and present the local government as non-partisan. This finds its expression in the use of the 'innocent', illiterate boy in the public ritual of the lottery draw. There is a sense that the boy symbolises the general good over partisanship, and his action signals a special relationship between those chosen and the town. They are, in the words of Marcus Kishlansky, endowed with the town's 'corporate identity'.[10]

The existence and longevity of the Yarmouth inquest is difficult to understand without reference to a wider perspective on the selection of officers and parliamentary representatives in pre-civil war England. The main thesis of Kishlansky's 1986 *Parliamentary Selection* is that most communities of this period sought consensus rather than competition in their choice of representatives. He draws the valuable distinction between 'standing for a seat' where the individual would see himself as a representative of the whole community, and 'running for a seat' in which candidates could be seen as representing a particular constituency within the wider community.[11] Contested elections in this period were the exception rather than the rule.[12] There was little or no political content in the processes of selection and there was genuine agreement that contests could be disastrous for the community.[13] Kishlansky notes how this conception of the political process grew out of complex notions of 'honour,

---

[7] Saul (1975) p. 6.
[8] Manship (1854) p. 24.
[9] This is also reflected in other features of Yarmouth local government such as the employment of twenty-four Common Councillors to 'have a syght of merchandize' in 1386. We do not know how they were chosen, however. Palmer (1856) p. 45.
[10] Kishlansky (1986) p. 36.
[11] *Ibid.* p. 11.
[12] *Ibid.* p. 12.
[13] *Ibid.* p. 15.

standing and deference', and a conception of the harmonious community which was seriously shaken by the upheavals of the mid-seventeenth century.[14]

The work of Thomas Gataker

In contrast to this very practical example, Gataker's 1619 thesis *Of the Nature and use of Lots* is an important benchmark for how lot was understood in intellectual circles in the early seventeenth century.[15] Thomas Gataker (1574–1654) was a fellow of Sidney Sussex College in Cambridge and held a lectureship in Lincoln's Inn. Later he became rector of Rotherhithe and was internationally recognised as one of the leading classical and theological scholars in the country. He was an important puritan cleric and part of a group of 'Westminster Divines' who regularly preached in Westminster Abbey.[16] These details give us some indications as to his readership and influence.

Of the Nature and use of Lots is a contribution to contemporary debates on divination and gambling and in it Gataker draws a clear dividing line between 'lawful' use of lot to achieve valuable human ends, and its use in gambling and forms of divination which he characterises as superstition.[17] We can interpret the term 'lawful' to mean morally permissible, but we should also recognise that Gataker's use has theological overtones. 'Lawful' means permissible according to God's laws. Gataker is well aware that lot is, in itself, a neutral phenomenon which can be used for good or evil purposes,[18] and he warns that 'lots determine no rights', and that no issue of 'right or wrong may be grounded upon lots.'[19] On the other hand he recognises that lot can be used valuably and legitimately as a means of settling disputes in the cause of 'peace and quietnesse'.[20] He further emphasises this point by quoting Proverbs 18.18 '... lot staieth or stinteth contentions or suites and maketh partition amongst the mighty.'[21]

---

[14] *Ibid.* p. 12.
[15] Gataker (1627). This treatise was first published in 1619.
[16] *Oxford Dictionary of National Biography*.
[17] Gataker (1627) p. 362.
[18] *Ibid.* pp. 5, 360
[19] *Ibid.* pp. 148–9.
[20] *Ibid.* p. 148.
[21] *Ibid.* pp. 61, 118. This constitutes, in fact, a biblical endorsement of its greatest political potential.

Gataker devotes a major section of his thesis to the use of lot for political purposes. He discusses the instances of sortition in classical Athens and Rome, ancient Israel and contemporary Venice in great detail, drawing on a wide range of sources. This is undoubted proof, if proof is needed, that these matters were thoroughly and securely in the public domain at this time. On more particular political issues Gataker sees lot and preference voting as interchangeable means by which candidates can be selected for office:

> No doubts or controversies are by any lawful lot resolved or decided, but such as it is in the power of man to resolve and decide otherwise. In election of officers that is done by lottery with some, that may be done, and with others is as well done, by the greater part of voices.[22]

At the same time, however, he recognises that, despite its use by democracies to establish an arbitrary form of equality, sortition is a powerful aid to the stability of government:

> Most common in Democracies or popular Estates (because they seemed justly to carry the most equality and indifferency that might be with them, as they do questionless, though such indifferency indeed is not always allowable, nor such equality, stand ever with equity) but no strangers in any kind of state or forme of government whatsoever is yea much used in the most flourishing and best ordered Estates, nor rejected but admitted and approved by such state-masters or state-wrights ... as they deemed would be for the best and like longest to continue.[23]

Again this is testament to the ability of lot to uphold and sustain political consensus, but this work also shows that among those of classical education in early seventeenth-century England the political role of lot was well known, in theory, and its potential and limitations were recognised and discussed. At the same time the controversy engendered by this work indicates there was clearly considerable apprehension about the use of lot amongst members of the puritan community.

While Gataker removes some of the moral and religious barriers to the use of lot to achieve beneficial political ends, there is a sense in his work that lot should be handled with care, and should not be used if a rational mechanism could achieve the desired results. He also suggests that a lottery will be more lawful when all parties partake willingly.[24] In general Gataker sees lot as more legitimate if

---

[22] *Ibid.* p. 59.
[23] *Ibid.* p. 68.
[24] *Ibid.* pp. 111, 49.

those in the pool are already equal: 'the less danger of inqualitie, the lawfuller the lot.'[25] In the use of sortition for choosing office holders, he also suggests that lot is, 'not lawful if it may be of consequence whether one have the office or the other.'[26] He does, however, make an exception to this: 'unless for some greater inconvenience enforce it.'[27] While he does not go on to explain what some of these greater inconveniences might be, this is, in fact, an admission that lot can be used in such a way as to make a positive virtue of its arationality. He describes lot as the 'most equall and indifferent course that can be and no corruption or partialitie can be charged upon it', and this again indicates that he understands its potential, even if he does not discuss or develop these ideas further in a political context.[28]

Gataker's work shows us that questions of lot were part of early seventeenth-century intellectual and theological discourse. This discussion, however, is not presented as part of a specifically political agenda, although, undoubtedly it was read in political circles. Puritan reservations and non-conformist antipathy to the idea that the arational could be used to perform rational tasks must have inhibited the acceptance of the political use of lot in England. Gataker's thesis is a reminder of the strength of this tendency, and of the cautious English approach to such matters, rather than an indication that the barriers to the greater political use of lot were about to be swept away.

English Parliamentary Committees

My third example from the pre-civil-war period is somewhat of a mystery, but it certainly substantiates the idea that lot was a practical option for political thinkers and practitioners during this period. On 3 March 1626, during the first session of parliament in the reign of Charles I, a committee of the House of Commons was asked to meet on the following day to 'consider of an indifferent course for the naming of committees'. The group of twelve consisted of renowned parliamentarians such as Sir Dudley Digges, Sir Thomas Hoby, Sir Edwin Sandys, Mr Herbert, Sir Miles Fleetwood and Sir Francis Barrington. The mover of the proposal, according to the journal of committee member Henry Sherfield, was Sir Dudley Digges, an ambitious MP and a vociferous opponent of the Duke of

---

[25] Gataker (1623) p. 73.
[26] *Ibid.* p. 238.
[27] *Ibid.*
[28] Gataker (1627) pp. 205–6.

Buckingham.[29] The diary goes on to give noted detail of the discussion and the full text of the proposal. The names of all the members of the house were to be written on small scrolls of paper and placed in a box under the table near the clerk. When a bill was to be committed the House would agree the number to be on the committee and the clerk would then draw out names amounting to half the number required. These would be the nominators, and they would be required to name one member each to go on the committee. Each committee member would then select another. The member drawn by lot could not be selected by the committee member he had chosen himself, but could be named by another nominator or committee member. According to custom, those who had spoken against the bill in question could not serve on the committee.

Sherfield's journal lists a number of objections that were made against this proposal. These included the length of time it would take to settle the committee membership, the possibility that those not named could be offended, and that members who did not want to serve could be named. Another objection was that the most eminent men might be named and so the 'business be carried in a few hands', a circumstance that the original proposal was designed to avoid.[30] It was also suggested that the papers near the top of the box might be taken out more frequently than the others.

The next item in the journal consists of an alternative proposal coming, it seems, from a different meeting consisting of a larger number of less prestigious Members of Parliament. This suggests that the House be divided up into ten equal parts, each consisting as far as possible, of the same number of 'lawyers, knights of the shires, of port men, of midland men, of merchants, and of tradesmen and others.'[31] These divisions would be numbered from one to ten and would be called to form the appropriate committee, in order, as was demanded by parliamentary business. The committees would have the power of co-option and could also decide whether those co-opted could have a voice or not. They could also summon any member of the house or send for any necessary information. Every committee would be open to all members of the commons to attend, but only those named as committee members would have a voice.

Both the schemes go some way towards establishing a fair and impartial procedure for selecting Parliamentary Committees. Both

---

[29] Bidwell and Janssen (1991–5) pp. 196–200.
[30] *Ibid.* pp. 198, 197.
[31] *Ibid.* pp. 189–200.

also have problems. The first advocates a complex mix of randomness and choice, while the second favours a proportionate solution for the make up of the Committees. The overall rationale for both schemes is to prevent those with a vested interest from packing the Committee designated to deal with that interest, and to spread committee work more equally amongst members of the House. In the first scheme the random element is compromised by the number of personal choices that those selected would make. Factions and slates could easily operate within this scheme. It is a scheme that sets out to prevent anyone from manipulating or controlling the make up of the Parliamentary Committees and this characterises it as a strong application of lot because it makes a positive use of the blind break. Unfortunately the scheme itself is badly designed and leaves scope for the manipulation it is ostensibly trying to eradicate.

Despite the fact that this second proposal does not use sortition, the strict method of rotation by consecutive number introduces an element of randomness into the procedure similar to the use of lot. It also has the potential to spread participation amongst the members of the House to a far greater extent than the first. It is a proportionate scheme, however, and addresses the question of the balance within each Committee in a way that is not possible by random selection. The list system is cumbersome, however, and could lead to distortions in the parliamentary timetable, and the question of who should decide on the criteria for the mix and who should then decide the particular personnel of any Committee is one that could elicit accusations of favouritism or corruption. A lottery within each stratification or category of the second scheme could solve this difficulty. The problem of allocating Committees could, likewise, be solved by holding a lottery after the debate had taken place. The latter proposal would combine a strong use of lot for inhibiting factional activity with the idea of rational balance and proportion contained in the original proposal. The idea of co-opting non-voting experts could also be useful in this context and would prevent a lottery choice from hampering the efficiency of any committee by excluding those with something to offer.

Harrington's *Oceana*

James Harrington's *Oceana* is an important link between the older republican practices of Renaissance Italy and the new republican thought of the English, American and French revolutions. What is important for this inquiry is that *Oceana* advocates a Venetian-style electoral system for the English nation-state and in so doing brings the idea of sortition into a new political landscape in the context of a total scheme of republican government. *Oceana* certainly presents a lot-based system, but it is difficult to assess exactly how Harrington views sortition. On the one hand the text is replete with instances of lot, both as part of the electoral system and for a number of other functions within the republic. Harrington clearly recognises that lot brings some value to the type of polity he is describing. On the other hand, there is no explanation or exploration of the use of lot. *Oceana*, therefore, presents us with the same set of problems that we faced with the use of lot in Athens and medieval Italy: how to understand the rationale for its deployment. This, however, is complicated by the fact that *Oceana* is a fictitious work that is both a response to contemporary events and an exposition of an ideal governmental structure. At one level it is very much a product of its political environment and at another, considerably abstracted from it.

Oceana is based on a number of ruling ideas or principles that Harrington presents explicitly in the preliminaries to the constitution and in fictional speeches in the second half of the work. These are the notion of 'natural aristocracy', equal possession of land as the material base of society, and the idea that a popular government, or one that involves substantial participation by the people, is natural, stable, and reflects the general human interest. These principles or ideas find their practical manifestations in suggested structures or procedures. The political role of the natural aristocracy is guaranteed through the division of labour between the senate, who deliberate, and the people (or representatives of the people) who resolve. The Agrarian law of Oceana, by which a ceiling of £2000 per annum is put on the possession of all land, is the means by which Harrington's ideas on equality and the material basis of society find their expression. The universal application of the ballot — the integrated Venetian-style process that involves nominators chosen by lot followed by preference voting — and the rigorous rotation of all offices are the means by which the links between people and government are to be maintained.

We should also note that *Oceana* is an ideal impartial republic. Political parties are forbidden. Although Harrington does not develop arguments on the dangers of factionalism in the manner of Nedham — who describes factionalism as 'that grand cankerworm of a Commonwealth' — arguments for impartiality occasionally surface in the text of *Oceana*.[32] A commonwealth is not a party,[33] he insists, and anyone declaring themselves to be partisan should have no place in the new regime.[34] No party should be excluded from government but: 'A Commonwealth consisting of a party will be in perpetual labour of her own destruction.'[35]

Harrington prescribes, and we presume advocates, the use of balloting for all representatives and officers at Parish, Hundred, and Tribal levels and nearly all officers elected by the senate. Candidates are to be nominated by proposers or electors selected by means of balls drawn from specially prepared urns at huge public gatherings. Those who draw gold balls from amongst the silver balls would make the choice of candidates, and these candidates would then be voted on in a secret ballot. This was to be performed by the use of a special box constructed with two internal compartments or divisions and a single aperture in the top into which the voter could place his arm. Each voter was to place a cloth ball or pellet in one of these compartments to signify their approval or disapproval of the candidate in question. These balloting procedures are described by Harrington in all their ritualistic detail.

There are many variations and refinements to the basic model. In the election to the Galaxy (Senate and Tribal Prerogative) lots were thrown to designate which file of potential nominators should approach the urns first.[36] In the elections to the Hundred offices, several sets of balls were available, each set identified by a letter engraved on every ball in the set. Lots were drawn before the main ballot to determine which set was to be used.[37]

Harrington suggests a number of different nominating processes to operate at different electoral levels. Parish representatives, amounting to one-fifth of all elders, are all to be nominated by one proposer chosen by lot.[38] In the election for the seven officers of the Hundred, seven nominators are to be chosen by lot and each asked to nominate three candidates for one of the posts to be filled. Their choice would then have to be ratified by a simple majority of the

---

[32] Nedham (1656) pp. 28–9.
[33] Harrington (1992) pp. 123, 63.
[34] *Ibid.* p. 215.
[35] *Ibid.* p. 62.
[36] *Ibid.* p. 90.
[37] *Ibid.* p. 86.
[38] *Ibid.* p. 78.

seven electors before the names went forward to the secret ballot.[39] At tribal level, four groups of electors are first to be chosen by lot and each group member charged with nominating for one office only. The choice has then to be approved by a majority of the group before the names could go forward. The final vote would then be held between the nominees of the four groups for each office in turn.[40]

The only exception from the combination of nominators chosen by lot followed by a secret ballot is the election of committee offices by the senate. In this case one candidate would be nominated 'by scrutiny' for each post, i.e. by the choice of respective committee itself. The final vote would be between the committee's candidate and four chosen by the senate 'in the usual way'.[41] Harrington's designation of a different word for the election of these candidates, who are to be chosen by preference voting without the operation of lot, indicates the extent to which he regards the sortive element as an integrated feature of the ballot as a whole.[42]

In addition to the selection of proposers and electors in the process of balloting, Harrington stipulates that a number of other tasks should be undertaken by the use of sortition. The research tasks for the drawing up of the constitution are assigned by the use of lot,[43] tribes are allocated names,[44] captains assigned to horse or foot,[45] soldiers sent to do military duty in the colonies of Marpesia and Panopea (Scotland and Ireland),[46] and officers assigned to their legions in time of war[47] – all by the use of lot. This indicates that Harrington sees lot as having a wider potential beyond the confines of the balloting procedure. The idea that lot should be used to allocate military command is a particularly strong application because it uses the arationality of lottery distribution to inhibit the build-up of factions inside the armed forces.

If we look at *Oceana* as a balanced piece of political literature, moreover, we can see that the drawing up of the constitution of

---

[39] *Ibid.* pp. 83–5
[40] *Ibid.* pp. 91, 95. Note that these could have been included as examples of various design possibilities .
[41] *Ibid.* p. 124.
[42] *Ibid.*
[43] *Ibid.* p. 69.
[44] *Ibid.* p. 87.
[45] *Ibid.* p. 88.
[46] *Ibid.* p. 194
[47] *Ibid.* p. 208

Oceana itself is framed by instances of sortition. The research topics for the drawing up of the Constitution are chosen by lot to initiate the preparation of the constitution, and lots are drawn to decide who will present the people's vote on the constitutional proposals to the senate as the final act of the process.[48] The most feasible interpretation of this is that he is using lot to stand for the idea of the citizen's consent to the impartial procedures of the new republic. Those who consent to the lot give up personal ambition and accept whatever role is assigned to them out of a sense of duty and service to the greater good. Agreement to the lottery symbolises an agreement to abide by the rule-governed authority of the polity.

In the early preliminaries in *Oceana*, in the speeches during the debates on the constitution and in a number of other works, Harrington alludes to and sometimes discusses the use of lot in Classical and Hebrew History. There are no major gaps in this knowledge and since Harrington's sources are, in most cases, the same as those used by Gataker, we can presume that there was a common understanding of the political use of lot amongst those with classical education in seventeenth-century England.[49] What is of more interest, however, is Harrington's attitude to these historical instances of sortition, especially those in ancient Athens. The Athenian lottery system, he claims, contributed to the decline of that city:

> ... in regard that the Senate, chosen at once by lot, not by suffrage, and changed every year not in part but the whole, consisted not of the natural aristocracy nor sitting long enough to understand or be perfect in their office, had sufficient authority to withhold the people from perpetual turbulence in the way which was ruin in the end.[50]

Athens was, he claims again, lost for lack of a viable aristocracy;[51] the people were 'too often deliberating',[52] and the people's access to the senate a 'mischief'.[53] These criticisms find their outlet in Harrington's scheme of a strict demarcation between the functions of the senate and of the people. If the people debate, anarchy, not democracy will be the result.[54] Lot in Athens, despite being as popu-

---

[48] *Ibid.* p. 252.
[49] *The Prerogative of Popular Government* and *Brief Directions*
[50] Harrington (1992) pp. 37–8.
[51] *Ibid.* p. 136.
[52] *Ibid.* p. 28.
[53] *Ibid.* p. 140. There are many examples of similar statements, for instance Harrington (1992) p. 142, and Harrington (1977) p. 477.
[54] Harrington (1977) p. 479.

lar as suffrage[55] and despite being representative of the people[56] violates this necessary division that Harrington, recasting Aristotle, sees as essential to democracy.[57]

> ... while, according to my principles (if you like them) debate in the people maketh anarchy, and where they have the result and no more, the rest being managed by a good aristocracy, it maketh that which is properly and truly to be called democracy, or popular government.[58]

It is clear, therefore, that Harrington is cautious about the democratic use of lot. What he is criticising in this, however, is not the arational process of lot itself, but the pre-lot decisions about who should be in the pool and which governmental tasks those who are chosen might be required to undertake.

Throughout *Oceana* Harrington emphasises the principles of rotation and the franchise. In relation to these, lot is portrayed in a decidedly instrumental, supportive role. An indication of how this operates is to be found in a speech by one of the main political actors in *Oceana*, Lord Epimonus:

> ... there is in this way of suffrage no less than a demonstration that it is the most pure; and the purity of the suffrage in a popular government is the health if not the life of it, seeing the soul is no otherwise breathed into the sovereign power than by the suffrage of the people.[59]

Here Harrington, in the guise of one of his main fictitious voices, places a clear political priority on the notion of electoral purity. The complex rituals of *Oceana* corroborate this focus and emphasise the essentially public nature of the electoral procedures. Although it is also apparent that the use of lot to select nominators plays a major part in this, Harrington does not find it worthy of mention. It is as if he is interested in the high principle rather than the lowly mechanism.

The urgency of this call for electoral purity, however, becomes more apparent when we consider the historical context of *Oceana*. In the recent English revolution Harrington had seen at first hand the dangers of absolute monarchy, arbitrary military rule, and the factional disintegration of the body politic. He also witnessed the vulnerability of parliament to corruption. Although *Oceana* is a

---

[55] *Ibid.* p. 549.
[56] *Ibid.* p. 481.
[57] Harrington (1992) p. 10.
[58] Harrington (1977) p. 479.
[59] *Ibid.* p. 118.

fictitious work, its real subject matter is the English civil war and the precarious republic that followed it. The procedures and institutions of Harrington's model are his response to the very real problems of the late interregnum matched with a solution drawn from his personal experience of Venetian stability. These problems, the hidden context of Harrington's application of sortition, reveal a consistent strong advocacy of lot as one of a number of measures designed to protect the process of election, and, by implication, the procedures and institutions of any possible new British republic.

If we take into account the extreme uncertainty of the period during which *Oceana* was conceived and produced, it is not unreasonable to consider it also as a plea for national unity. Leveller demands are addressed in the long-term operations of the Agrarian Law, the abolition of the House of Lords accommodated by the notion of natural aristocracy, while the need to appease the upper echelons of society is manifest in the exclusive political rights of the senatorial class. The dangers of military dictatorship are countered in the election of army officers and the use of lot to assign them to their regiments. Furthermore the exercise of arbitrary power, a concern for both pre-civil war parliamentarians and anti-Cromwellians during the interregnum, is thwarted in the proposals for rotation in office, regular elections and the top-to-bottom system of representatives and officers.

This interpretation goes some way towards explaining Harrington's ambivalent attitude to sortition. The rituals of the ballot are public shows of national consent to the new demonstrably non-partisan commonwealth, and within this context lot is used to symbolise submission to rule-governed procedures—an ethos at the heart of Harrington's vision of republican consciousness. While it contains concrete political proposals, we should be aware just how much of *Oceana* is also a piece of rhetorical political literature.

Although we can understand *Oceana* as a response to the events of the time, the model republic was not the type of work that could easily translate into political action — especially not in England during the late 1650s. It was presented to a public that was unfamiliar with most aspects of Italian republicanism—lot included—and was highly unlikely to commit itself wholeheartedly to complex foreign rituals. Thus while sortition was advocated in theory, the practical expertise and understanding that existed in Italy—the product of several hundred years of trial and error—was missing. There is a sense, therefore, that *Oceana* is as much an essay in possible ideas and a fable that explores the ethos of republicanism, as the advocacy of relevant, applicable, solutions. It puts forward a fully-grown republican model at a time when republican practice in England was in its infancy. As part of this picture, Harrington transplanted the idea of sortition into a new environment; but there was little chance that its potential could be realised in its new home.[60]

Harrington's importation of Venetian sortition to late interregnum England shows that he knew something of its applicability to the problem of how to defend a republic. But *Oceana*, in fact, tells us little more of the potential of sortition as a mechanism than we knew from its original Venetian context. As we turn to examine the influence of Harrington on the constitutions of the proprietary colonies of America, we see an inversion of this process as attempts are made to take Harringtonian sortition out of its very particular theoretical environment and put it, once again, into political practice. Nonetheless elements of *Oceana* did emerge in the New World and some have stood the test of time. The ballot continued but lost the element of lot in the choice of nominators; lot, on the other hand, became merged with the English jury form. What was lost, however, was the integrated vision of the Venetian style polity, in which lot was used to protect the public process of selection for major office holders from corruption and private control. Harrington certainly understood that sortition had potential in this respect, but he did not develop a critique of a type that could help those who followed. This omission was not solely responsible for the demise of lot as a central element in republican practice, but probably made it harder for later generations to understand its value.

Sortition and the American proprietary colonies

Although it is difficult to prove the direct influence of Harrington, the constitutions of such colonies as New Jersey, South Carolina and Pennsylvania were drawn by writers from Commonwealth or radical Whig circles in Britain where *Oceana* would have been well known.[61] They also contain features that are strongly reminiscent of

---

[60] The idea that Harrington's advocacy of sortition had no English heir is challenged by an anonymous constitutional proposal of 1701 entitled *The Free State of Noland*. This advocates the use of lot for the selection of electors for the Shire Councils. See Noland (1701) pp. 55–6.
[61] See Cotton (1980), Gooch (1917), Russell-Smith (1914) and Robbins (1959) for the fuller Harringtonian circle. In this respect we should also note that

the *Oceana* model, especially Agrarian law, the division between a deliberating senate and a resolving representative body, the secret ballot and the use of lot. Furthermore these were the first attempts at constitution-building in the early modern era and they show an obvious debt to the most significant contemporary theoretical model of that process.

The proprietary states were short-lived, and their original constitutions even more so.[62] Of the original nine colonies of this type only three, Pennsylvania, Maryland and Delaware had not reverted to Royal Colony status by the time of the American Revolution. The constitutions of East New Jersey and South Carolina proved unworkable in practice within a few years of their introduction, and in Pennsylvania many of the key features of Penn's original *Frame of Government* were revoked by the turn of the century. Moreover the proprietary form was a curious hybrid. These colonies owed their existence to Royal patronage, which granted the right to govern to a single proprietor or group of proprietors. They needed to attract new settlers and capital investment, and with their constitutions often following commonwealth lines, they seemed to face in a number of directions at the same time. This essentially private form of government provided a window of opportunity for late seventeenth-century republican thinkers to put their ideas into practice, but the effectiveness of this experiment was compromised by irresolvable conflicts of interests on the ground. The established settlers saw their new proprietary overlords and their officials as a threat to their freedoms. The proprietors, on the other hand, found themselves sandwiched between the need to provide favourable conditions for incoming landowners and industrialists, and the need to assuage the antipathy of entrenched local élites — many dominated by religious loyalties. Faction in the colonies was also directly encouraged by the mother country — especially after the Restoration when late Stuart patronage networks spread across the Atlantic. Local oligarchs were tolerated by English governments where it was useful to do so, and local dissidents could be encouraged if their governor or proprietor was out of favour in England.[63] There was a sense, therefore, that the new constitutions were some-

Harrington's printer, John Streater, published an account of the constitution of Ragusa, a state that used lot for nominations in a style similar to Venice. See Streater (1659). The constitution of E. New Jersey has been linked to Algernon Sidney. See Karston (1967).

[62] See Osgood (1924). In particular p. 58 and pp. 74–5 for the rise of assemblies.
[63] See especially Olson (1973) pp. 66–7.

what of an abstract political exercise and were not at all a response to local conditions. This accusation has especially been made against the constitution of South Carolina.[64]

South Carolina

Long considered to be the work of Locke, and also associated with his employer Shaftesbury, one of the proprietors,[65] the *Fundamental Constitution of South Carolina* of 1669 gives the first impression of being thoroughly aristocratic with the avowed aim of avoiding a 'numerous democracy'.[66] Taking their lead from Harrington's Agrarian law the drafters of the constitution proposed to divide the population into several strata, based on their ownership of land, and to organise the decision-making institutions of the colony according to that division. Legislation was to be proposed by a Grand Council of fifty (only fourteen of whom were representatives of the people), and resolved by a parliament of proprietors, landgraves (a new proposed class of hereditary nobility), caciques (middle rank owners of between 12,000 and 24,000 acres), and wealthy commoners. Compared to the earlier charter, which gave considerable rights to the elected assembly, this new constitution offered little to the settler population, many of them experienced wealthy planters from Barbados. The *Fundamental Constitution*, however was probably meant more as a means to encourage new settlers of the right quality than to please those already in situ. It did this primarily by guaranteeing rights and freedoms, especially religious freedom, within the context of stable government and rule by a new 'natural' aristocracy.[67] While its reputation as 'visionary, crude, incomplete and impracticable'[68] is probably unjustified, *The Fundamental Constitution* was almost certainly 'too elaborate for immediate application'.[69] The proprietors were faced with an uphill struggle to implement their new scheme in the face of organised local opposition, and, in 1705, gave up after the fifth attempt to draft an acceptable document. The popular assembly was given greater powers in 1682, and in 1693 the right to initiate legislation was

---

[64] See, for instance, Weir (1983) p. 54.
[65] Russell-Smith (1914) p. 159.
[66] *Ibid.* p. 157.
[67] The right to create nobility was part of the original charter, as long as the titles differed from those of England. See Weir (1983) p. 50.
[68] Edward McCready quoted in Edgar (1998) p. 42.
[69] Weir (1983) p. 58.

granted to both houses.[70] Apart from the provision to rotate the portfolios of the proprietors by lot, there is no mention of sortition in the original constitution.

Although every version of the constitution was rejected, some of the clauses in the later drafts found favour with the assembly and were included in the body of colonial law. The most significant of these was a measure in the third version of 17 August 1682, which stipulated that juries were to be drawn by lot. A list of all eligible jurymen was drawn up and the names written on separate pieces of paper. A child would then draw the names from the box.[71] It seems as if South Carolina was the first state to introduce this method and it probably marks the first instance of a legally constituted randomly-selected jury in the history of the jury form. It also proved remarkably successful and remained in force until after the American revolution.[72] It is interesting to note that this was not only a response to local conditions, coming in a revised draft written in the colony itself, but it was also a popular measure and temporarily united parties otherwise locked in factional struggle.

West and East New Jersey

In 1676 New Jersey was divided into two separate proprietary colonies. William Penn, 'fresh from his study of Harrington and Moore,' acquired an interest in West New Jersey, the constitution of which provides us with a couple of measures which bear some relation to our study.[73] There is provision for a group of 'seven honest and respectable persons' to defend the constitution by making an accusation against anyone introducing treasonable legislation. This is similar to the right of the Ancient Athenian citizen to challenge Assembly decisions. The West New Jersey *Concessions and Agreements* of 3 March 1676 also stipulates that balloting boxes or 'trunks' are to be used at elections 'for the prevention of partiality, and whereby every man may freely choose according to his own judgement and honest intention'.[74] No indication is given as to whether, in the Venetian style, sortition was to be used for nomination of candidates, but the brief apologia indicates that the ballot was seen as a means of combating factionalism.

------

[70] Russell-Smith (1914) p. 161.
[71] Sirmans (1966) p. 37.
[72] *Ibid.*
[73] Russell-Smith (1914) p. 162.
[74] New Jersey Statutes (c.1700) p. 405. See also Russell-Smith (1914) p.162.

It is in the *Fundamental Constitution* of East New Jersey, however, that we find an elective system that includes nomination by sortition.[75] According to Russell-Smith, the East New Jersey Constitution of 1683 is the 'most complete of all attempts to introduce *Oceana* in the colonies', and its introduction coincided with the take-over of the colony by a new group of twenty-four proprietors.[76] These included William Penn, James Drummond Earl of Perth (a prominent freemason)[77] and a number of leading Scottish Quakers.[78] Under the terms of the constitution the governor was to be elected by the proprietors for a three-year period and would be forbidden to serve consecutive terms of office. The Governor's Council of the twenty-four proprietors (or their proxies) plus twelve freemen chosen by ballot by the Grand Council had no legislative power on its own, and was divided — as was *Oceana*'s Senate — into committees for administrative duties.[79] The Grand Council itself was to consist of the twenty-four proprietors plus seventy-two freemen who had to be property holders.[80] These were to be divided into three groups. One-third was to retire after each year and each office-holder was ineligible for re-election for another two years.

Significantly any member of the Grand Council could initiate legislation, and here the constitution differed both from the earlier South Carolina and the later Pennsylvania constitutions.[81] Members of the Grand Council were to be elected by first choosing fifty from each county by lot — drawn 'by a boy under ten years of age' — and then another twenty-five from that fifty. Only these twenty-five would be eligible for office, and the twenty-five left in the hat would be charged with nominating either eight or twelve candidates from these, depending on how many places were to be filled.[82]

---

[75] Leaming and Spicer (1758). The actual authorship of the document is unclear, but Whitehead's *East Jersey under the Proprietary Governments* suggests that the new deputy governor Gawen Laurie was responsible for its introduction

[76] Russell-Smith (1914) p. 163.

[77] Schuchand (2002) p. 729.

[78] See Landsman (1985) and Stevenson (1988) p. 203 on the mix of Scottish Freemasons and Quakers in East New Jersey.

[79] Russell-Smith (1914) suggests that this could mean by lot (p. 165). This is another instance of how it is difficult to interpret the term 'ballot' where no further details are given. See below pp. 162–3.

[80] Of fifty acres in the country or three in the boroughs. Leaming and Spicer (1785) p. 155

[81] *Ibid.* p. 155.

[82] *Ibid.*

A consistent approach to sortition in this constitution is established in the proposed use of lot to choose jurors[83] and to select the members of the Court of Appeal.[84] This consisted of four proprietors and four freemen. The names of sixteen proprietors would go into a box, eight would be drawn out as eligible candidates, and the eight remaining given the job of selecting four from those eight. The choice of freemen, we are told, was to proceed in a similar manner, but it is unclear how these were to be nominated. In both jury and Appeal Court lotteries the draw was to be made by a ten-year-old boy. In the constitution this measure is justified as being 'for the full preventing of all indirect means'.[85] Since the question of bribery is addressed earlier in the clause, we can presume that the term 'indirect means' refers to more organised conspiratorial methods.

Given the problems in South Carolina we can view this measure similarly as a direct challenge to those who had forged local power-bases in the assembly, and its inclusion was possibly one reason why the *Fundamental Constitution* was never adopted. There could have been other reasons, however. New Jersey historian Richard P. McCormack suggests that the constitution was 'fanciful' and 'doctrinaire' and was an unwelcome threat to the ancient rights of the inhabitants.[86] The rejection of the new constitution can therefore be seen as part of an ongoing defence of local self-rule.[87] This is a reasonable interpretation: the inhabitants of East New Jersey had never really accepted the legal status of the proprietary government itself, and they had recently waged a struggle against Governor Andros of New York who had tried to take over the colony in 1680. William A. Whitehead's account of 1851 sheds a different light on the issue, however. Apparently the privileges that came with the constitution were only to be extended to those who would undertake a re-survey and reappraisal of their original grants and who paid their quitrent arrears, some of which were substantial.[88] Faced with non-compliance, and fearing the

---

[83] *Ibid.* p. 163.
[84] *Ibid.* p. 164.
[85] *Ibid.* p. 155.
[86] McCormick (1964) p. 32. Pomfret (1973) p. 33, notes that judges were elected prior to 1683.
[87] See Pomfret (1973) p. 59.
[88] The quitrent was a sum of money to be paid to the proprietor by every lot-holder. McCormack (1964) p. 25, places this at either one penny or one halfpenny per acre per annum for the province, depending upon when the setters had arrived. Non-payment was rife.

prospect that two parallel systems of colonial government might emerge, Governor Laurie backed down and put no effort into implementing the constitution.[89]

We can, however, read the 'fanciful' constitution as a piece of advertising. Given the need to find new settlers amongst the Scottish fraternity, it was important to assure them that they would not be excluded from political participation in their new environment. The proposals for the rigorous use of lot can therefore be seen as an attempt to do just this. Unfortunately, if we follow Whitehead, it seems that the price for the participation of those already in situ was set too high.

The election to the Council in the proposed *Constitution of East New Jersey* is of interest on a number of counts. First we have to understand it in the context of the role and make up of the Council. This, unusually, was to be a group that included the twenty-four proprietors, but included them in a minority, considerably outnumbered by the freemen of the colony. All members of the Council also had the right to deliberate and to initiate legislation.

The use of lot to select both the nominators and the candidate group is unique amongst the schemes we have looked at. Its particular value is that it is a full citizen lot scheme that also involves preference election, but it is one that does not divide the citizenry between those who vote and those who govern. Its aim, commensurate with the need to integrate new settlers into the colonial government, is to distribute office in such a way that small groups or cliques cannot dominate the proceedings. Sortition is used strongly against potential concentrations of power, and in order to give all freemen an equal stake both in the process of nomination and in the entitlement to be nominated. While it seeks to combine the notion of preference with a widening of opportunity, choice on the basis of experience or merit can only be made relatively rather than absolutely—from a randomly-selected temporary *reggimento* of twenty-five. It is, in this respect, a good example of how lot can be used in a rotational scheme in such a way as to effectively, but temporarily, *exclude* all but a small group of citizens from office. The danger of excluding those with governmental experience is offset in this constitution by the presence of the proprietors in the Council,

[89] Whitehead (1875) p. 133.

and by the idea that a wider range of freemen would gain experience than if a purely preference scheme were adopted.

Pennsylvania

The early history of Pennsylvania is valuable for us because it shows
a written constitution in action. It is also important because we can
see the adjustments made by Penn after the problems in New Jersey.
Firstly, sortition is used in practice to select juries. Secondly, there is
a comprehensive system of rotation established for the members of
the governor's legislative council. Finally, in Pennsylvania we see
the secret ballot used for all elections to government offices and all
elections within government.[90] Although it has little impact on
political development of the new colonial government, a draft
scheme for dividing the council by lot in order to instigate the first
cycle of rotation gives us an indication of how inappropriate
sortition can be when used to remove members from government
office.

   Penn's *Frame of Government*, published in May 1682, lays great
weight on the right to trial by jury, but gives little indication of how
juries are to be selected. In an earlier draft of the *Laws Agreed upon in
England*, Penn suggests that juries should be 'returned by the sheriff',[91] but his Dutch friend, Benjamin Furly, in his comments upon
these drafts, suggests that sortition could be used:

> … especially where life is concerned … Let God rather than
> men be entrusted with this affaire in the first place, that all cor-
> ruption in packing of juries to hurry men out of the world
> (without) just cause may be prevented. To which purpose let
> the names of all freeholders as such as are capable of serving, be
> written in papers, and let 48 draw, which done let the prisoner
> have his liberty still to accept, giving sufficient Reasons to the
> Court, that so things may go squarely on both sides.[92]

   Penn seems to have acted belatedly on this advice for on 1 March
1683, possibly influenced by events in South Carolina, the statute
was passed by which juries were to be selected by lot from a list of
freemen in each county.[93] This statute was later declared a funda-

---

[90] Beckman (1976) p. 160.
[91] Penn (1982) vol. 2, p. 206, doc 59.
[92] Penn (1982) vol. 2, xi p. 232.
[93] The freemen were first to be summoned by the sheriff and their names
      written on small pieces of paper and placed in a hat. Forty-eight freemen
      thus selected would act as a pool from which the first twelve accepted by the
      prisoner would serve. Staughton (1879) p. 129. chap.LXIX.

mental law, but was abrogated by William and Mary in 1693.[94] Furly's comments also suggest that Penn's decision was a highly conscious one.

Penn's establishment of a bicameral system of government in Pennsylvania followed Harrington's principles, in that the council alone had the right to initiate legislation, and the assembly was charged only with its approval.[95] The assembly was to be elected by ballot from the freemen, and all freemen were eligible to stand. The freemen members of the council were then elected by secret ballot from the assembly. One-third of council members would be re-elected every year.[96] In an early draft of the constitution Penn suggests that the initial reduction was to be made by lot. [97] It seems, however, that in the final scheme, the initiation of the rotation cycle was actually achieved by a different arrangement: the election of three sets of councillors, one to serve for one, one for two, and one set to serve for three years.[98]

The question at issue here is the extent to which the problem requires an arational solution. There is little in the circumstances of this proposal to suggest that the use of an arational mechanism could be justified, and the make-up of the three groups is probably best left to be decided by the candidates themselves. The draft proposal is therefore a weak use of lot, and a rational decision-making process would be far more appropriate. The suggestion of lot to effectively de-select elected councillors also undermines the integrity of the electoral vote. This use of lot, however, was common in the first constitutions of the American states following independence.[99] We also find it in France under the Directory, where the problems of using lot to remove sitting officers had more serious consequences.

---

[94] Beckman (1976) p. 9.
[95] Initially, Penn envisaged a Council of seventy-two and an Assembly of 200, but this was scaled down in practice to eighteen and thirty-six respectively. Russell-Smith (1914) p. 168.
[96] Pole (1996) pp. 82–3.
[97] Penn (1982) vol. 2, p. 145, VII, and p.165.
[98] We can see in this a faint reflection of the scheme described by Milton, but in that description the removal of councillors by lot is not connected with the idea of starting a scheme of rotation. See Milton (1660) p. 9.
[99] See Poore (1878): for Maryland p. 823; Kentucky p. 675; New York p.1333; N. Carolina p. 1411; and Virginia p. 1911.

The secret ballot in Pennsylvania

As we saw in the constitution of West New Jersey, the secret ballot was perceived as a means of establishing electoral impartiality. Penn was certainly enthusiastic about this new procedure and its potential to allow the voter to come to an unhindered decision. He explains that the ballot is: 'To prevent that corruption which men not guided by a just principle are subject to for fear or favour'[100] and he alludes both to the practice in Venice and the use of the ballot box by the Royal Society at Gresham College.[101] Details of the balloting procedure and descriptions of the box are to be found in some of the tracts published by Penn to encourage settlers from England and continental Europe.[102] Here again the idea of impartiality is mentioned. There is, however, no indication that Penn included nomination by random selection, and there is, in fact, little detail in the statutes and constitutional drafts about how nominations were to be made.[103]

Penn can certainly be credited with implementing Harrington's vision of the secret ballot as a universal political tool. It was not universally popular, however, and for some council members it suggested the presence of secret deals and underhand methods.[104] It was specifically excluded from Markham's new frame of government for the colony in 1696; it is also absent from the 1701 *Charter of Privileges*. If we date the loss of the secret ballot to the mid-1690s this places it alongside a number of other measures of this period which gave the assembly greater power over the proprietary council. These include the loss of the randomly-selected jury, the end to strict rotation in office and the granting of the right to initiate legislation to the assembly. Penn was absent from the colony during this period, and he was also unpopular with the new regime in England. Penn attributes the loss of the secret ballot to the leader of the assembly dissidents, David Lloyd, and in a letter to Logan in 1704 he berates this loss:

> I acquiesced, having first showed my dislike: as at their disliking the model of the elected council to prepare, and an assembly to resolve. And 2 as throwing away the use of the ballot,

---

[100] *Ibid.* vol. 2., p. 147; see also New Jersey Statutes (c.1700).
[101] Penn (1982) vol. 2, p. 166, note 12.
[102] Shumway (1925).
[103] See particularly Staughton (1876) and Beckman (1976).
[104] Shepherd (1896) p. 266.

which their children, as I told them, will have perhaps cause
sufficient to repent of their folly therein.[105]

Sortition and the secret ballot

This is a good point in the chapter to look at the relationship
between sortition and the secret ballot. We have already seen them
both in operation together in the later version of the *brevia*, which
formed the basis of the Venetian voting system. In this type of system lot was used to select nominators for governmental or political
posts. The secret ballot was also used by the Athenian *dikasterion*,
not for the selection of personnel, but for voting on the final verdict.
The aim of this was to ensure that each *dikastes* reached his decision
independently.

   Among the definitions of the word 'ballot' in the Oxford English
Dictionary there are two relevant meanings: to vote by some secret
method, and to select by lot.[106] That two distinct processes should
emerge under the same name suggests a common origin, and we
could be justified in placing this at the point when English writers
began to take an interest in the Venetian electoral process, which
encompassed both procedures. Inevitably the picture is a complex
one. While works such as *Oceana* and the later pamphlet *The Benefit
of the Ballot* present nomination by lot and secret preference voting
as part of an integrated process under a single name, there was also
considerable interest in secret voting as a procedure in its own right
during this period.[107] The Royal Society at Gresham College used
the secret ballot, as did the Royal College of Physicians, the Virginia
Company and other early commercial organisations.[108] In 1677 the
first attempt to use the secret ballot for parliamentary elections was
held in Lymington in Hampshire, but this seems to have been a relatively isolated experiment.[109] The interest in secret voting was also
reflected in contemporary pamphlet publications. *Chaos – or a discourse wherein is presented the view of a magistrate*, published in 1659,
advocates secret ballots with votes registered in writing.[110] By 1701,

---

[105] Penn (1982) vol. 4, p. 348.
[106] Second edn (1989). The *OED* cites Thomas' 1561 *Historie of Italie* and
Raleigh's *Remains* of 1618 as early instances of the first and second meanings
respectively.
[107] *Benefit* (post 1688). Published after 1688 this was thought to have been the
work of Andrew Marvell.
[108] Russell-Smith (1914) p. 39.
[109] *Ibid.* p. 139.
[110] *Chaos* (1659) p. 39.

when the influential pamphlet *An enquiry into the inconveniences of public and the advantages of private elections with the method of the ballot* was published, the term clearly begins to refer to a secret vote which does not necessarily include nomination by lot.[111] The word 'ballot' continued to be employed to describe a lottery, and was especially used when draws were held to select men for military duty.

The use of the secret ballot in the proprietary colonies of America, especially Penn's Pennsylvania, marks the first stage of its now universal application in western-style liberal democracies. With this use we begin to see the separation of the secret voting procedure from the lottery for nominators which had previously been part of the same process. The combined procedure achieved two objectives. The selection of nominators by lot was used where only a small, fixed, number of candidates were to stand for election. The role of lot was to prevent any individual or party from controlling the selection procedure by using party slates or setting up straw candidates. The secret ballot then prevented bribery or intimidation from influencing the vote that followed.

Both aspects served the same overall function of preventing those with power and influence from dominating the electoral process. The 1676 *Concessions and Agreements* of West New Jersey saw the new balloting trunks primarily as a means of preventing 'partiality'. This suggests that the main reason for the use of the secret ballot was to inhibit the rise of factions. The protection of the individual voter's 'honest intention' is presented, at this stage, as a secondary objective.[112]

There are many reasons why the process of selecting nominators by lot might have been lost in the transition from Venice to the New World. The scattered rural population of the American colonies probably made the large meetings that were so central to the Venetian and Harringtonian systems impracticable. In both these systems, moreover, the drawing of the lottery was very much a public process, witnessed by the whole community or *reggimento*. To the puritan settlers this could have seemed a very foreign, bizarre public ritual which smacked of superstition—even Catholicism. The secret ballot, on the other hand, conformed to the Protestant ideal that the private individual should be alone in his judgement and answerable only to God. In circumstances where the secret ballot, sortition and rotation (indeed even citizen participation in govern-

---

[111] Russell-Smith (1914) p. 139.
[112] New Jersey Statutes (c.1700) p. 405. See also Russell-Smith (1914) p. 162.

ment) were all untried innovations, a lottery could have been seen as the least acceptable mechanism.

If we now think of the secret ballot alongside the process of open acclamation, which, in some cases, it replaced, we get another perspective on how it was used. As well as protecting the individual citizen's judgement from interference, the secret ballot also protects the body politic from the type of open division which makes it clear who supports which candidate, and who, potentially, would take their side should open conflict arise. The secret ballot, therefore, seeks to retain unity by keeping the fault lines in the body politic less open, less pronounced.

The secrecy of the ballot can also extend beyond the task of protecting the citizen and come to characterise the process of election as a whole. When a voter's opinion is turned into a mark on a paper and placed in a ballot box, it becomes anonymous: abstracted from the person who created it and the reasons why it was made. It becomes a quantitative, rather then a qualitative, act of political expression. Thus while the secret ballot provides the voter with the safety of numbers, it also hides the rationale for that opinion from the public gaze. This idea of 'hidden' opinion characterises the secret ballot as a private process, even though it is used to elect public officers.

Although each lot-selected nominator was charged with making an individual, personal decision, the process of selection was public in so far as everyone in the pool had a stake in the process of selection. When the secret ballot became detached from the use of randomly-selected nominators two things happened. First, the nomination process became more vulnerable to corruption and manipulation: it became, in all essentials, lost from public ownership. Second, the election process as a whole became less of a public event in which every citizen could, potentially, have a qualitative input, and became dominated by the private quantitative act of secret voting.

The nominators drawn from the Venetian Grand Council and the communal citizens selected by the *brevia*, moreover, were *required* to perform the function for which they had been selected. This signifies a sense of the common ownership of the process of selection in all its phases and an ethos of citizen participation. When the lottery element was lost from the election process in transition to the New World, this sense of citizen obligation to the polity was also lost. These changes also accelerated the division in the body politic between the relatively passive, private voters and the active, career-based political caste. Thus, while the secret ballot protects the citizen's vote, it has also come to place that activity firmly in the private sphere. The secret ballot on its own, outside its original republican context, becomes a defence of the individual's political conscience; within its republican context and assisted by sortition, it is a means of protecting the shared values of the public polity.

Standalone examples from the American revolutionary period

Paine's Common Sense

Paine's proposal in *Common Sense* is straightforward. Each colony would need to be subdivided into districts in order to elect delegates to Congress. He suggests thirty from each colony. At the meeting of Congress itself, a lottery would determine the name of one particular colony and the delegates of that colony would then vote for one of their number to be president for a year. The colony providing the president for any year would then be omitted from succeeding lotteries until after thirteen years when every colony had elected a president. At the end of his proposal Paine suggests that: 'He that will promote discord under a government so equally formed as this would join Lucifer in his revolt.'[113]

Paine presents his scheme with remarkable simplicity, but it serves a complex purpose. His aim in writing *Common Sense* is to make an independent America seem both desirable and possible; but he was also a democratic republican and understood the impact that a new American republic would have on the *anciens regimes* of Europe. In this there is a sense also that Paine is using lot for its political symbolism as well as constituting part of a genuine proposal. He is flying a particular sort of kite. To take his readers over the threshold and let them see what a new America can be like, Paine has to address what he considers their greatest fears. These are first that the colonies possess no natural unity, and second that any future government would be dominated by the powerful few in the most powerful states. In this sense this proposal constitutes a strong advocacy of lot. The arationality of the process ensures that no qualitative distinction is made between the states in the choice of president. The use of lot also makes it clear that the future co-ordinating body of the states is to be an impartial body.

---

[113] Paine (1976) p. 96.

The exact context of the proposal for the election of the president in the text of *Common Sense* is significant. It comes immediately after a powerful polemic against the British monarch and monarchy in general. Although he recognises the need for a single figurehead, Paine also talks down the status of the office to make it more of a chairman than a chief executive. Rotation and lot are also used as a guarantee that one powerful individual cannot dominate the process of selection — it is a guarantee that there will be no American monarch. At the same time, lot is presented as a complement to, rather than a substitute for, choice based on merit. By advocating lot Paine is playing the modern Kleisthenes. He is demonstrating in advance that unity of purpose is possible, that powerful separate interests can be curbed, and the energies of all channelled into this new co-operative venture. This proposal is, in fact, the embodiment of the idea that government is an agreement among individuals about how best to govern themselves, which, in fact coincides with Paine's conception of the social contract as he develops it in *Rights of Man*. [114]

The Articles of Confederation

Our second example of sortition from this period follows the same theme: the need to establish Congress as impartial vis-a-vis the thirteen states. On Monday 27 October 1777 the Continental Congress (meeting in York) voted on Clause Nine of the *Articles of Confederation* – effectively the first constitution of the United States.[115] The clause laid out a procedure for settling inter-state disputes and replaces an earlier draft by Dickinson[116] which proposed to give Congress the 'sole and exclusive Right and Power of settling all disputes and differences now subsisting, or that hereafter may arise between two or more colonies concerning Boundaries, Jurisdictions, or any other Cause whatever.'[117]

The new clause reduced the role of Congress by making it the last resort of appeal in all such disputes. On receiving due notice of any such dispute from either party, Congress would summon both parties to a special court hearing. If agreement could not be reached, Congress was to make a list of three people from each state in the

---

[114] See Paine (1945) p. 278.
[115] See Nilsen (2004) p. 21.
[116] The Delaware delegate responsible for the first draft of the *Articles*.he was known to be a strong advocate of central government.
[117] Library of Congress (1907) Vol. 5, p. 550

United States, and each party would alternatively strike off one name each until thirteen remained. From these thirteen, up to nine, but no fewer than seven, would be chosen by lot in the presence of Congress. Those drawn, or any five of them, would act as judges to hear, and finally determine, the case. A majority was sufficient to do this.[118]

Article Nine is essentially a very practical measure, but it also carried political overtones. Debate had been intense in Congress over the role of any central governmental organisation, and there were fears, expressed by R.H. Lee, amongst others, that the sovereignty of individual states would be compromised. Article Nine, however, was approved by sixteen of the delegates, with four opposing and three abstentions. Only one state, New Hampshire, opposed, New Jersey and South Carolina were divided and Connecticut, significantly, had two of their delegates abstain and one oppose the measure.[119] Given the earlier acrimony a remarkable degree of consensus was reached. The measure therefore, achieved its twin objectives, of being undeniably even-handed while at the same time setting a benchmark for the role of Congress that could be accepted by almost all present. It was to have—as it needed to in these instances—superior authority to the individual states, but at the same time the authority it wielded had to be understood to be impartial.

James Wilson's proposal to the Constitutional Convention

My third example from the revolutionary period of American history comes from the Constitutional Convention, which met in May 1787 to devise a replacement for the *Articles of Confederation*. In a long and arduous debate, which extended intermittently from early June until late July, the delegates had become seriously bogged down on the issue of the election and powers of the chief executive, or president. The debate pivoted around the relationship between the president and the newly-proposed bicameral legislative body.

James Wilson and Gouverneur Morris, both from Pennsylvania, had already moved that the president should be directly elected by the people and they had hoped that this could act as a check on the power of the legislature. On 17 July, however, the proposal was

---

[118] Library of Congress (1907) Vol. 9, p. 841–843. See also Jensen (1940) p. 180.
[119] On account of the long-running boundary dispute between Pennsylvania and Connecticut over the Wyoming Valley. See Jensen, Kaminski, Saladino (1981) pp. 1414, 1418.

heavily defeated, with only Pennsylvania in support. Nonetheless arguments were still being made for a greater separation of powers, and during the next few days the convention vacillated between proposals for a weak executive dominated by Congress and proposals for a strong, independent executive — which raised fears that a monarchy was being created in all but name.[120] Then, on 24 July, as the debate seemed to drift into acceptance of the view that Congress should elect the president, Wilson introduced his gambit. Madison's note reports the speech as follows:

> As the great difficulty seems to spring from the mode of election, he wd suggest a mode which had not been mentioned. It was that the Executive be elected for 6yrs by a small number, not more than 15 of the national Legislature, to be drawn from it, not by ballot, but by lot, and who should retire immediately and make the election without separating. By this mode intrigue would be avoided in the first instance, and dependence would be diminished. This was not, he said, a digested idea and might be liable to strong objections.[121]

Before Wilson made this a full resolution, a motion to postpone considerations on the executive was moved and lost. Wilson with his Pennsylvania delegation voted for the motion. Wilson then moved the resolution on lot, it was seconded by Mr Carrol of Maryland and a discussion ensued.[122]

In opposition Elbridge Gerry of Massachusetts suggested that: 'This is committing too much to chance. If lot should fall on a sett of unworthy men, an unworthy executive must be saddled on the country.'[123] Rufus King from Massachusetts was worried about the prospect to lot producing a majority from the same state and commented that: 'We ought to be governed by reason, not by chance', and that since no one was satisfied, a postponement was in order. Wilson seconded the postponement and Gouverneur Morris then suggested that the chance of a majority of electors from the same state being drawn was almost infinite.[124] The resolution to postpone was then carried unanimously. Wilson's proposal on lot seems to have been lost during the next few days, for on 26 July, as the arguments were being summed up prior to the issue being sent to a committee, Col. Mason of Virginia made the dry comment: 'Among

---

[120] Collier and Collier (1986) pp. 297–310.
[121] Madison (1987a) p. 359.
[122] *Ibid.* p. 361.
[123] *Ibid.*
[124] *Ibid.* p. 362.

other expedients, a lottery has been introduced. But as tickets do not appear to be in much demand, it will probably not be carried on, and nothing therefore need be said on that subject ...'[125] Although Madison's notes on the convention are full, Farrand's account, which draws on the secretary's notes, suggests that a more detailed discussion of Wilson's proposal took place. A scrap of paper found amongst the secretary's papers actually mentions that balls, some gilded, would be used for the draw.[126]

It is difficult to be entirely sure what Wilson was trying to achieve by making his proposal. His justification that 'intrigue would be avoided and dependence would be diminished' correlates with his general line on the purity of government institutions, for later he talks of reducing 'cabal and corruption' and is worried about the 'influence and faction' of a permanent senate.[127] Although 'undigested' it is a far more sensible proposal than some modern commentators have suggested, and we can be sure that he was searching for a principle or formula by which the power of the legislature could be moderated and the influence of key individuals and factions neutralised.[128] There is a sense, also, that his motivation for moving this quite extreme resolution at that moment was to bounce his fellow delegates into a greater awareness of the dangers they faced. The final outcome of the debate — that the president should be elected by electors from the states in equal numbers to their members of Congress — did not close the door on the possibility of a popularly elected president and so was indeed a concession to Wilson.

Gerry's response to the proposal and the brief altercation between King and Morris over the probability of drawing electors from one state are also revealing. Gerry's contention that elected members of Congress might be 'unworthy' can hardly be taken to mean that they might be intellectually incapable of making a good choice. But while his remarks can easily be seen as familiar aristocratic arguments about who should govern, the context suggests another interpretation. The term 'unworthy' was used by Freemasons during this period when they rejected candidates to the fraternity.[129] If we follow this line of reasoning, Gerry has either made a slip of the tongue or is warning his fellow brethren (this would include both Washing-

---

[125] *Ibid.*, pp. 370–1.
[126] Farrand (1966) vol. 2, p. 99.
[127] Madison (1987a) p. 578.
[128] Rossiter (1966) p. 199.
[129] Barratt, Sachse (1908) pp. 361, 399, 362 etc.

ton and Franklin) of the consequences of Wilson's proposal.[130] By the same token, Wilson might well have been aware of the (undigested) bombshell he was dropping and the likelihood that it would gain him concessions.

Morris' assertion that the chances of drawing a majority of electors from the same state would be 'infinite' indicates that he either knew something of probability theory or that he had given the matter prior consideration. It also leads us to a consideration of the efficiency of the proposal as a means of achieving unity and resolving potential conflicts and therefore its appeal to the state delegates at the convention. Within this scheme there is a high probability that a mixture of electors from the northern and southern, seaboard and interior, small and large states could have been produced. Within an electoral group of fifteen, moreover, this scheme offered much to the smaller states. Delaware and Rhode Island would have about a one-in-thirty chance of having an elector from their state, North and South Carolina and Connecticut one-in-seventeen. These states would have known that they could potentially hold the balance of power in certain circumstances, thereby tempering any tendency for the executive to be dominated by competing power blocks.[131]

James Wilson's 'undigested' proposal for the choice of president by a randomly-selected enclave is a typical weighted-lottery conflict resolution scenario. We can define it as a weighted lottery because the proposal to use randomly-selected individuals is made in a context dominated by groups or groupings of individuals. In this case the groups are the Congressmen selected from each state. It was suggested to give all parties a proportionate stake in the outcome, and thus to facilitate an agreement that otherwise might have proved elusive. To do this it relies on the idea that all parties can make a rough calculation of their chances of success, and therefore also of the risks that they would take if they supported the proposal. The success of the scheme as a means of reaching agreement is therefore premised on notions of ratio, rather than arationality and randomness. It is therefore a weak use of lot in which the lottery process provides the proceedings with an anonymous, objective

---

[130] Morse (1924) pp. xi, 68, 72, 110. See p. 61 for the Masonic influence on the Continental Congress.

[131] These calculations are derived from the following congressional quotas: Virginia: 12; Pennsylvania, Massachusetts: 10; New York, Maryland: 8; Connecticut, N. Carolina, S. Carolina: 7; New Jersey: 6; New Hampshire, Georgia: 5, Delaware, Rhode Island: 3. See Collier and Collier (1986) for a fuller discussion of voting patterns at the Convention.

mode of choice by which the relative chances of success for each state or group of states can be realised by proportionate calculation.

The Convention had been dominated by the intractability of state positions with very little breaking of ranks by individuals, and it is in context that Wilson's proposal derives its potency. The unpredictability of lot threatened to break the monopolies that the powerful states might exercise if majority voting was used. Instead each state would have a stake in the outcome proportionate to the numbers of their congressmen in the draw. No state would be excluded.

While Wilson's proposal might have solved some of the short-term disagreements that surfaced at the Convention, we can read it as a substitute for a more workable, long-term proportionate solution that was evading the delegates. With a relatively small pool of professional politicians it could easily become corrupted or could become the object of increased intrigue and horse-trading as groups of congressmen forged alliances in order to increase their chances of influence.

Paine's proposals for the militia

At this point it is useful to take a look at another scheme involving lot which emanated from the pen of Thomas Paine. Probably around 1780 he produced a plan for recruiting members of the American armed forces by lot. Pools of thirty potential conscripts would be drawn up with the object of producing one militia member by sortition. The other twenty-nine, however, were to have a charge levied on them to cover this one soldier's expenses and equipment. In this eminently sensible scheme Paine is aware of the potentially divisive nature of choice by lottery and seeks to maintain unity by sharing the burden between all participants.[132]

Whether it be for burden or reward, choice by lottery unites the pool in anticipation of the outcome. It also unites them because no individual amongst them is charged with the choice. Where the

---

[132] Paine (1945) pp. 208-9. This scheme is a kind of inversion of the insurance schemes used against the ballot call up for the English militia during this period. Groups of those subject to conscription would form savings clubs to pay the fine for avoidance or sponsor a replacement should one of their members be chosen. (Both these expedients were allowed under the various militia acts.) See Western (1965) p. 253. While the question of recruiting militias was a central part of the long-running debate on the political implications of the standing army, the English scheme differed fundamentally from its American counterpart in that it was designed to avoid a general arming and training of the people. See Western (1965) p. 127.

rewards or burdens are to be rotated amongst those in the pool and the lottery merely determines the order in which they are distributed, this sense of unity can easily be sustained. Where the burden imposed by lot is that much heavier or the duty more onerous, a wider division between those selected and those not selected can open up. Paine's notion of bringing those not chosen into support roles for their comrade is designed as a means of re-establishing the sense of community involvement and responsibility after a potentially divisive draw.

In general terms the use of lot to choose members of a militia, while unpopular, is a strong use of lot in so far as it prevents those with influence from engineering exclusion from service. It is also the type of choice that would be the subject of a huge number of conflicting moral claims were it left to an individual or group of individuals. It is also a very good example of lot being used as a surrogate choice. It is made on the grounds of expediency — simply because it would take too long to balance all the claims and in this sense we can think of it as a weak use of lot. Paine's scheme cleverly creates a new moral framework, which makes the rationale of the final choice less important than the idea that this is a shared project in which both winners and losers shoulder some of the responsibility.

The randomly-selected jury

The jury prior to random selection

The last section of this chapter looks at one of the flagship institutions of the Anglo-American tradition: the jury. Despite the efforts of the eighteenth-century writer Pettignal to establish a direct link between the English jury and its Greek and Roman counterparts, the picture is far from simple.[133] The Athenian *dikastai* are completely different from any judicial institution in later Europe, both in form and function, while the Roman *judices* differ from the English jury by their being selected from only the upper echelons of society. While some Roman influence cannot be discounted, the origins of the English form, where ordinary members of the community play a temporary judicial role, are undoubtedly Scandinavian.

Thorl Grund Repp, in his 1832 study of Icelandic and Scandinavian jury forms, suggests that the English jury is an amalgamation of two judicial forms practised from the ninth century onwards.

---

[133] Pettignal (1769).

These are the Scandinavian jury and the 'wager of law'. The latter consisted of a number of men named by the accused to render assistance against accusations brought either by another individual or by prosecuting magistrates.[134] According to Repp this was the most democratic, but also the most barbarous of these forms of community jurisdiction, in contrast to the more aristocratic, but more impartial, jury. Repp's characterisation of the wager of justice as 'barbarous' is probably because it was confrontational; the juries at this time were usually selected from amongst the more educated members of society, and would therefore be perceived as aristocratic. Repp claims that the Anglo-Saxon juries, so admired by seventeenth and eighteenth-century radicals, were, in fact, wagers of law. The membership of the wager of law was chosen by the accused and was obviously partisan. On the other hand there is no direct evidence to suggest that lot was regularly used to choose early Scandinavian juries. They were usually hand-picked by magistrates or judicial officers.

While the Saxons used lay members of the community in support of the accused in this manner, petty juries under the Norman kings of England had the role of bearing witness, usually, but not necessarily, in support of the prosecuting authorities. Their task was to supply the touring assize judges with local knowledge concerning the likely innocence or guilt of the accused parties, and in this they were expected to come to decisions favourable to the judge. Despite this they could be considered as a counterweight to the Grand Juries, which had the role of bringing prosecutions.

Although English medieval petty juries were not selected by lot, the traditional right of the accused to mount as many as thirty-six challenges to proposed jurors was a guarantee of impartiality and encouraged the sheriffs to be even-handed in their initial selection of jury members.[135] In the first years of the system, petty juries were made up of knights or men of high social standing in their communities, but this began to change during the later Middle Ages when jury qualification became linked to the ownership of freehold property.

That the English jury symbolised justice embedded in the community and a bulwark against arbitrary power is clear from its inclusion in the Magna Carta. It was only after the abolition of the Court of Star Chamber in 1641, however, that the jury began to have

[134] Repp (1832) p. 18.
[135] Green (1985) p. 134.

a practical political impact, as crimes against the state, and hence the existing political order, ceased to be treated by inquisition and became the subject for public trial. By the second half of the seventeenth century, therefore, accelerated by a series of key trials, the jury had rapidly established itself as the most representative institution in the realm and the strongest line of defence for the individual against the coercive power of the state.[136] Two cases deserve special mention. First the acquittal of Lilburne in 1653, and second the Penn-Mead or Bushel case of 1670, which established the jury's immunity in cases where they challenged the bench.

The case of Lilburne is significant because it confirms in practice the Leveller premise that the jury was, in essence, a law-making body. Lilburne was acquitted by jury in 1649 and again in 1653. The second trial is of considerable interest since Lilburne had returned home from exile, but, by doing so, he had broken the terms that had been imposed on him by Parliament. He was therefore brought to trial. As a major plank in his defence he challenged the constitutional legitimacy of Parliament's original decision. Moreover, in asking for the jury to acquit him, Lilburne was, in fact, claiming that the jury as an institution should take precedence over Parliament in interpreting the law. In this way he portrayed the jury as having more authority than the Rump that had exiled him.[137]

The jury's right to interpret the constitution and to make law was, from the Leveller perspective, an essential means by which pre-existing common rights and the process of common law were to be defended against the tyranny of Parliament. In *An agreement of the Free people of England* of 1649 Lilburne had also insisted that the selection of juries was an important aspect of this role. Juries, he explained, were, 'to be chosen in some free way by the people and not picked and imposed as hitherto in many places they have been'.[138] For the jury to be a body that stood for the people, suggests Lilburne, their selection cannot be left to the under-sheriff. He is looking for a way in which popular sovereignty can be manifested in practice, but he does not specifically advocate the use of lot, and therefore does not make the link between the role of the jury and Athenian democracy or Italian popular republicanism.

The Penn-Mead case of 1670 marks a watershed in the relations between judge and jury that was instantly incorporated into English

---

[136] Cockburn and Green (1988) p. 182.
[137] Green (1985) p. 173. State trials 4.1320–73 and 4.1379.
[138] Green (1985) p. 161.

Common Law and is still very much part of modern practice.[139] Under the 1664 Conventicles Act, part of the Clarendon Code, non-conformist religious meetings were deemed unlawful. There was, however, some confusion as to whether seditious intent needed to be proved, and this point was quickly taken up by a number of Quaker tracts of the period.[140] William Penn and William Mead were both arrested for preaching in the street and the jury, while admitting to the material fact, acquitted both defendants against the recommendations of the bench. In addressing the jury Penn had assumed that they had a right to go beyond the judgement of fact alone: 'The question is not whether I am guilty of this indictment, but whether this indictment be legal.'[141]

Once the jury had reached their decision, however, the judge fined the jury for ignoring his opinion. Some were imprisoned. One juryman, Bushel, however, moved a writ of Habeas Corpus to the Court of Common Pleas and secured a reversal of the judge's action. There is a certain parallel between the Penn-Mead and the Lilburne cases. Parliament had, two years previously, debated the issue of jury-fining and had prepared a bill which was to outlaw the practice. The bill, however, died in committee.[142] The ruling on Bushel by Vaughan in the Court of Common Pleas was a recognition in law of the jury's right to interpret the law independently of the judge. It was also, in effect, a legislative decision in lieu of a failure by the supreme legislative body to address the issue of jury fining. In this period the jury was clearly forcing the pace of its own rights and functions against the inertia of Parliament.

These successes for the jury system were achieved before sortition was used for the selection of jury members. It owed its success to the notion that it was considered to be an impartial institution, and this was achieved by judicious selection and the right to multiple challenges from the accused. The system was open to abuse, however. Jury-packing often took place and it was often difficult to find people willing to serve on juries. It was thus in the interests of all to find an efficient means of selection that could guarantee its continued impartiality. Before I return to look at the role of the jury in the later part of the eighteenth century, I need, therefore, to describe precisely how the change to random selection of jury members took place.

---

[139] *Ibid.* p. 274. See also Nilsen (2004) p. 21.
[140] Green (1985) p. 203.
[141] State trials 6.958. See Green (1985) p. 223.
[142] *Ibid.* p. 219.

The origins of the randomly-selected jury

The pattern is easy to discern. As we have seen, randomly-selected juries were proposed in some of the proprietary colonies in the late seventeenth century. While in East New Jersey and Pennsylvania their success was short lived, in South Carolina the system became an established part of the colony's judicial operations for most of the next century. English juries were selected by lot after the *Bill for Better Regulating of Juries* of 12 March 1730.[143] Five American colonies followed suit between 1736 and 1758,[144] while a further two states, New Jersey and Maryland turned to random selection between Independence and 1800.[145] Pennsylvania finally returned to a system of drawing juries by lot in 1821, and was joined in this by Maine. Virginia still used its traditional method of selecting half the jury from the 'ablest and nearest' bystanders up to 1796.[146]

The provisions in colonial and state legislation and the brief report on the English act by Tindal are revealing. In the law of 20 August 1731 confirming its 'ancient practice', the South Carolina statutes comment that:

> ... the equal, indifferent and impartial method of drawing juries by ballot, used and approved in this province for many years past, hath greatly contributed to the due and upright Administration of justice, and is the surest means to continue the same.[147]

The draw for the jury was to be carried out in court by a child under ten, and public notice of the draw was to be given '... by the Beat of Drum in the most public streets of Charles-town, on the same day the said jury is to be drawn.'[148]

Such a public demonstration of their ancient institution is in contrast to the sober measures of the English act of 1730. The bill passed without opposition and was approved by the Lords. Tindal's commentary states that this is a 'most excellent act'. It had two clearly

---

[143] Cobbett (1811) col. 802.

[144] These were Massachusetts: 1736; New York: 1741: Connecticut: 1742; New Hampshire: 1758. See Massachusetts (2000) Ch. 234 § 7; New York (1894) pp. 183, 189; Connecticut (1750) pp. 102–3; North Carolina (1751) pp. 163–4; New Hampshire (1771) pp. 189–90.

[145] For New Jersey see Wilson (1784) pp. 344–5. For Maryland see Kilty (1799) Ch. 87 § 8.

[146] Virginia (1727) Chap. XXIV, p. 9. The system was introduced in 1662. See below note 156.

[147] Trott (1736) p. 503.

[148] *Ibid.* p. 506.

stated aims. The first: to ensure that 'men of substance' could not get out of jury service, leaving the juries full of 'indigent people; which opened an easy way for corruption in most capital cases'. The second: to prevent jury packing by 'knavish lawyers'. To achieve this two measures are described. Petty Constables would make up lists of those qualified to serve and post them on the 'church door two or more Sundays before Michaelmas to allow for objections'.[149] A draw by lot for the twelve members would then take place in Court on the day of the trial.[150] If anything the act was designed to put a brake on the type of radical expansion of the jury's role as an organ of popular government that was seen in the previous century. The overall thrust was to make juries reflect the sober middle strata of English society. Lot in these circumstances was a means by which this burden could be fairly spread, and as a protection for the rich against unscrupulous sheriffs who would call the same persons over and over again in order to obtain bribes.[151]

Most colonies and states emphasise how lot will provide an 'indifferent' and 'fair' means of selecting juries. Most involve the sheriff in the drawing up of the original panel and specify that this choice should be governed by some explicit criteria in terms of the good-standing of the prospective jury members. Some states (New Jersey 1793, Maryland 1799) changed from sortition to a struck jury in which the contending parties would delete a number of names alternatively from a list of potential jurors.[152] In other states this was advocated for civil cases or boundary disputes.[153] The method of appointment of the sheriff varied from colony to colony, and in Massachusetts, for instance, the freemen of the town were responsible for selecting the juries before sortition was introduced in 1736.[154] In two colonies, New Hampshire in 1761 and North Carolina in 1756, special juries were chosen to decide on the routes of new high-

---

[149] Cobbett (1811) col. 802. This process is almost identical to the procedure used to select the militia by ballot on a county by county basis after the English militia act of 1757. See Western (1965) p. 247. This is an intriguing parallel. The 'church door' list is clearly designed to place the notion of public duty in the heart of the community.

[150] Cobbett (1811) col. 803.

[151] *Ibid*.

[152] For Maryland see Herty (1799) pp. 313–14; for New Jersey see New Jersey (1800) p. 261.

[153] North Carolina (1765) p. 356.

[154] Massachusetts (1814).

ways, an indication of the potential of juries for wider legislative activity.[155]

With the exception of South Carolina, the advent of sortition in the jury system seems to have been a very down-beat, business-like affair, with many colonies or states commenting on the efficiency of the system rather than any political or democratic potential it might have. Nearly half the states had already used sortition for jury selection for a good number of years by the time that the right to trial by jury was incorporated into the Bill of Rights. In the ratification debates it was clear that the prerogative of states to develop their own best practice for selecting juries was to be respected, and those states, such as Virginia, which used different methods of selection, were not required to change.[156]

The law-finding role of the jury – the seditious libel crisis

The tendency to view the jury as having a 'law-finding' role had been enhanced during the early years of the century by the practice of jury-based mitigation, in which acquittal was used as a means of commuting excessive sentences for petty crimes.[157] A practical understanding was thus emerging that the jury could be made to make up for deficiencies in legislation and provide a flexible community-based system of justice. It was against this background that a protracted struggle for the freedom of the press took place in the latter half of the eighteenth century. The main weapon in the hands of the government was the law of seditious libel, and the main defence of the writers, publishers and booksellers faced with this catch-all legislation was to appeal to the jury. This could only be effective, however, if the jury based their judgement, not on the fact of publication, but on the general case of whether the accused was guilty of sedition. This naturally involved a value judgement as to whether the content of the publication in question was actually seditious, or was merely a justifiable act of public criticism of government incompetence or corruption.

A gradual build-up of cases during the middle years of the century (including Zengers in New York in 1735, and Owen in London in 1752), led to a climax in the campaign in the 1760s and 70s as the

---

[155] For North Carolina see North Carolina (1765) pp. 90 and 269. For New Hampshire see New Hampshire (1761) p. 115.

[156] Jefferson in fact presented a petition in October 1798 to have this changed to election. See Jefferson (1943) pp. 126–8.

[157] Green (1985) p. 270.

government attempted to prosecute Wilkes under the act in 1763 and then sought prosecution in 1770 for the publication of the Junius Papers—tracts which criticised British policy towards the American colonies.[158]

In his successful defence of the bookseller Owen for bringing out a tract critical of the House of Commons, Camden had argued that the right to criticise was fundamental.[159] This was the essence of the crisis. Other issues were inevitably raised, however, and these included a serious constitutional debate on the role of the jury. At the height of the Junius trials, Solicitor-General Thurlow had raised the spectre of jury control over the law,[160] while in the other side of the struggle the Wilkites portrayed the jury as the people's best guarantee of liberty under a corrupt and unrepresentative Parliament.[161] While remnants of the Leveller arguments that law flowed from the community via the jury were still in evidence, Blackstone, among others, adopted a more instrumentalist approach that the jury constituted a 'watchdog' against the excesses of corruption and tyranny.[162] The controversy finally came to an end with Fox's Libel Act of 1792, which granted the jury the right to bring in a general verdict in seditious libel cases.[163]

Within this context a wealth of publications and tracts were produced. A number of these are important for our purposes in so far as they allude to the relatively new use of sortition for jury selection and relate this to the political role of the jury. George Rous produced his 1771 pamphlet *A Letter to the Jurors of Great Britain* in response to Lord Mansfield's published opinion on the Junius case. Like much of the pro-jury literature of this period, Rous' viewpoint is bound securely to his view of popular, open government: 'While the trial by juries subsists in its proper vigour, the criminal judicature thereby remains with the great body of the nation, no avenue will be open to oppression.'[164]

Civil liberty, he claims, can be preserved only by the rule of law, but the 'laws themselves are preserved by a sense of common inter-

---

[158] *Ibid.* p. 322.
[159] *Ibid.*
[160] *Ibid.* p. 324.
[161] *Ibid.* p. 327.
[162] *Ibid.* p. 332–3.
[163] *Ibid.* p. 330.
[164] Rous (1771) p. 3.

est'.[165] A judgement on the complex issue of seditious libel, where public safety and freedom have to be weighed in judgement, can be made only, he suggests, if we 'enter into common life' and 'imbibe the sentiments of the people.'[166] In this respect, therefore, random selection is a means whereby this common sense is made accessible to the judicial system: 'Juries taken by lot from among the people are *particularly* the proper judges in cases of libel.'[167]

The non-partisan and amateur status of the jury, moreover, is a guarantee that corruption, where it takes place, will have a limited effect: 'Jurors, therefore, are taken by lot from the people, and having tried a *particular* cause return immediately to the common mass.'[168] Rous is then able to combine the argument for the incorruptibility of the people in rotation via the institution of the jury, with his notion of popular sovereignty: 'I sincerely believe the PEOPLE to be the only legitimate source of power. The only source which cannot be corrupted.'[169]

A similar viewpoint is presented by Robert Morris in *A Letter to Sir Richard Ashton*, a pamphlet produced in 1770. Morris presents the question of popular sovereignty and the role of the jury in the context of a social contract argument. The fact that juries are literally drawn from the people is significant to this: 'Who is more interested than juries (for juries are composed of the people) to preserve the peace and order of the state? It is for their[170] security that government is established.'[171] For Morris, therefore, the randomly-selected jury is the most fundamental means by which the original agreement for self-government can be manifested in practice. He also sees sortition as valuable because it prevents corruption:

> Everything which may, nay which must be uncertain, in the particular case, is left to the judgement of another tribunal, a tribunal, to be taken by lot and by rotation from among the people; which is therefore perpetually changing; which, if corrupted, the evil can only be extended to the oppression of a single individual.[172]

---

[165] *Ibid.* p. 5.
[166] *Ibid.* p. 51.
[167] *Ibid.*
[168] Rous (1771) p. 60.
[169] *Ibid.* p. 65.
[170] i.e. the people's.
[171] Morris (1770) p. 42.
[172] *Ibid.* p. 53.

It is in these pamphlets that we find the nearest thing in the Anglo-American thought of this period to a philosophy of popular sovereignty that is linked to the principle of random selection. It is a development of the Leveller argument that justice flows from the community but now, with the advent of sortition and rotation, there is a sharper focus on issues of impartiality and incorruptibility. Rotation and sortition came into Anglo-American politics via Harrington, but unlike Harrington, the integrity of the vision of Rous and Morris relies on the idea of direct selection from the people as a whole rather than the use of lot as part of an indirect system of election. It would also be fair to say that these developments arose from the failures of the legislative body in Britain.

The political role of the jury

One feature of this narrative is the similarity between the role of the jury in the 1680s and 90s — that is, prior to the adoption of random selection — and its role in the latter part of the eighteenth century, during the judicial battles over the question of seditious libel. In both cases the jury was the organ of government at the forefront of the defence of freedom of political expression against the state. In the acquittals of Lilburne and the seditious libel cases the jury showed its potential as an institution of community justice. It was an organ that allowed a section of those who were the subject of legislation — the governed — to disapprove or approve of the actions of those who sought to govern them.

While these events show the potential of the jury as an organ of community justice, they also show its limitations. The type of political role that we have seen the jury assume is reactive and defensive. The jury comes into political prominence when the state acts in such a manner as to bring it into conflict with the political sensitivity of its subjects. In this sense, and commensurate with its origins in the early Norman period, the jury has always belonged to the state as a form of government, rather than to the republic. It emerged as a means by which the community could support the state judicial machinery, and only later developed as a guarantee against the abuse of state power. In this respect, therefore, we should be careful not to over-estimate its political potential. Nor should we think of it as bearing anything beyond a passing resemblance to the Athenian *dikasterion*, which, in its heyday, was charged with both approving legislation and passing judgement on political and public interest cases, usually brought by individual citizens.

We can therefore view the jury as operating in the space between the central state authority and the community. It is a governmental organ, and is organised and controlled by central government authority; but, at the same time, it involves members of the community who, at least after the Penn-Mead case, are free to find a verdict independently of that authority. The jury is also an institution that suits both the community and the state. A centralised government finds it easier to uphold justice if it enlists the co-operation of the community; while the community benefits from the authority, organisation and physical protection that central government brings to the institution. The process by which jurors are selected, therefore, stands at the interface between state and community — at the heart of this reciprocal relationship.

We can see, moreover, how the use of random selection endorses and strengthens this necessary sense of compromise. We have seen various expressions of this. Lilburne called for greater impartiality in the selection of jurors; the citizens of South Carolina reached a rare agreement with their new proprietary government over the question of jury selection by lot, perhaps because it clearly favoured no single party. We also saw how the British Parliament was unanimous in the need to define the responsibility of its citizens more precisely and to curb the power of the under-sheriff. Finally we saw the Wilkite pamphleteers stressing how the use of lot defines the jury as an institution of the people. There is a genuine sense, therefore, that randomly selected jurors were acceptable both to the central authority and to the community at large.

We saw how the jury's role as an organ of community justice *before* the adoption of random selection was almost identical to its role in the late eighteenth century — after the introduction of lot. Nonetheless, there is a distinct difference in the terms in which it operates compared to any other form of selection. It derives greater authority as an institution because no individual or organised group of individuals can control the selection of its members. In criminal cases this means that neither the defence nor the prosecution can manipulate the selection of the jury to serve their own ends. In cases where the state is challenged on a particular political issue, or where a citizen is defending herself against state prosecution on political grounds, random selection means that the make up of the jury cannot be manipulated either by the state, or by the enemies of the state. In this sense, therefore, the role of the jury as a point of mediation between the state and the community is enhanced by random selection.

Random selection also defines the relationship between the citizen and the jury system. All in the citizen body — or at least all those in the portion of it from which juries are drawn — have a potentially equal stake in the system as a whole. The blind break ensures that no one is included or excluded in conscious preference to any other, and, in principle — and certainly in the tenor of the 1730 act — responsibility is spread amongst those in the pool. This defining of the public obligation through the process of sortition, together with the idea of public ownership inherent in the randomly-selected jury, is more than the strengthening of the jury's community role or its representative function — as suggested by the Wilkite pamphleteers.

We can, in fact, think of the randomly-selected jury as an institution of republican or public government. It is in public, rather than partisan or state ownership; it is operated by citizens, whose political obligation it defines; and while it reflects the community, it is not merely an organ of community justice, but part of public governance. Its members, even under a monarchy, act as citizens, not subjects. The point in 1682 when South Carolina adopted the randomly-selected jury was the point when the jury became such an institution. This was not only because this act linked the English form of community justice with the republican practice of sortition, but also because sortition has the potential to organise the role of the citizenry in public government.

Conclusion

This chapter dealt with a period in which the type of republican polity that used sortition extensively was in decline. It shows us that while sortition has political potential, the realisation of that potential is not inevitable. Reasons why the potential of lot might not be realised include a lack of familiarity with the practice of using the mechanism in a political environment, the failure of political theory to understand and explain how it works, pre-judgement against the use of lot, and its use in badly designed schemes. Sortive schemes might also be rejected if a faction in power, or contesting power wished to retain some level of control over the selection of office-holders. These reasons often combined to make sortition appear as a less attractive option amongst a range of alternative mechanisms.

The story of how the political use of lot was received in northern Europe, away from the circumstances in which it developed, is the story of how these factors came into operation. In early seventeenth-century England, republicanism itself was little known in practice, and the political use of sortition even less so. The use of lots in general, moreover, engendered the natural suspicion of the puritan community, despite the input of classicists such as Gataker who had acquired a greater knowledge of its ancient use in the political arena. We saw how lot played a major part in the procedures for the selection of officers in Harrington's *Oceana*; but how no explanation was advanced as to exactly what it contributed to the polity and its ideals. In East New Jersey we saw an inclusive constitution that used sortition rejected because it was seen as a threat to local self-government. In the colonies the secret ballot and the use of rotation were adopted in preference to sortition and were used to fulfil some of its functions—such as preventing voter intimidation and inhibiting the growth of powerful cliques. In the proposed scheme to select English Parliamentary Committees the role of lot was so compromised by preference choices as to lose its effectiveness. In the proposal to divide the Pennsylvania council into three by lot as a preliminary to rotation lot seems to have been suggested as a matter of convenience rather than because an arational scheme was needed. Both these examples indicate that the understanding of how to use lot effectively was limited.

On the other hand, Paine's scheme for the election of the president of a new, united, independent, America, and the actual application of lot in the Articles of Confederation, suggest how lot could be usefully used in the political consolidation of a unified polity. In this respect there are obvious comparisons with the use of lot in Athens as a device to bring disparate parties into the same political process on an equal footing. The proposal by James Wilson at the Constitutional Convention belongs in this context in so far as it concerns the use of lot to bring parties into some form of procedural agreement. It shows how the weighted lottery form can be used to broker deals between contending groups. The story of this proposal also intimates how secret, or semi-secret societies, such as the Freemasons, would have regarded sortition as a threat. This is an obvious, but nonetheless significant potential of sortition, and is a consequence of its function of protecting the public nature of the selection of political officers. In Paine's militia proposal lot has two functions: to prevent the subversion of the selection procedure, and to avoid the complexity of competing claims for exemption. It is an important example of how to make a potentially divisive lottery decision less so by strengthening the community of interest of those in the pool.

Of the stand-alone examples the most intriguing is that of the Great Yarmouth inquest. Its existence and longevity would seem to contradict the idea that lot was an alien and unfamiliar election mechanism in England. It clearly served the governmental and economic needs of the community well — otherwise it would have been replaced. It stands as a reminder of how the intuitive invention of lot can operate locally even when the mechanism is not part of a national political culture.

We also saw in this chapter how with the loss of the random element from the integrated Venetian-style balloting procedure the public aspect of the process of selection was diminished. A far more private electoral process took its place — one that placed fewer obligations of participation on its citizens. Although the secret ballot in its new form was destined to become the key mechanism in the new form of representative republicanism that grew from these American roots, it is useful to recognise how much of the public nature of the process was lost in transition from its Italian origins.

In this chapter, however, it is the randomly-selected jury that tells us the most about the political potential of sortition. In the story of its origins and the examination of its role we have seen how the introduction of a broad-based sortive scheme for an institution of government can promote certain relationships that operate in respect to that institution. Lot can help to define the role of the citizen, and can define his or her obligations to the polity in a structured and organised manner. Sortition can also protect the public nature of their political activity by protecting the process of selection of official personnel. Institutions chosen in this way command authority because their personnel are chosen impartially. For these reasons we can think of the potential of sortition as the potential to create republican institutions: institutions that have republican characteristics, whether or not the context in which they exist is republican in its general orientation.

Bibliographical notes

The range and scope of this chapter required that I search through a wide range primary material for instances of sortition. I also had to pull together many small scraps of material from different origins in order to form a picture of how sortition was understood and used.

Of the authors who were eliminated from my inquiries, special mention needs to be made of the English Republicans, Nedham, Neville, Sidney, Milton, Vane and Ludlow, whose major works I consulted. This is not to say that further references to sortive schemes will not surface in shorter tracts or journal articles by these authors. I did, however find some interest in Venetian-style sortition in the work of Streater — Harrington's printer, whose *Observations, Historical, Political and Philosophical upon Aristotle's First book of Political Government* of 1654 and whose 1659 *Government described. Viz what monarchie, aristocracie, oligarchie and demoracie is. Plus a model of the commonwealth or free state of Ragaus* (published under the initials J.S), I cite.

For the proceedings of the early Stuart Parliaments I used Bidwell, W. B. and Janssen, M. eds *Proceedings in Parliament 1626.* Vol. IV. Yale University Press.(1991-5); and Wallace N. *Commons Debates for 1629 Critically Edited with an introduction dealing with Parliamentary Sources for the Early Stuarts.* (1921). For the American Constitutional Convention I used Farrand, M. ed. (1966) *Records of the Federal Convention of 1787* Vol. 2 Yale University Press, supplemented by Madison's notes published by Norton in 1987. For the Continental Congress I used the Library of Congress *Journals of the Continental Congress* published in 1907, and for the statutes of individual colonies, a series of microfilm compilations available from the Oxford University Law Library. References from these are cited under the particular volumes from which they are drawn. For the State Constitutions Poore (1878) provided the best source.

I consulted Harrington's works in the editions of 1992 and 1977 edited by Pocock, Penn's in *The Papers of William Penn*, edited by Dunn, R and Dunn, M.M. and published by the University of Pennsylvania Press in 1982, and in individually published works. Citations from Paine come, for the most part, from the 1945 Foner edition, but I use the Penguin Classics *Common Sense* on occasions. For Jefferson I used the Princeton edition of his collected papers and the 1943 *Complete Jefferson* edited by Padover.

Of the most valuable secondary sources I must include Kishlansky (1986) on early Parliamentary selection, Osgood's thorough 1924 *The American Colonies in the Eighteenth Century*, and Robbin's 1959 *The Eighteenth-century Commonwealthman*. My exploration of the jury was aided considerably by T.A. Green's 1985 *Verdict according to Conscience*, Repp's ancient but remarkable *A Historical Thesis in Trial by Jury, Wager of Law, and other Co-ordinate*

Forensic Institutions in Scandinavia and Iceland of 1832, and Forsyth's classic 1852 *The History of Trial by Jury*. The links between English and American republicanism were admirably served by Pocock's *Machiavellian Moment*, Gooch's *English Democratic Ideas in the Seventeenth Century*, Russell-Smith's *Harrington and his Oceana*, and Olson's excellent *Anglo-American Politics. 1660-1775. The Relationship between Parties in England and Colonial America* of 1973.

My appreciation is also extended to the numerous local historians without whose hard work the threads of this chapter could not have been pulled together. These include McCormack, Pomfret, Shepherd and Whitehead for New Jersey; Edgar, Ramsey, Sirmans and Weir for South Carolina; Nash for Pennsylvania and Palmer for Great Yarmouth.

Chapter Six

Sortition During the French Revolutionary Decade

In this chapter I look at a number of examples of sortition during the decade 1789–99 in France. Although sortition only plays a minimal role in the story of revolutionary change, it does occur, and its use and advocacy is instructive to our understanding of how its political potential can be realised in practice. It is instructive, however, in a largely negative sense. We see in France during this period the very problems of factional discord and arbitrary rule that sortition was employed to inhibit in Italy and Athens. At the same time we see in most of the instances where lot was used or advocated only a partial understanding of why it had been previously used—a failure to grasp its full potential.

When Rousseau and Montesquieu discuss sortition their evalua- tion owes more to an eighteenth-century interpretation of classical democracy than to an understanding of more recent practices. This tended to identify sortition too strongly with revolutionary egalitar- ianism and to minimise its potential for impartiality. We also see this tendency in a major constitutional proposal of 1792 that I explore in this chapter.

On the other hand, it was difficult for many of those in the centre ground of French republican politics who believed in the primacy of reason to embrace an arational procedure. The view of lot as a dem- ocratic measure that might bring the uneducated into government made it even less acceptable to this enlightenment ethos. Thus while Sieyès and Lanthenas recognise that lot could be used in the new voting system to prevent its corruption by factions, their endorse- ment of this mechanism is considerably reserved. Thus, while the use of lot for the selection of juries and for a number of other, mainly judicial, functions seems not to have encountered any opposition, and while its potential for inhibiting the development of factions was known at local level, there was little consideration of lot as a means of selecting members of the national legislature or executive.

There are exceptions, however, and these belong to the period when the dangers of uninhibited partisanship were becoming more apparent. One is a scheme for dividing the legislative assembly into two by lot to create two temporary assemblies for the purpose of improving the quality of debate. This was presented as an adjunct to the ill-fated Girondin Constitution of 1793. The other is the actual use of lot and rotation immediately after the fall of Robespierre and under the Directory government of 1795–9. In these circumstances the need for measures that could restore the impartial authority of government became more pressing, but while some applications of lot contributed to this end, others were problematic and show that there was little exact knowledge about the true potential of this mechanism.

Montesquieu and Rousseau on the use of lot

Although Montesquieu approves of the idea of using rotation as a means of preventing corruption[1] and favours the use of juries some-what on the lines of the Athenian or English systems, he does not make the link between sortition and the idea of protecting public office from subversion.[2] His brief exposition on the subject in Book II of the *Spirit of the Laws*: 'Just as the division of those having the right to vote is a fundamental law in the republic, the way of casting the vote is another fundamental law. Voting by *lot* is in the nature of democracy; voting by *choice* is in the nature of aristocracy.'[3]

In this way Montesquieu tends to bracket sortition firmly to democracy, a system which he equates with the ideology of equal-ity, and one, moreover, which is constantly in danger of corruption by what he calls extreme equality.[4] He values lot, however, as a non-competitive means of selection and one that encourages citizen participation: 'The casting of lots is a way of electing that distresses

---

[1]   Montesquieu (1989) p. 17.
[2]   *Ibid.* p. 158.
[3]   *Ibid.* p. 13.
[4]   *Ibid.* pp. 43, 112.

no one; it leaves to each citizen a reasonable expectation of serving his country.'[5]

In general, however, his overriding interest in the citizen's act of electoral choice leads him to see lot as an imperfect method of selection. It can only be usefully used in combination with voting or if controlled by the use of measures such as the Athenian *dokimasia*.[6] Because he is limited by his use of the Athenian citizen lot polity as his only example, and because he sees in this a form of dangerous extreme egalitarianism, Montesquieu presents sortition merely as a kind of problematic precursor to his new model of representative government. In this respect he fails to address the fuller potential of sortition, particularly its capacity to establish the type of impartial republican institutions that he advocates elsewhere in the *Spirit of the Laws*.[7]

The same omissions are also to be found in Rousseau, although his presentation is more complex and his attitude towards democracy more favourable. Rather than viewing sortition as a means of facilitating the consolidation of republican institutions, he tends to see lot as a mechanism linked exclusively to democracy. Moreover he does not see sortition as a means of creating conditions where democracy can prosper, but sees it as an appropriate measure only after democracy has been established: 'Elections by lot would have few drawbacks in a true democracy in which, all things being equal both in morality and talent as well as in maxims and fortunes, it would hardly matter who was chosen. But I have already said that there is no true democracy.'[8]

There is a sense in this that Rousseau sees the potential of lot as the distribution of office between pre-existing equals, which contradicts the idea that lot can be used to establish a form of political equality between citizens of differing abilities and aptitudes. Implicit in this viewpoint is the idea we found expressed by Montesquieu: sortition is an inherently flawed means of selection and its use can be justified only when the impact of these flaws is minimised. Lot is valuable only when its arationality is made more rational.

Rousseau, along with Montesquieu, approaches sortition from the point of view of the possible products of the lot, rather than con-

---

[5]   *Ibid.* p. 13.
[6]   *Ibid.* p. 15. Montesquieu does not mention the *dokimasia* by name.
[7]   See especially Part 2 Books 11 and 12. Montesquieu (1989) pp.154–213.
[8]   Rousseau (1988) p. 153.

sidering what it can contribute to the procedures of government. Thus when he comments on the idea of using lot for some offices and election for posts where different talents are required, he makes a useful point about the design of constitutions, but does not consider the potential of the arational:

> When elections by choice and by lot are combined, the first method should be used to fill positions which require special talents, such as military posts; the second is suited to those in which common sense, justice and integrity are sufficient, such as judicial offices, because in a well-constituted state, these qualities are common to all citizens.[9]

What this shows is that neither Rousseau nor Montesquieu can see beyond the identification of sortition with egalitarianism based on a particular reading of classical democracy. Beyond this, and the few managerial points made from that perspective, the positive political potential of sortition — the value of the blind break — remains a mystery. It is likely that this outlook derives from a straightforward reading of Aristotle, Herodotus and Xenophon, none of whom explain the full role of lot. It is also an indication of how the newer political thinking of the eighteenth century tended to assess political innovation from the point of view of classical precedent.

The new French voting system

During the early years of the revolution it would be fair to say that a head of steam had built up behind the new system of preference voting. In fact the abiding theme of the politics of 1789 was that of representation. The calling of the *Estates General* , the *Cahiers de Doléances*, the early struggle for the National Assembly and the demand for political rights for the third estate in proportion to their numbers, were all part of the same essentially representative agenda.[10] What is more, this was accompanied by a considerable interest in the mechanisms of voting — the work of Condorcet in the pre-revolutionary period especially springs to mind.[11] In the immediate aftermath of the fall of the Bastille there were debates as to whether a direct or repre-

---

[9] *Ibid.*
[10] Forsyth (1987) p. 128; Doyle (1989) pp. 86–111.
[11] See Condorcet (1994). Of particular note are the 1789 essay 'On the form of Elections' and the essay 'On the Constitution and functions of Provincial Assemblies'.

sentative form of government should be adopted. The size of France was the determining factor in the decision in favour of representation.[12]

In his 1996 study Malcolm Crook talks of 'a wonderfully diverse, sometimes bizarre experiment' with elections, and draws our attention to the sheer magnitude and complexity of this undertaking.[13] Every official post, save that of the King, became elective after 1789; twenty rounds of elections were held in the space of the revolutionary decade; the basis of suffrage was modified four times and the mechanism for voting amended 'almost annually.'[14] Referenda were held on the Jacobin Constitution of 1793 and the Thermidorian Constitution of 1795. Despite the efforts of Condorcet and others to find a workable electoral mechanism that genuinely reflected the judgement of the electors, electoral methods at this time were 'antiquated', and still adhered to quasi-feudal structures and relationships.[15]

For the most part, elections were indirect.[16] Primary Assemblies at local level would elect electors who would meet in Secondary Assemblies to elect both local and departmental office-holders.[17] While this empowered the upper sector of the third estate, it also preserved the power of parochial elites, since many electors were themselves office-holders.[18] Membership of Primary Assemblies was conditional on a property qualification,[19] and since there were no declared candidates, electors were usually members of the local community who were already well known.[20] The result of this was to create what the Marquis of Villette called an 'invisible aristocracy'.[21] This also contributed to an inevitable tension between the declared right of all citizens to office[22] and the actual situation on the ground in most of provincial France.

---

[12] Crook (1996) p. 30.
[13] *Ibid.* p. 5.
[14] *Ibid.*
[15] *Ibid.*
[16] There was considerable opposition to this, particularly from Robespierre, Antoine and La Croix who saw the Primary Assemblies as vulnerable to cabals and contrary to the notion of popular sovereignty. See Crook (1996) p. 96.
[17] Crook (1996) p. 29.
[18] Forty to sixty per cent, according to Crook (1996) p. 176.
[19] Known as the silver–mark qualification. See Crook (1996) p. 36.
[20] *Ibid.* 177.
[21] *Ibid* p. 178.
[22] Article 6 of the 1789 *Declaration of the Rights of Man and of Citizens*.

The vocal ballot was abolished in 1789 only to be re-instated by radicals in 1792 and abandoned again in 1795, when the Thermidorian Constitution stipulated that the secret ballot be used.[23] Voting was by a 'cumbersome'[24] double-list system, which was often abandoned by Primary Assemblies.[25] Property and fiscal qualifications were swept away in August 1792 after the fall of the King, but while the primary and municipal elections in the second part of 1792 were the most democratic of the decade, the promise of universal manhood suffrage, enshrined in the suspended 1793 Constitution, was never honoured. [26] The 1795 Constitution restored the property qualification.

As well as the fact that the indirect voting system favoured the rising 'natural aristocracy', there were other problems. Voter fatigue seriously affected turnout, and figures as low as ten or fifteen percent were recorded in some instances.[27] Another major problem was voter manipulation, and although political parties were disallowed and candidates were not declared or named in advance, electoral pressure from factional sources was inevitably applied. Possibly in order to counteract the system's inherent bias in the favour of local élites, the Jacobin clubs were especially guilty of electoral manipulation, circulating slates and publishing lists of 'unpatriotic' citizens.[28] These practices took a more ominous turn with the onset of the Terror, but were adopted again by royalists and other anti-Jacobins seeking revenge after the fall of Robespierre. The Directory government, trying to maintain stability in the face of agitation by both Jacobins and resurgent royalists, also indulged in electoral fixing in the period immediately prior to the Consulate. [29]

The revolutionary decade can be described as a prolonged crisis of political legitimacy. In it voting played a somewhat ambiguous role. The composition of the National Assembly, Convention and Legislative Assemblies was clearly critical in determining the overall course of the revolution, but it is useful to reflect that during the revolutionary decade every pivotal change of political direction

---

[23] Crook (1996) p. 19.
[24] Brissot is quoted to this effect : Crook (1996) p. 87.
[25] *Ibid.*
[26] All freemen over twenty-five were to be entitled to membership of the Primary Assemblies. Crook (1996) p. 103.
[27] Crook (1996) p. 94; pp. 119–20 for the voting on the 1795 Constitutional referendum. Note that in these referenda voting was both for and against.
[28] *Ibid.* p. 89.
[29] *Ibid.* pp. 140, 153; Aston (2004), pp. 58–9.

was achieved by direct means. At the same time, however, and for a different class, the voting system was slowly consolidating habits of regional political participation.

What this shows is that the new voting system was experimental and brought with it as many problems as it did solutions. It was particularly vulnerable to manipulation and inevitably brought the competitive political contentions of the capital into local politics.

Sortition within the voting system: Sieyès and Lanthenas

There are some instances where lot in conjunction with voting was proposed or discussed. [30] Sieyès, prior to 1789, had suggested that Primary Assemblies should be abandoned and secondary electors should be selected by lot from a pool of known electors. This was, it seems, to prevent local intrigue. The Primary Assemblies, he remarks, are too full and would be 'prone to factional problems, anti-social motives'. [31]

In a more discursive paper *Des élections et du mode d'élive par listes épuratoires* of 1792 Fr. Lanthenas devotes two pages to the question of elections by sortition. In his opening remarks Lanthenas feels he must respond to an existing discourse on the subject: 'Some people, struck by the valid criticisms made of all the modes of election, have no difficulty in *seriously* proposing the use of lot to decide the outcome of all elections.' [32] He further suggests that this was motivated by misplaced egalitarianism. [33]

Lanthenas holds the view that the interests of the Republic are best served if only the most virtuous and enlightened citizens are electors. [34] To favour sortition, however, is to believe that nature, rather than reason, should be the deciding factor, and this springs from the belief that: '… one will encounter (in sortition) that very thing which is to bring safety, in the midst of the infinite variety dis-

---

[30] While Mont–Gilbert (1793) p. 23, suggests that there is no reason why one citizen should be chosen over another for public office, he does not develop the implications of this in terms of a citizens-lot scheme.

[31] 'inconvénients des cabales, de l'espirit antisocial …' Guéniffey (1933) p. 120, cites the Bibliotheque National reference AN, 284 AP, 3 no.2 liasse 1.

[32] Lanthenas (1792) p. 39. *Quelques personnes, frappées des justes reproches à faire tous les modes d'élire employés jusqu'à présent, n'ont pas–fait de difficulté de proposer sérieusement le sort pour décider de toutes les élections.*

[33] *Ibid.* p. 40. *..un amour mal–entendu de l'égalité.*

[34] *Ibid.* p. 39. *…le plus vertueux et le plus éclairé.*

played by nature.'[35] He does admit, nonetheless, that if enough men of upright spirit and character were available, the choice between them would be of little consequence.[36] If it was known that some sort of intrigue was afoot, then this could be countered by adding more people to the electoral lists and drawing the office-holders by lot. This, he insists, would be 'a method of last resort to break intrigue and counter factions.' [37] Lanthenas has faith that 'pure men of benevolence'[38] should be able to make the right choices, but suggests that sortition can be usefully employed in conditions where corruption and ambition are rife: 'It is when society is run through by bad and ambitious men, capable of sacrificing everything, that sortition can be combined with elections in order to combat their criminal aspirations.'[39] Sortition for Lanthenas is thus a default position, to be used when humanity is not as enlightened as it should be.

The views of Lanthenas are revealing. They show us how the potential of lot to protect the electoral process was well understood by Girondin opinion, but his remarks also indicate why this sector of the political spectrum could be reluctant to embrace sortition more comprehensively. Sortition was arational, and its extensive use — even for good reasons — would tend to undermine the ethos of reason that was so central to the politics of the new natural aristocracy. Lanthenas' opening remarks indicate that his contribution to the subject was a response to pressure from a more democratic direction. He is, therefore, lukewarm in his advocacy.

Lanthenas' view of sortition as a corrective measure of last resort, conveys the idea that arationality should only be used when reason has failed. There are, however, difficulties with this idea. One immediate question concerns the timing of such a move: when would be the right time to switch to the use of lot? Furthermore, who would be responsible for making the decision? Again, this attitude indicates how lot was seen as an imperfect or surrogate measure rather than an arational tool that could be applied rationally in a preventative capacity. While he understands the value of lot on a

---

[35] *Ibid.* p. 40, ... l'on rencontrera justement ainsi ceux qui conviennent à sa santé, au milieu de la variété infinie des substances qu'étale la nature.

[36] *Ibid. Le choix soit indifférent.*

[37] *Ibid. C'est un dernier moyen de rompre l'intrigue et de tromper les cabales.*

[38] *Ibid.* p. 41... *des hommes purs, de bonne volonté.*

[39] *Ibid. C'est quand la société est traversée par des méchans et des ambitieux, capables de se tout sacrifier, que le sort peut, concourir aux élections, afin de tromper leurs criminelles espérences*

local level, Lanthenas does not see its political potential as a major means of inhibiting factional discord, or as a more permanent means of protecting the voting system. There is some irony of hindsight to this given the direction that the revolution would take. Compared to the Italian republicans, the French had, at this stage at least, less experience of the dangers of competitive factionalism.

The draft constitution presented by Lesueur

It could be that Lanthenas' remarks about a wider debate on sortition were referring to a constitutional scheme sent as a paper to the National Convention in September 1792 by one Theodore Lesueur. 184 copies were circulated to the deputies, but it does not seem to have elicited any discussion in the Convention itself.[40] Lesueur's presentation of the proposed constitution to the Convention in September 1792 was on behalf of an anonymous writer. A copy of the document, which is entitled *Idées sur l'espèce de gouvernement populaire*, was first discovered in the British Library by S. B. Liljergen, who immediately drew a parallel between the constitution's structures and procedures and those of *Oceana.* [41]

A fundamental feature of the constitution is the selection by lot of a body of 100 citizens every year from each electoral district of 1,000. This grouping of one citizen in ten, known as a Civic Century, was to form the pool of citizens from which all the District Officers and higher level representatives for that year would be elected.[42] Apart from the selection of a president and censors by lot from this body, all other posts were to be filled by election or by a combination of election and lot-nomination in the Venetian style. On the initial selection of the Civic Century by lot the author is unambiguous: 'Assembled in this manner, the 1000 citizens of the order of virility, who composed the local District, elected from amongst themselves *by lot* and not by election, *ONE* citizen from every *TEN*.'[43]

In a later section of the document, moreover, there is an account of the exact procedure to be followed for the sortive and elective proce-

---

[40] Lesueur (1932) p. 83.

[41] See Lesueur (1932). A major portion of Liljergen's introduction is concerned with this theme.

[42] Hammersley (2005) p. 126; Lesueur (1932) pp. 97, 116.

[43] Lesueur (1932) p. 116. Note that the emphasis was in the original. *Assemblés de cette manière, les mille Citoyens de l'ordre de virilité, composant un District local, éliront entre eux, par la voie du sort et non par la voie des suffrages, UN Citoyen sur DIX.*

dures. This is to take place in a special purpose-built building.[44] In the pre-amble to this section the author makes it clear why such steps are necessary: 'The greatest of all vices is when too much permanent power is held in the same hands; and this permanency, which ends up being absolute, is always the result of the ease with which scheming, ambitious and rich men come to get themselves elected.'[45]

In the scheme itself the entire population was to be subdivided into 8,000 Districts,[46] each consisting of 1000 citizens of the 'order of manhood', and 101 'Circles', which was the name given to the higher administrative division.[47] The Tribe was to be the higher political unit, consisting of twenty-five Civic Centuries.[48] Each Circle was to be administered by a combination of Tribal and judicial officers, all of whom came from the original randomly-selected Civic Centuries. Each Circle was to elect twelve members of the National Legislative Council, and one member of the National Executive Council. Strict conditions applied to this procedure. Of the twelve members of the Legislative Council elected by each Circle, four were to belong to the upper economic class — the *plus possidentes* of income above 1500 L per annum — while eight were to come from the lower economic class or *minus possidentes*.[49] The Executive Council was to be made up entirely of *minus possidentes*.[50] Tribal officers, or officers from the Circle were forbidden to stand for these posts. The electorate for the Legislative and Executive Councils was to consist of the Circle Assembly plus half the deputies from the Civic Centuries.[51]

In her recent study of the influence of English Republicanism on the French Revolution, Rachel Hammersley identifies a distinct strand of Harringtonian thought emanating from the Cordeliers Club during the early years of the revolution.[52] This was based

---

[44] *Ibid.* pp. 150–2.

[45] *Ibid.* p. 149. *Le plus grand de tous ces vices est la trop grande permanence de pouvoir dans les même mains; et cette permanence, qui finet par être absolute, est toujours la conséquence des facilités qu'y trouvent les hommes intrigans ambitieux et opulans de parvenir à s'y faire élire.*

[46] *Ibid.* p. 115.

[47] *Ibid.* pp. 115 and 119.

[48] Ibid. p. 117.

[49] Ibid. p. 122. See also Hammersley (2005), p. 127.

[50] Lesueur (1932) p. 123.

[51] *Ibid.* p. 119–20

[52] Hammersley (2005), p. 83.

around the figure of Jean Jacques Rutledges, who produced a journal called *Le Crueset*. Hammersley describes this as a 'Harringtonian
text'.[53] The 121st issue of *le Crueset*, indeed, includes the description
of the Venetian balloting system complete with the diagram of the
balloting room, which also appeared in John Toland's original publication of *Oceana*.[54] Hammersley, with justification, suggests that
Rutledges was, in fact, the author of the constitution presented by
Lesueur.[55]

Both Hammersely and Liljergen highlight how this proposal differs from Harrington's *Oceana*.[56] The main points in this respect
relate to the greater democratic potential of the Lesueur proposal.
First is the yearly exclusion of nine-tenths of the citizens of each district by lot, which was most probably designed to prevent the
build-up of powerful local cliques. Second is the stipulation that
two-thirds of the legislature and executive should be *minus
possidentes*. Third is the fact that the Lesueur proposal is unicameral,
compared to the bicameral arrangement, which plays such a central
role in Harrington's political outlook.[57] All three of these factors
place the Lesueur constitution outside the parameters of the mixed
polity paradigm of *Oceana* which specifies that there should be a
division of political labour between those who deliberate and those
who vote. We can, on these grounds, accurately categorise it as one
of the first modern nationwide republican constitutions that advocates genuine rule by the masses.

Of considerable interest for this study is the role that lot plays in
the Lesueur scheme, and how it works in combination with the electoral elements and with the measures concerning the two National
Councils. As with Machiavelli's 1520 scheme, lot operates at the
lowest point of entry into the pyramidal body politic. It ensures a
regular rotation of new citizens into office and allows for further
selection by choice — with the notable exception of the Century secretaries and censors. Lot, therefore, plays the important double role
of inhibiting local factions and encouraging participation. At the
same time, however, it allows those with greater experience and

---

[53] *Ibid.*
[54] *Ibid.* p. 108. Note also that the Cordeliers Club were also calling for a citizen
army and greater participation for Passive Citizens during this period. *Ibid.*
p. 104.
[55] *Ibid.*, p. 135.
[56] Hammersley (2005), pp. 126–7, Lesueur (1932).
[57] Hammersley (2005), p. 127. Hammersely notes that there would be '… no
place for a natural aristocracy to reside.'

ability to be elected for offices further up the system.[58] There is no stipulation as to economic class applied to these District level offices, and it would be expected that the Civic Century would include citizens of ability from a variety of social backgrounds. It would therefore be seen as both impartial and inclusive.

At the National level, however, we see the use of quotas as a direct affirmation of the right of the masses to self-government. The upper stratum is not completely excluded, but the aim was clearly to ensure that the national government never became the exclusive political domain of the rich. It is thus partisan at a National level, but, through the use of lot, impartial in its original selection of the annual *reggimento*. Thus the imposition of arbitrary quotas contradicts the idea of a citizen-based polity which the author has already established by the original use of sortition at the point of entry into the political system. It is as if the author does not have sufficient confidence in the potential of sortition to generate a new politically active citizen body in the longer term.

In terms of its immediate political environment the use of quotas places the proposal in the democratic camp, and this could have meant that it would have been perceived as partisan in terms of the political divisions of 1792. It is worth noting that without the quota arrangement the scheme would have offered something to all parties and given the new active citizens time to develop political experience. From a theoretical point of view this proposal is remarkable in that it combines the structure and methodology of *Oceana*—drawn from the long-standing Venetian tradition — with the radicalism and egalitarianism of revolutionary Paris. Its aim is to create an active citizenry and to give them a permanent place in the body politic. It is bold and far-reaching, and it entails a considerable reworking of the geo-political infrastructure. In this respect, however, it is no different from some of the complex electoral schemes which were actually implemented — in fact it is far more straightforward than many proposals of this period.[59] While its author was clearly aware of the democratic potential of limiting the electoral influence of the rich and powerful, less awareness of its potential for establishing impartial republican institutions is in evidence.

---

[58] Thus calling the bluff of both Socrates and Guicciardini. Arguably it is more meritocratic than traditional aristocratic constitutions in that it encourages greater equality of opportunity while still allowing choice based on ability.

[59] The Girondin Constitution of 1793 was particularly complex. See Condorcet (1793).

The Jury system and the Girondin Constitution

The advocacy and use of lot between 1792 and 1794 is piecemeal, but it is worth considering two areas where it is to be found: first in the jury system, and second in the draft Girondin Constitution. This was a document drawn up in 1793 by a committee that included Condorcet, Paine, Brissot, Sieyès, Lanthenas, Pétion and Danton. The draft was, however, rejected when the Jacobins took power.

Alongside the question of representation, the reform of the criminal justice system was a central concern of the early phase of the French Revolution. In 1790–1 a number of important measures were introduced which included uniform sentencing for each category of crime, oral cross-examinations in public courts, and trial by jury.[60] The main impact of this last measure was to effect a transition from a system reliant on complex legal proofs to a system where common sense and moral proofs became the primary means by which justice was delivered. Court judges and justices of the peace were now elected and a grand jury system for indictments was set up.

The trial jury of twelve had sovereign power over the case they were selected to try, and needed a majority of ten to two to convict. In cases of a split decision the judge could add more to the jury.[61] Grand jurors from each district were selected by lot, from lists of thirty, and trial jurors were selected in the same manner from a list of 200 for each department. The jurors had to have the same property qualifications as the electors.[62] The drawing up of the lists was initially the sole responsibility of the procurator syndic of each department and in December 1793 this role was passed to the *Agent National* of each district who was charged with calling up one name per 1000 inhabitants. During year II (1793–4), however, these district agents became increasingly pressured into selecting those with Jacobin sympathies.[63]

In March 1793 measures were put into place to deal with offences of a specifically political nature. A main Revolutionary Tribunal was set up in Paris, and other local tribunals on similar lines were set up in major centres of population. These used juries, but the jurors 'differed little from functionaries of the revolutionary government, being a permanent corps of citizens appointed directly by

---

[60] Woloch (1994) p. 356.
[61] *Ibid.* p. 359.
[62] *Ibid.* p. 363.
[63] *Ibid.* p. 364.

the convention'.[64] Revolutionary Tribunals also had the right to prosecute without either juries or defence lawyers, and to carry out sentences in twenty-four hours without the right of appeal. After the fall of Robespierre, the jury system—now ostensibly less political—was nonetheless put under severe strain as jurors in some localities began to acquit citizens who had committed crimes of revenge in the aftermath of the Terror.

From its initiation there was a certain emphasis on establishing the jury as a professional body rather than a means of embedding justice in the community. Sièyes had favoured a majority of lawyers on every jury. This measure, he stressed, would only be interim, until the people became more enlightened.[65] In a similar manner Condorcet's deliberations on the probability of a jury reaching the correct verdict introduced the factor V which stood for the level of 'enlightenment' of the jury member.[66] Condorcet's preference for enlightened, professional juries is further emphasised in his *Essai sur l'application d'analyse* where he suggests that a two-thirds majority in a tribunal of 'enlightened men, practised in discussion' would be more reliable than a unanimous decision by a jury picked at random.[67] Also in *Justie et Police* he proposes that from a pool of 64 jurists, 16 could be challenged by the accused and then 16 of the remainder drawn by lot to make up the trial jury. Not so high a number, he specifies, as to 'have recourse to the services of uneducated men'.[68] The idea of judgement by one's peers seems to be absent from this line of thought. Condorcet also favoured a fixed period of jury service rather than having juries selected on a trial by trial basis.[69] It seems as if Condorcet's reservations about the use of lot are primarily on the grounds of capability, and he does not seem to suggest that the use of the lottery process itself could add anything to the selection procedure.

This tendency of the French to define a jury as a group of specialised individuals is corroborated by the proposals made by Sieyès in August 1795 for a 'Constitutional Jury'. This was to be a specially selected group of 108 experienced politicians appointed to act as a 'Court of Constitutional Appeal' to check whether constitutional

[64] *Ibid.* pp. 365–6.
[65] Clapham (1912) p. 109.
[66] Condorcet (1994) pp. 34–40 of the introduction.
[67] Baker (1975) p. 449 n. 156.
[68] Williams (2004) p. 188.
[69] Woloch (1994) p. 188.

power had been exceeded, to review proposed constitutional amendments for referenda, and to act as a kind of equity court to judge exceptional cases. This last task was to be performed by a smaller group of one-tenth of the whole jury who would be selected yearly from the main jury by lot.[70] One third of the group would be renewed annually, chosen from the ranks of retiring members of the legislative body by the members of the jury themselves. The first Jury was to be chosen by the Convention.[71] Sieyè's Constitutional Jury would have had a specialist role, status and composition remarkably similar to the U.S. Supreme Court, and may have influenced the final form of that institution.[72]

A curious caveat on the relationship between the elected and the randomly-selected jury occurs in Condorcet's speech introducing the Girondin constitution of 1793. After commenting that the jury system would be undermined if lists were drawn up by public officials, Condorcet suggests that those on the original lists should be chosen by simple plurality from the Primary Assemblies. This suggestion is not unusual, and, in fact, corresponds in certain respects to proposals made by Jefferson and to the practices in some American colonies in the early eighteenth century. What is interesting, however, is Condorcet's justification.

> This is not, of course, a true election; but the formation of a list of jurors should not be an election. A jury must not belong to the majority alone, because although the majority is the sole interpreter of the general will, the universal laws of justice prevent it from extending its powers over a citizen's individual rights. Our method ensures that no jury can ever be completely dominated by a single party or even by one political opinion: the apparent imperfection in the election method assures the impartiality which is the sacred and distinctive characteristic of this beneficial institution.[73]

The surprise here is Condorcet's suggestion that it is the very imperfection of the simple plurality vote that makes this form of selection more impartial than one where an absolute majority is required. For Condorcet, of course, a plurality vote based on a long list was so imprecise as to be a form of chance, but it is still not quite the same as selection by lot. Despite his awareness of the dangers of partisan majority control in the distribution of justice, he seems

---

[70] Clapham (1912) pp. 170–73.
[71] Forsyth (1987) p. 188.
[72] Clapham (1912) p. 265.
[73] Condorcet, (1994) p. 211.

unaware of the partisan opportunities offered by a simple plurality system to a determined party with an organised slate.[74] Jury lists selected by lot would be less susceptible to this type of intervention. It seems that Condorcet, coming to political practice from the assured ground of mathematics and faith in reason, was unwilling to admit the value of sortition, and at the same time was unaware of the fast developing art of electioneering.

The context of the Girondin Constitution provides some further explanation for the nature of Condorcet's argument. This constitution can be read as an attempt to bridge the gap between direct and indirect political means by bringing popular protest under the constitutional umbrella. All citizens were given the right to attend the Primary Assemblies, and these were to be given a new deliberative role with the right to challenge legislation. In these novel circumstances there were no doubt concerns about arbitrary majoritarian rule from the centre. We can also read the Girondin Constitution as a last-ditch attempt to save the enlightenment project in the face of mounting class partisanship. As such its faith in genteel deliberation belies a basic lack of trust in the judgement of the people at large on the one hand, and an unfamiliarity with the rawness of partisan interest on the other.

Despite this tendency there are two instances of the advocacy lot worthy of note. The first is the proposal to use of sortition to select provincial representatives to the legislative bureau; the second is the idea of creating a temporary division in the legislative body by lot to aid debate.

The first proposal is fairly straightforward. A bureau of thirteen members of the legislative body was to have the important role of reporting on legislation during its passage through the Assembly. It could also re-draft legislation, but had to indicate where this had been done in its reports.[75] The membership of this bureau was to be elected every month by drawing thirteen Departments by lot and then asking each of these to nominate one of its members. Thirteen other names nominated by the Legislative Assembly would be added to make a list of twenty-six, and the final thirteen then chosen by preference vote.[76] This measure ensured that the nominations

[74] A 'determined minority' see Crook (1996) p. 95.
[75] Condorcet (1793) p. 35.
[76] *Ibid.* pp. 35, 36, Title VII section IV . While rotation is not specified it seems likely that departmental members would be excluded from the lottery until all departments had been drawn.

were spread between the Departments by the simplest and fairest method, at the same time it was also a challenge to the hegemony of Paris. The Girondins, in measures such as these, recognised the problems that factional control of governmental committees had caused in the previous years and were taking direct measures to prevent or hinder their reoccurrence.

The split legislature scheme

The story of the split legislature is instructive. Between the 16 and 20 of February 1793 rumours circulated in the popular press that the Constitutional Committee, which had just presented its draft constitution to the National Convention (on 15 and 16 February), were planning to create a bicameral system. This referred, in fact, to two loosely made proposals in Condorcet's verbal report.[77] The first was a scheme to facilitate debate by splitting the legislative body into two temporary chambers that would then return together to take the final vote as one body. The second was the creation of a small separate body charged with checking the constitutional integrity of measures passed by the legislature. Amid fears that a senatorial upper house would be created by stealth, a debate was held on the 20th.[78] There were objections that the proposal had not been read to the Convention, but also assurances that the measure would not compromise the integrity of the new legislative body. It was also pointed out that the proposal had already been mentioned in Condorcet's report when the original draft had been presented on 15th February. This, unchallenged, would mean that it had accrued some level of political legitimacy. On the understanding that this proposal would have the status of a *project de constitution* and would not form part of the Constitution itself, the Jacobin opposition was satisfied. To confirm this status the two schemes were published as annexes to the main draft of the constitution.[79]

There was probably some justification for their concerns, however. Condorcet's verbal report makes no mention of exactly how the division of the legislature in the first scheme was to be carried out. The written annexe, on the other hand, confirms unambiguously that the legislative body should be divided by the use of sortition—it even specifies how it should be carried out.[80] In addi-

---

[77] Mavidal (1862–) vol. LVIII, p. 589.
[78] Alengry (1904) p. 248.
[79] Condorcet (1793b).
[80] *Ibid*. p.105.

tion the wording is clear that *all* debates should be held in this way and that a new draw for the division should be held every two months. The annexe further stipulates that the groupings formed by the division should have no independent powers and were to be of equal status—there would be no aristocratic senate, either by accident or design. By failing to specify the mode of the proposed division in his presentation, however, Condorcet merely aroused the suspicions of the opposition.[81]

The scheme for a bicameral legislature divided by lot from an elected pool has a good pedigree. Paine proposes a similar scheme on two occasions,[82] and Jefferson makes an almost identical proposal much later in 1824.[83] Both specify that lot should be used and that this would help to inhibit factions. As a general idea this type of proposal is eloquent in its simplicity, but has far-reaching implications. It is one of the most constructive of the sortive schemes we have considered where lot is used from an elected pool. It has a clear purpose and a clear entrance qualification, it is inclusive and is directly linked to the actual practice of debate.

The division is based on the principle that a smaller chamber will allow more views to be expressed and a greater sharing of ideas. This operates in both a preventative and a positive perspective. From the preventative point of view, sortition inhibits the deliberate packing of the chambers to predetermine how the debate should go. If the split is effected immediately prior to each debate there would be little opportunity for powerful members of the pool to marshal their support. Likewise the regular rotation of members of each group would make it difficult for factions to organise on a permanent footing. The use of lot further signals that the body organising the debate is non-partisan, or impartial. Nobody could complain that they had been manipulated, treated unfairly, or discriminated against.

---

[81] Condorcet had, in fact, produced a short essay on the merits of making such a division back in 1789, but again, he fails to specify exactly how this division should be made. He states that for the purpose of the exposition we should presume that the chambers be equal in all respects. Condorcet (1789) p. 10.

[82] These can be found in an address to the citizens of Pennsylvania in 1805, (Paine (1945) p. 1001); in the *Rights of Man* Part II (*Ibid.* p. 390); and in his *Answer to four questions.*(*Ibid.* p. 526). He seems to favour the idea that the Assembly be split into two or three sections, and that those not debating should listen to the debates of the other sections before contributing themselves. In *Answers to four questions* lot is not actually referred to as the means of effecting the division.

[83] Jefferson (1943) p. 294–5. Jefferson's paper is dated 5 June1824.

On these grounds alone the application of lot is strong. It is a decision taken out of the hands of the rational human judgement of any
individual or group, and it cannot be predicted in advance. It is not a
proportionate solution in that it does not divide the pool according
to the abilities of its members, the constituencies that they might
represent, or their ideological loyalties. These factors could become
a problem if the division was to be permanent, but the system operates on the principle that random mixing over a period of time will
create a spread of different combinations within the mechanics of
debate and deliberation. If consistently used in this manner its main
positive advantage is that it allows new patterns of discussion, new
working relationships (such as those between experienced and
inexperienced members) and new independent (literally non-
dependent) voices to emerge.

All three versions of the scheme (Paine's, Jeffersons and the 1793
Annexe) were also clearly designed to counter the idea that a bicameral solution to the problems of debate should necessarily involve
an upper and a lower house. In this respect, significantly, they stand
in opposition to the Harringtonian ideal of a natural aristocracy.
Above all they articulate the idea that the political process should be
a commonwealth of shared ideas and opinions.

Sortition under the Directory

Many in the socialist tradition of historiography have portrayed the
Thermidorian coup of July 17–28 1794 as a triumph of reaction, the
end of the Revolution.[84] Recent authors, however, have recognised
the difficult and demanding role played by the Thermidorian government as it sought to stabilise the French Republic after the Terror.[85] Its attempts to promote impartiality are especially useful for
our study of lot.

After the fall of Robespierre the National Convention found itself
in the unenviable position of coming to terms with its own role in
the Terror, while recognising that too contrite a purge of their own
ranks could put the gains made by the revolution in danger.[86]

---

[84] Baczko (1994) p. 259. Trotsky's *The Revolution Betrayed* likens Stalin to the
Thermidor government. The socialist–inspired historians include Jaurès,
(1972) vol 6 p. 518; Leffeve, (1964) p. 137; Mathiez (1962) p. 501 and (1975) pp.
1–4; Soboul (1968) p. 147.

[85] Aston (2004) pp. 43, 50. Aston states that 'Scholars now queue up to acclaim
most aspects of the 1795 settlement.'

[86] Baczko (1994) p. 115.

Above all, trust in the legitimate organs of government had to be restored and this meant returning the Convention to its constitutional role as the sole locus of sovereign government.[87] Jacobin clubs were progressively closed, the Paris Commune and Sections disbanded, and the question of how to break up concentrations of power in the governmental committees was rigorously addressed.[88] While the Thermidorians seemed to have no strategy save that of preserving the revolution by preventing a slide into post-terror blood-letting and anarchy, a certain consistency of tactics can be seen in their approach to governmental institutions. Put simply, they used the 'Harringtonian' principle of rotation, and to institute that rotation they used lot.[89] The use of lot in the Thermidorian context, moreover, was as rhetorically pointed and utopian as its use in *Oceana*. It seems to have been designed to signal the determination of the new government to break with the past. The new broom should be seen as less opportunist and less desirous for power and position than the displaced order. [90]

In the first months of the regime, that is, prior to the instigation of the year III Constitution of 1795, attention was given to the old revolutionary apparatus. The jurors on the Revolutionary Tribunal were now to be selected by lot and renewed every three months.[91] The Tribunal was now to be split into two sections and judges assigned to each section monthly by lot. In addition, when a suit was brought to the Tribunal, the section to which it was to be assigned was likewise to be chosen by lot.[92] The infamous Committee for Public Safety was also to be rigorously rotated with one quarter of its members retiring by lot every month. Those going out would not be eligible for re-election.[93]

---

[87] Aston (2004) p. 46.
[88] Doyle (1989) p. 281–2; Baczko (1994) pp. 104, 105, 110–5. Baczko emphasises the parallel power of the Jacobin organisation. Symbols of National Unity were also used to help foster a spirit of unity, Baczko (1994) p. 118.
[89] This was not a new idea, however, and because many of the new State Constitutions in the United States had done this.
[90] The new government also used sortition for a number of other tasks where demonstrably impartial choice of personnel was needed. The extent that they needed to preserve the gains of the revolution should not be underestimated. Too much of a break would be dangerous.
[91] Stewart (1951) p. 542 *Decree Reorganising the Revolutionary Tribunal 28th Dec. 1794 Title V section 27.*
[92] *Ibid.* p. 541, *Title V sections 14 and 17.*
[93] Doyle (1989) p. 28; Clapham (1912) pp. 166–7.

The new Constitution prescribed the use of sortition for the make up of two important areas of government: the bicameral legislative assemblies and the seven-man executive council – the Directory. The new legislative body was to be made up of a lower house of 500 to initiate legislation and a 250-strong *Conseil des Anciens* to approve or reject it. A controversial new law stipulated that two thirds of the entire legislative body (i.e., both houses) should be made up of existing members of the National Convention – a somewhat arbitrary measure designed to preserve continuity. From the combined numbers of 500 from the Convention and 250 newcomers the two houses were to be chosen by age and lot. Those over forty years old would be assigned to the Council of Elders and the numbers suitably reduced or enlarged by lot.[94] In addition one-third of each house would be randomly selected to retire and be replaced by election each year.[95] The lower house would be charged with nominating fifty candidates for the Directory, and the Elders would then vote for the final five members.[96] One member of the Directory would be chosen by lot to retire every year.[97] Although this was designed to establish a rotational system, the Directory did not last long enough to establish its first cycle.

Amongst the uses of sortition by the Thermidorians one instance of great import should be noted. On 1 November 1794, 21 members of the Convention were chosen by lot to form a commission of investigation into the crimes of Jean Baptiste Carrier.[98] As *agent en mission* for Nantes during the Terror Carrier had been responsible for widespread atrocities in that region. The commission in charge of drawing up his indictment was also selected by lot, and he was tried by the Convention itself.[99] Carrier's trial and execution marked an important stage in the attempts made by the new regime to come to terms with the Terror. The public statement of choosing the commission by a demonstrably impartial method signalled the end of the arbitrary and subjective practices of the Terror years. Revolutionary justice was now a crime.

In addition the Thermidorian government devised a system of seating arrangements for the new legislative assemblies by lot. This,

---

[94] Aston (2004) p. 48; Clapham (1912) pp. 167, 176–7.
[95] Stewart (1951) p. 581 *Title V section 53*.
[96] Aston (2004) p. 48.
[97] Stewart (1951) p.589, *Title VI no. 137*; Doyle (1989) p. 319.
[98] Baczko (1994) p. 146.
[99] *Ibid.* p. 166.

no doubt, symbolised their desire to break from the factional divisions of the previous era. The scheme was, however, ignored in practice.[100]

Despite these measures the Thermidorian government found the task of delivering a post-revolutionary settlement too difficult.[101] Perhaps it was a reflection of their lack of political experience, vision and direction. The task of establishing security and stability was finally bequeathed to the Consulate. Napoleon Bonaparte took control via the safe hands of that great gate-keeper of the revolution, Sieyès, in 1799.

There are a number of ways that the use of sortition under the Directory can help us to understand its political potential and how that potential can be realised in practice. The first point to note is how sortition and rotation were used for major committees as a response to the need to establish greater trust in the institutions of government. Rotation was clearly introduced as a means of breaking up concentrations of power, and lot was used, it seems, mainly as a supporting mechanism to this end. In this respect there seems to have been little attention given to what the lottery itself contributed to the process as a whole. This applies particularly to the distinction between selecting personnel by lot to serve on public bodies, and de-selecting them randomly from an existing body.

Cases such as the selection by lot of the commission to investigate the crimes of Carrier fall into the type of category we are familiar with. Lot is used to establish the idea that the body is impartial and to ensure that no one can manipulate the process of selection. It is a strong use of lot, and the arationality of the process serves a definite positive role. Cases such as the regular random de-selection of one quarter of the Committee of Public Safety and the random de-selection of the Directory are more complex.

As we saw with the draft proposals for the Council of Pennsylvania, the use of lot for de-selection in order to kick-start a rotational scheme is a weak use of lot. It does not utilise the arational blind break beyond the delegation of responsibility to an anonymous agency. While the deleterious consequences of this type of application can be marginal in some cases, they can be more severe in others. In the case of the Committee for Public Safety the overall emphasis of the new arrangement was to create a rapid rotation of

---

[100] Guéniffey (1933) p. 486.
[101] See Aston (2004) pp. 58-9; Crook (1996) pp. 140 and 153 on the Directory's failings and their desire to control elections.

temporary office holders. The rationale for this was clearly to develop a greater sense that the Committee was no longer a seat of unaccountable executive power, but was in the common ownership of the National Convention. The use of lot to deselect for the first few phases of the rotation would have little effect on the operations of the Committee because the Committee itself was to be subject to a rapid turnover of personnel. If there was little disadvantage to using lot in these circumstances, there was also little advantage. Its application can therefore be seen as fulfilling a largely rhetorical function.

The case of the Directory, however, raises a number of important questions about the difference between selection and de-selection by the use of lot. The best way to look at this is in terms of the aims of the Directory-led government. These consisted of the apparent contradiction of effecting post-Terror reconciliation while at the same time defending the revolution against royalist restoration. A strong executive was needed for the latter task, while at the same time there needed to be safeguards against the re-emergence of concentrated arbitrary government — there could be no going back to the Terror. The decision to use rotation for this function seems the logical way out of this dilemma, but the use of lot to deselect seems entirely at odds with the aim of establishing strong and stable government.[102] The longer time-frame and the political significance of the experience of individuals in such a small but strategically important body meant that the use of an arational means of de-selection could be damaging to the process of government. A more satisfactory solution would have been to adopt the solution used by Penn in Pennsylvania and elect members for different stated lengths of service.

While it would have been equally inappropriate to select such a body by lot, lot could have been used for the nominating process, or to select a temporary rotating member of the executive with a similar role to Machiavelli's Provosts. These measures could have provided checks against the arbitrary partisan power while still providing continuity in government.

In general, the use of lot under the Directory shows that lot and rotation were called upon to establish greater impartiality in government and to break up potential concentrations of power follow-

---

[102] See Sydenham (1974) p. 127. The lotteries were apparently held in public. Sydenham describes this measure as 'One of the most inane provisions of the Constitution of 1795.'

ing the Terror. This shows an intuitive understanding of the value and potential of these mechanisms, but at the same time the actual application of sortition shows how little its potential was really understood. We can think of its use as being high on rhetoric, but low in efficiency. It is also possible that greater use of sortition at a lower level of the electoral process - in the Primary Assemblies for example - could have been more productive in the longer run and moderated some of the local tensions that dogged the latter stages of the Directory government.

Conclusion

In this chapter we have seen examples of the advocacy and application of sortition during a period of rapid revolutionary change in a major nation state. The prevailing impression, however, is that little was known about the full political potential of lot, and where something of its potential was known, the idea of developing lot-based election schemes was only tentatively embraced.

The main reason for this is that little of the extensive practical experience of the use of sortition had filtered through from fifteenth-century Italy to late eighteenth-century France. We also saw how the close identification of sortition with egalitarian democracy meant that the potential of sortition to establish impartial governmental institutions and protect electoral procedures from manipulation and subversion was obscured. This is evident in the accounts of sortition offered by Rousseau and Montesquieu. On the other hand, Lanthenas understands the electoral potential of lot, but expresses what was probably a common view of the time: that its arational nature makes it incommensurate with the new rational republican polity. He shares with Rousseau and Montesquieu the idea that lot is an imperfect mechanism. We also saw a general tendency for those who were critical of sortition to focus on the question of capability in office, rather than seeking to understand how the arationality of the lottery process itself might be useful to the polity. This, however, was contradicted by its acceptance as a means of selecting members of juries or other judicial bodies. For certain areas of the body politic, therefore, its value as an impartial mechanism of choice was recognised.

Two well-designed schemes emerge from this period. The first is the draft constitution circulated by Leseuer in 1792. This proposes that lot is used at the point where the citizenry enter the political arena—the Civic Centuries. In this context sortition is primarily used as a means of ensuring that political participation is not the exclusive domain of those who already exercise power or influence. The design of the constitution creatively combines lot with preference voting and its author recognises the potential of lot as a means of protecting the selection procedure from manipulation. The use of quotas of different classes of citizens in order to give the masses a greater proportion of members of the National Councils, however, contradicts the impartial, citizen-based nature of the constitution established by the use of lot. This characterises the scheme as an exercise in democratic republicanism, rather than a proposal designed to promote unity and facilitate political consolidation. The second scheme is the proposal to divide the legislative assembly by lot into two temporary sections. This is a strong use of lot to address what were clearly problems in the conduct of debates. It allows new voices a greater opportunity to be heard and promotes the idea that independent, non-partisan, opinion is to be valued.

The use of lot and rotation under the Directory indicates again that the French were aware that Italian republican mechanisms could be used to establish greater public ownership of key political institutions. The best example of sortition from this period is the use of lot to select the commission to investigate the crimes of Carrier. Here the use of sortition gives the commission greater authority because the process of selection is free from partisan influence. It also acts as a rhetorical statement of the post-Terror regime's intention to re-establish an impartial system of justice. The least successful example is the use of lot to deselect members of the Directory. Here the weak application of lot had severe consequences for the continuity of government. The use of lot in this manner indicates that little was actually known about the potential of lot and how to realise that potential in practice.

One of the most significant features of the French Revolution is the speed at which factional centrifugal forces within the body politic and in the country at large inhibited the development of stable authoritative institutions of government. France stumbled from crisis to crisis as it tried to find new forms and procedures that would hold the slide to all-out civil war. To this extent we can think of the revolutionary period as a learning process in which the idealism of the early years continuously came up against the hard realities of division, chaos and bloodshed. It is from this clash between forms of government that stem from ideals and forms that are created by the demands of practice that we can learn the most about the political potential of lot from this period. Sortition belongs to the latter category. It is not an ideal form; it is primarily problem-driven.

While there are considerable differences between the social, ideological and geopolitical contexts of the Italian city republics and the later attempts to develop a nation-state republican solution in France, the political problems that both faced were remarkably similar. In the main these revolved around how to establish authoritative rule-governed procedures of public government, and how to avoid the twin dangers of factional division and the exercise of arbitrary power. In the pursuit of these objectives the learning process of the Italian city republics was protracted and took over two hundred years of twists, turns, crises and setbacks. During this time the dangers to the body politic became well known, as was the repertoire of measures that could be used to counter them. The French revolutionaries considerably underestimated the complexity of this process, and had little direct experience of the range of mechanisms used by the Italians to defend their republican forms of government — including sortition. This is evident in Lanthenas' characterisation of lot as a measure of last resort rather than a more permanent preventative measure. Not only was he unhappy with the possible widespread use of an arational mechanism, but he failed to understand the need to protect the public process of selection more comprehensively.

This perspective affects the way we approach the relationship between the older form of lot-based polity and the newer forms of representative polity based on preference voting. In France, the new experimental form of representative democracy was not designed to replace an older, outmoded republican form that involved selection by lot. The French Revolution was a revolt against feudal absolutism, not an attempt to improve an older republican model. From this we can argue that there is no major structural or ideological divide between old and new republicanism that specifically excludes a mix of older and newer mechanisms. The gap between the older lot-based republics and the newer forms of the eighteenth-century is, I would suggest, primarily a gap in the knowledge and experience of their respective political actors.

Bibliographical notes

For the events of the decade I relied primarily on Doyle's comprehensive *Oxford History of the French Revolution* of 1989. In addition I need to mention a number of more specific studies from the period which gave me some of the detail that I needed to write this chapter. These are Aston's 2004 study *The French Revolution. Authority, Liberty and the Search for Stability*; Crook's 1996 account of elections during the French Revolution; Hammersley's recent (2005) book on the influence of English Republicanism; Baczko's 1994 *Ending the Terror*; Woloch's 1994 *The New Regime. Transformations of the French Civic Order. 1789-1820*; and Woronoff's (1984) *The Thermidorian Regime and the Directory, 1794-9*. Forsyth's 1987 *Reason and Revolution: The Political Thought of Abbé Sièyes* provided both a thorough commentary on the life and work of Sièyes and an insight into the ideological struggles of the decade.

For the work of Condorcet I used the 1994 edition edited and translated by McLean and Hewitt; the citing from Rousseau was from Ritter's translation of 1988 and for Montesquieu I used the Cambridge edition of *The Spirit of the Laws* of 1989. In addition, Stewart's 1951 *A Documentary Survey of the French Revolution* proved to be an invaluable source of legislative and constitutional detail. It is also worth noting that while the reference to lot for the split-legislature is to be found in an annexe to the Girondin Constitution, this is not included in most versions of the Constitution. It can, however, be found in the original printed edition of 20 February 1793 (Condorcet (1793b) Le 38/ 1766 D).

Chapter Seven

Conclusion

I open this concluding chapter with a summary of the characteristics of sortition as a body of political practice. This leads me to the defining point of the study: how we are to understand the political potential of sortition and its wider potential. This is a drawing together of the earlier evidence and argument and it takes the form of the combination of the analysis of lottery form and the historical practice of sortition that I have used throughout. I end with a short discussion of how the principles I have developed can contribute to the possible modern application of sortition.

Sortition as a body of political practice

The most significant shape to emerge from the historical narratives is that there exists a body of political practice concerned with the selection of governmental and political officers by lot. What is more, this body of practice is considerable—particularly in terms of its longevity. The use of lot for political purposes in ancient Athens extends from at least the seventh century BCE right up to the end of democracy in 312 BCE and beyond. In Venice the combination of sortition and election lasted from the thirteenth century to the fall of the republic in the closing years of the eighteenth century. The Florentine system was used from 1328 until the fall of the First Republic in 1434. As we saw, it was restored for many offices in 1466 and for the *Signoria* during the Second Republic. Even our local example, the Great Yarmouth Inquest, lasted over three hundred years. The randomly-selected jury in Britain has been in operation from 1730 until the present, and dates from 1682 in South Carolina. These achievements should be set against the relatively short period in which universal franchise voting for political parties has been the practice in western representative democracies and elsewhere. To this longevity should be added the fact that when any sortition-based system was discontinued, this was more often as a result of the overthrow of the regime from the outside rather than from dissatisfaction on the part of the citizens. Above all this study has revealed that those polities that used sortition made a considerable political investment in it as a mechanism for selecting public officers. This investment was, in the main, highly organised, purposeful and committed.

While this study has concentrated on the use of lot in Ancient Athens, late medieval and Renaissance Italy and in the American and French Republican movements, there are indications that it was more widely used. It was certainly used in Ancient Rome to allocate government postings, and in many of the Swiss Cantons, even up until recently. The full extent of its practice is not, as yet, known, and is quite possible that it was used in guild elections throughout Europe in the medieval period.[1] From the evidence I have considered it would be fair to say that its consistent application for the selection of government officers took place in geographical pockets where local custom and practice was well developed. We should, however, understand the lottery process itself as a principle distinguished by its universality, and as a mechanism for the distribution of land and resources it was used throughout Europe from ancient times up until recently.[2] It is best, therefore, to view lot as a universal human invention that has crossed into the political sphere at particular times and under particular conditions.

However, we should distinguish two main lines of use rather than one unbroken tradition. The first is that of Athens and some of its near neighbours in the ancient world; the second is that of the European medieval communes and post-medieval republicanism in Europe and America. The commune-builders of the Middle Ages did not refer to Athenian practice, but used lot spontaneously to address the particular problems that they were engaged upon. There is some self-conscious reference to Athenian use of lot, once this was known about, but the local practice was not originally modelled on any ancient example. However, as I hope to have demonstrated, there is a tenuous, but very real, connection between Venetian republican practice and the Anglo-American ran-

---

[1] The English term ' scot and lotte', signifying the obligation to pay guild fees and the liability to bear office, indicates that sortition could have had widespread use as a means of selecting guild officers in the medieval period. See Smith, Smith and Brentano (1870), p. 346.

[2] See Green (1910) for the use of lot to allocate pasture in Yarnton near Oxford up to the early 1900s. See also Ostrom (1990), pp. 19–20, 65, 67, 77.

domly-selected jury. This link operates by way of English Republicanism: through the works of James Harrington and the Harringtonian constitutions of the New World.[3]

In terms of the governmental forms explored in this study, the most consistent use of sortition was found where there was open public government and the rule of law; where citizens were regularly assigned specific governmental responsibilities; and where there was a distinct ethos that the general good should take precedence over sectional interests. It is in political communities that aspired to these ends that we have seen sortive institutions at their most inventive and developed. In this respect, therefore, I feel justified in drawing another dividing line. This time the line falls between two distinct types of polity: those which employed sortition systematically and developed lot-based institutions to a high level of sophistication, and those where lot was used occasionally or for very particular institutions only. On the one hand we find Ancient Athens along with the *popolo* communes and the later republics of Florence and Venice. On the other stand the republics that were constituted in the late eighteenth century: the United States and France. In these later political landscapes preference voting unassisted by sortition became the dominant means of selecting political officers; citizens were less regularly or systematically engaged in government; and the problem of factions was addressed in a different—sometimes less successful—manner. Although we saw how sortition had the capacity to re-assert its value in new circumstances, as it did with the jury, its use in the major organs of government did not cross this dividing line.

Another aspect of sortition to emerge from the study, and one that has a possible bearing on its later decline, is its relation to practical political experience. As we have seen, sortition commands little attention from political writers and features relatively little in the transference of ideas via the written word. In the case of lot necessity seems to have been the mother of invention and its use tended to derive from the problem at hand rather than because it conformed to any written notion of the ideal polity type. Thus in two of our examples, the Florentine Republican *risorgimento* of 1465–6 and

[3] See Nilsen (2004) p. 22. Nilsen identifies three main sources for the use of random selection as a 'fundamental institution of modern government' : Ancient Athens, medieval Italy — reflected in Harrington's *Oceana* — and the Anglo–American Jury. The early use of random selection for juries in S. Carolina — a 'Harringtonian' constitution — effectively shows that there is an historical link between the last two of Nilsen's categories.

the British seditious libel crisis of the second half of the eighteenth century, reference to classical precedent took place only *after* the potential of lot was realised as a result of local practice and experience. Another example, that of East New Jersey, suggests that the passage of the idea of lottery *from* theory *into* practice can often be a transition fraught with difficulties.

We saw in the last two chapters that as the practice of sortition declined, so too did the knowledge of what it could actually bring to the polity. Those who were aware of its efficacy in practice saw no reason to write about it, and many of those who came later, unaided by written accounts based on first hand experience, had little knowledge of exactly what it contributed to the body politic. We saw how Harrington omitted a full explanation of the role of sortition in his model republic of *Oceana*, and how Montesquieu and Rousseau, drawing primarily from classical sources, failed to explore its fuller potential.

In a similar manner the theoretical case for lot was weakened rather than strengthened by its association with democracy. Arguments against lot were often arguments against democracy, and because these arguments concentrated on the egalitarian aspects of sortition, understanding of its more general political potential became distorted. Herodotus' identification of lot with popular government was an observable fact of the political landscape in which he wrote, but, as we have seen, the use of lot is not exclusive to democratic regimes. Venice was an aristocratic republic, and the First Florentine Republic was, at times, a closely-knit oligarchy. We have also seen how sortition had the effect of moderating democratic excesses. Furthermore, it is not the action of the lottery that determines whether the outcome is democratic or not. If democracy is defined by the level of participation in government, then the democratic credentials of a lottery system are established by the pre-lottery rational decisions to extend the size of the pool or the qualifications for belonging to the pool, not the action of lot itself. The logic of this is to suggest that our focus of inquiry into the political potential of lot should be based not so much on the question of *who should govern* but more on the question of *how government should be conducted.*

In addition, the idea that lot was merely a levelling device that took no account of specialist skills or abilities became a particularly strong argument by which lot was discredited. This argument is closely linked to the aristocratic notion of government by the best.

We can trace this line of thought from Socrates, through to Guicciardini. We can also find an echo of it in Condorcet's preference for enlightened hand-picked juries. In contrast, the 1520 proposal for the constitution of Florence made by Machiavelli shows us that lot can be used in a way that is sensitive to different levels of ability. The use of directly elected magistrates for specialist posts in Athens also indicates that advocates of lot did not ignore the question of specialist selection based on capability. As with democratic participation, questions of capability are not decided by the lottery itself but by earlier rational decisions to match the general abilities of those in the pool with the requirements for the job.

One of the main arguments used against lot was that it denied rational choice and individual moral judgement. This was Savonarola's view, and it is a major plank of Guicciardini's attack on lot, both in his *Logrongo Thesis* of 1512 and in *Del modo di eleggere ...* It is picked up again in the early nineteenth century by Godwin in *Political Justice* where he describes Sortition as a 'desertion of our duty, and an act of the most 'contemptible cowardice.'[4] This argument portrays a lottery decision as a substitute for rational thought, rather than one that has a positive function precisely because it is arational. By portraying sortition as irrational in all its aspects, rather than an arational mechanism used rationally, these arguments against lot obscured many of the more compelling reasons why random selection was used. The study also showed that lot was nearly always used in highly organised political structures and institutions — some of them exceedingly complex. Within such environments it is noticeable that there is scarcely an instance where lot was carelessly introduced without consideration of how it was to balance with other constitutional elements. On the contrary, most of the constitutions where sortition was widely employed were highly structured and rationally organised. The idea that lot-based regimes are inherently chaotic must therefore be challenged.

In this study we have seen lot used in combination with other procedures and mechanisms. This tells us that sortition should not be considered in isolation. In all these cases, however, it has been important to ask what work is being done by random selection, and what is achieved by other elements in the same package. Rotation — the use of temporary offices — has a particularly close connection to the use of lot and I have not encountered one instance where lot was used to select a permanent office holder. While this is an effi-

---

[4]   Godwin (1971) pp. 241–3.

cient pairing of mechanisms, I hope to have shown that sortition is more than just a convenient way of establishing rotation.

Throughout the study we saw how sortition has always had very close connections with other forms of selection—notably preference election. Here it has been useful to explore the relationship between the secret ballot and sortition, and to see them both as part of the same drive against partisan interference in the selection of governmental officers. Sortition, moreover, was more often used in combination with election than in opposition to it. Some of the best designed constitutions that I have examined: Machiavelli's 1520 scheme for Florence, the ill-fated proposals for E. New Jersey, and Lesueur's proposal for the French constitution, all show an understanding of how lot can work with preference election. One exception to this is the call for lot in Florence in 1465-6; another is the reinstatement of lot during the Second Florentine Republic. In the first instance the voting system was almost totally discredited; in the second it was regarded with considerable apprehension. It would be wrong, therefore, to think of lot as an alternative to voting, or as a stage in political development that preceded or led up to the more 'perfected' democratic form of preference choice. In general lot and voting have worked together in the same political environments and have, for the most part, complemented each other.

The primary political potential of sortition

This overview of the body of political practice has enabled us to take a broad look at how and where sortition was used. In the earlier chapters, through a process of informed reconstruction, I have also been able to develop some form of critical discourse as to *why* sortition was used, and what was achieved by its use. In the historical narratives this proceeded, in the main, on a case by case basis. What now remains is to see whether it is possible to find a common link between these cases that could allow us to see the benefits of using sortition in some sort of logical relationship to each other. I do this in the first instance by identifying what I call the 'primary political potential' of sortition.

As we have seen, the lottery mechanism is able to contribute to the political community in a variety of ways. We now have to ask whether there is *one* function of lot that is more significant than all the others or one which we can recognise as the point of origin of all other political functions and benefits. To qualify for such a status this function of lot has to satisfy certain criteria. It has to be something that lot does well, and where it is applied to maximise its potency. In terms of the framework that I advance it has to be a strong use and make a positive use of the blind break. We can understand this by applying the analysis of Chapter One. Then it has to be something that has the capacity to make a difference to the body politic or polity in which it is applied and to the way that the participants view the political process. We should be able to extrapolate this from the active contexts of lottery use that we have examined. Then we should look at how often lot was used to select political officers and ask whether there is one reason above all others that is relevant to the greater part of this usage. Finally the primary potential of sortition has to be a function of lot that is grounded in the immediate context where lot is used — in the case of this study this is the process by which political officers are selected. This is important because it enables us to separate what happens in the first instance from secondary functions, consequences and effects.

The political potential of sortition also has to be seen against some sort of political ideal: a political community that sees itself as striving towards certain agreed beneficial goals. These can be described negatively — such as the prevention of fragmentation, the defence against tyranny, foreign invasion or the canker of internal corruption — but they can also be expressed positively in the idea of an open public polity where the institutions and procedures are regarded as commonly held, or shared. We can think of this sort of political community as being maintained or enhanced by the use of sortition. We can also consider how sortition can benefit the earlier process of establishing this type of political community.

Taking all these conditions into consideration, the most significant and fundamental reason that lot is used in the selection of public officers, *is to inhibit the power that any individual or group of individuals might seek to exercise over that process of selection.* This is the simplest, most immediate and direct statement about the way that sortition operates and what it has the capacity to do: its political potential. It defines sortition as a combative measure used by those who wish to establish a shared, rule-governed, public political process against its known enemies: those who might wish to subvert it for their own sectional, covert or private ends. We have seen in the narratives how this use of lot developed as a result of long, often bitter, experience.

This function of sortition makes a positive use of the blind break in the sense that those wishing to exercise control cannot easily place their agents in positions of influence with any level of consistency. Thus it has the effect of breaking up concentrations of personal or sectional extra-constitutional power within the body politic and defending the polity's status as a shared institution. For this reason it can have significant impact on the shape of the polity and the direction of its political development.

My contention is that this primary potential of the sortive process lies behind every application of lot that we have examined, even in those instances where another function was in the minds of those responsible for its immediate application. By far the most telling application of lot in this role is its re-introduction by the Florentines in 1465-6 as a means of challenging the Medici, who had gained immense personal power by controlling the systems of appointment and election. Its successful advocacy in these circumstances was a move to restore collective, inclusive, republican government.

The example of ancient Athens is revealing in that lot was used to counteract the threat of tyranny but also to prevent the development of competitive factions such as could threaten the unity of the *polis*. The Athenians understood that while the assumption of power by a single tyrant represented the end of the public political process, the scenario of rival parties seeking arbitrary power could be just as harmful to the *polis*, if not more so. These motives were also behind the use of sortition in the late medieval communes of northern Italy, especially where it was used by *popolo* governments.

The function of preventing private or individual control over the process of selection is also a major reason why random selection for jury members has been an enduring practice. We saw how the 1730 act of Parliament that introduced random selection was aimed at preventing the under-sheriff from misusing his power of selection. In the seditious libel cases, the jury was seen as a counterweight to the elected government because the government could not control the selection of personnel. We can also see this aim behind the suggestions of Sieyès and Lanthenas to use lot to prevent the packing of Primary Assemblies. Even Paine's proposal for the selection of the President by lot from each of the thirteen American states in turn carries an echo of this use. Paine hoped to inspire confidence in the process of unification and the idea of using lot would prevent a single state from dominating the selection procedure.

This primary potential is not the end of the story, however. Like the spreading of ripples after a stone has fallen on water, this initial point of inhibition, this 'taking away' of personal power at the interface between citizens and government has the potential to create a considerable expanding effect on the character and operations of the political community.

The secondary benefits of sortition — its wider potential

My conclusion that the greatest political potential of lot lies in the protection of the public process of selection from private control does not mean that there are not other possible uses, or that lot cannot be advocated for other, secondary, motives or to solve other, secondary, problems. I would claim, however, that when lot is used to select public officers, all roads lead back to the primary function and potential of lot to protect that process of selection from private control. These roads can be various and instructive, and the variations in the motivation for using sortition in different political contexts can tell us much about how the potential of sortition can be most efficiently realised.

If lot protects the polity from arbitrary power by keeping the process of selection out of the hands of ambitious individuals or lawless factions, by the same process it also strengthens the political community by *lowering the threshold to political office*. This is a strong use in the sense that the selection is not based on any criteria save that of belonging to the pool. No party can dominate the proceedings through their strength or influence, and no appointment can be based on discrimination, prejudgement, favouritism, friendship, enmity, or any other form of personal dependence. This creates a low threshold to political participation, and encourages a sense of equality between those taking part in government and those who are in the pool. In citizen-wide lot schemes, such as the Athenian *dikasterion* or the Anglo-American jury, lot has the potential to involve large numbers of citizens in important but straightforward political duties. This potential is also recognised in the schemes advocated by Machiavelli and Lesueur and could also have been the rationale behind the inclusion of sortition in the proposed constitution of East New Jersey.

Connected to the ability of lot to provide unconditional citizen entry into the body politic is the idea that lot can give all citizens in the pool a *potential stake in the office in question*. In a lottery process the number in the pool is always greater than the number selected; but all in the pool have a potentially active role because they *might* be chosen. In this way sortition can create a strong, active, relationship between the citizen body (or at least those in the pool) and those who are charged with making decisions on their behalf. The organisation of the pool, to this extent, defines the active citizen body, and the process of selection creates a direct, unmediated, relationship between the citizen and the polity in a way that appointment or election cannot. This is a strong use of lot, based on the fact that the outcome of a lottery cannot be predicted. In the practical political environment, however, it is also a consequence of the fact that no party can dominate the selection process.

Because no group or individual can take control of the selection process where lot is used, the agency that organises the lottery — in most cases the polity — *can be understood as neutral or impartial*. Thus sortition can help to resolve conflicts and help to create unified republics. These polities can be understood as belonging to all in the sense that they do not belong to anyone else — no smaller, select, or partial portion of the body politic is in control. Kleisthenes' use of lot to divide the *trittyes* shows how potentially harmful rivalries can be moderated because a lottery decision cannot be laid at the door of any individual. Similarly a major source of the jury's authority lies in the impartial nature of its selection. This neutral or impartial role of lot can also bring hostile factions together in greater trust because the filling of posts cannot be seen as the subject of conspiracy. It is therefore impartial in the very practical sense of inhibiting the power of partisan — literally *partial* — groups within a body politic striving towards unity. In terms of its potential for conflict resolution, the decision to use a lottery is always a compromise position in the sense that it gives all parties a chance. But it does so primarily because it prevents any one party from giving itself an advantage that the others might see as unfair.

In the use of lot to select magistrates in Athens in 403 BCE we saw the potential of lot to aid the process of reconciliation. Because lot is arational, a lottery choice cannot be subject to the type of *irrational fears and competitive passions* that can so easily dominate electoral choice. A lottery system, moreover, cannot inflate the pride of the victor or contribute to the disappointment of the defeated. This 'neutralisation' or 'de-personalising' of the selection process can have a valuable unifying effect on the political community especially during times of tension. In an active political context this neutralising effect is intrinsically connected to the way that lot prevents factions or parties from dominating the selection process. In a lottery-based decision there is no advantage in using threats, promises or other appeals to the emotions. The device of the 'box of possible epithets' is particularly useful in the understanding of this aspect of sortition.

The independence of the selection procedure from external control also means that *habits of independence* can develop within the polity and within governmental decision-making. The randomly-selected citizen owes nothing to party leader, patron or overlord for his or her position. For this reason there is every encouragement for public officers to think and act with more independence than under an electoral system. A polity that uses lot extensively, moreover, brings citizens together in new and unpredictable combinations in a way that can enliven debate and bring fresh viewpoints to any issue at hand. This is one of the reasons behind the proposals by the French Constitutional Committee, Paine and Jefferson to use lot to divide a legislative assembly on a temporary basis. The ethos of independence of opinion underpinned the role of the Athenian *dikastai*; it can also be linked to Chaitin's idea of randomness as complex independence that we saw in Chapter One.

While the primary political potential of sortition lies in its capacity to protect the process of selection and hence the polity itself from subversion, the secondary roles of lot all serve to reinforce this objective. Their operation, moreover, is often of a symbiotic nature. The direct and equal relationship established between the citizens and the polity by the use of lot activates the citizens in daily defence of their polity. The perceived neutrality of a lot-selected polity is a source of its authority, and the non-competitive, neutral nature of lot inhibits divisions that might arise if preference elections were used in its place. Independent citizens in government roles, moreover, can act to stem the rise of powerful partisan forces and add to the qualities of decision-making.

Weak use and the effects of good and bad lottery design

Lot should be used to its maximum effect if its full political potential is to be realised. Where this is compromised by weak use or by badly designed schemes this cannot happen. The use of sortition by the Athenians to demote the office of *archon* is a weak and inappropriate use because lot is applied to a task that does not require arationality. This use probably gave the aristocratic enemies of the *polis* the opportunity to portray lot as a crude levelling device. The practice of removing office holders by lot is, in most circumstances, also a weak use. We saw this in Penn's first drafts of the constitution of Pennsylvania where it was advocated in order to start a rotational system. There was no advantage gained from using an arational process to address this task — indeed the idea of electing three sets of officers was a far more appropriate solution. As we saw in the case of the Directory, the advantages of using lot to protect the process of selection do not transfer so readily to the task of removing individuals from office. Here the unpredictability of the lottery process seriously interrupted the process of government at the highest level during a period when strong government was needed.

Another problematic, and ultimately weak, aspect of sortition is the weighted lottery. A lottery can *become* a weighted lottery when the pool becomes divided into supporters of particular parties. If the pool is small, patterns of patronage and dependency can begin to create groups within the pool. In these cases the selection process, initially protected by lot, becomes more and more vulnerable to private control. The best example of this is the Florentine *scrutiny*, but the use of lot in Venice to choose nominators also became a weighted lottery as the allegiances of the council members became well known. James Wilson's proposal for the election of the U.S. president by a randomly-selected conclave is also a weighted lottery because the pool was based on congress members grouped by state. This scheme would have been vulnerable to manipulation and intrigue had it been implemented. Some weighted lotteries and lotteries that become weighted can be useful in the short term, and can bring parties together by providing a procedural agreement that all can agree to. This operates best while the outcomes remain relatively unpredictable. As the groupings develop and become known, however, any weighted lottery system can become increasingly vulnerable to wilful interference.

The idea that lot will produce a proportionate result is a modern one that comes from sampling theory. While it might be suggested that the motive for using a lottery in Ancient Athens or in Renaissance Florence was to produce a representative sample of the population in government, it is unlikely to have been the original rationale for its use. This suggestion would constitute a weak use of lot because the objective of creating a sample does not require or need arationality. Reading the republican use of sortition from the point of view of modern sampling theory detracts from the stronger uses of lot where its greater political potential lies.

In contrast to the weak use of sortition, the political potential of lot is facilitated by well-developed schemes that are sensitive both to the arational nature of the lottery and how it can complement rational elements in the design. The best examples of these are Machiavelli's 1520 proposal for the Florentine Constitution and the Leseuer's proposed French Constitution of 1792. In both these cases lot is used intelligently as a means by which the citizen's entry into the body politic could be achieved. Both use large pools, and in this way the citizen body itself becomes a means of protecting the process of selection from private control. Both these schemes owe something to the Athenian *dikasterion* in the sense that a considerable proportion of the citizen body is given a stake in regular political participation. Schemes that use large pools maximise the political potential of the lottery by preventing a lottery from degenerating into a weighted lottery.

The political context of sortition

In this study we have seen how the full realisation of the political potential of sortition is dependent on the overall context in which it is applied. We have seen it operating in what I would generally call republican contexts. Here the main political actors were seeking to establish forms of open public governance that were, to a greater or lesser extent, inclusive. In these circumstances, lot was often supported by a range of other measures designed to serve the same, or similar, ends. These included oaths of office, enclaves, ostracism, rotation, the secret ballot and the *dokimasia*. While lot can help prevent corruption during the process of selection, it is, however, no guarantee that those selected will remain immune from corruption. Other measures for ensuring accountability would be needed for this.

How, then, would lot operate in a less supportive environment? Does its impact in the political sphere depend, for instance, on its links to a certain type of republican polity? Certainly it is difficult to think of potential tyrants diluting their wilful power to appoint by introducing lottery schemes, or a potentially dominant faction opting for a lottery scheme rather than taking further steps towards achieving hegemony. It would seem as if the use of sortition is incompatible with concentrations of extra-constitutional or privately exercised power. I can envisage, however, a number of scenarios where lotteries could be used in contexts that were less than supportive of the aims of open public governance. Aspects of Florentine *scrutiny* would certainly fit into this category, as would a scenario where, for instance, a totalitarian government introduced randomly selected juries while at the same time controlling the dissemination of all public information and the fate of dissident jurors. Similarly if the institutions to which citizens were selected by lot had no power, or were subservient to a private seat of power, lot could only play a minimal role in the protection of due public process. It would seem, therefore, that lot can be a servant to those who desire an open political society, but it cannot fulfil its potential to protect the public polity if it is unsupported by wider political forces working towards that end.

If, however, we look at the immediate context in which lot is used, in none of these instances does a lottery actually *cease* to exclude those with power from exercising it in the selection of personnel. Within a tight-knit oligarchic grouping a lottery will still prevent one member from dominating the making of political appointments, even though the attitude of the ruling group towards the citizen body at large might leave much to be desired. Similarly, in the example of the totalitarian jury, the action of the lottery still has the potential to break up concentrations of power within its own field of operation, even though the effects of that dilution are contradicted by other measures. A lottery for a token institution is still immune from interference or manipulation even though the institution might command little power or real influence. We can therefore think of the primary potential of sortition as inherent in *all* instances where a lottery is used to select personnel, but that it can be more fully realised and can be given greater political relevance when used in a more fully republican context.

The future application of sortition

For the final part of this conclusion I consider the question of the future application of sortition, and whether the political potential that we have been discussing in respect to its past practice is transferable to a modern context. There are a number of approaches that can be taken to this question, but all must proceed on the understanding that, with the notable exception of the Anglo-American jury, sortition is a largely discontinuous practice. There are, moreover, considerable differences between the world of the Athenian or Florentine lot polity and the types of polity that are current in the twenty-first-century political world. The presence of this gap can cause us to react in several ways.

A first view is provided by the idea that since there is such a great difference between the tiny lot polity of the past and today's nation state, lot is a wholly inappropriate mechanism and just cannot operate in modern conditions. According to this view, the advent of political parties, a bureaucratic state apparatus, and universal suffrage leave no space for lot. Its role in protecting the polity is now taken by other, more rational, measures such as checks and balances, and the separation of powers. Lot is therefore seen as belonging to an earlier age when our political institutions were less secure and needed greater protection, and where politics was more face to face. This viewpoint has attractions. It certainly conforms to the post-enlightenment view that liberal democracy can adequately self-police without recourse to arational methods, and that regular elections between competing political parties provide an acceptable level of accountability. It is, however, a view that tends to see sortition and preference election as mutually exclusive rather than complementary mechanisms.

Another way of approaching the future use of lot is to envisage the revival of lot as the finding of a missing link in a chain stretching back to Athens. From this perspective, today's democracies in which citizens are increasingly alienated from the political process, despite their universal right to vote, are examples of unfinished business. The jury is, in this view, the last vestige of the former lot polity, a last guarantee for the individual citizen against the encroaching power of the state. The need to revive lot is thus linked to a normative impulse to develop more inclusive, more responsive government—to bridge the gap between those who rule and those who are ruled. This would suggest that lot could play a part in a new republican agenda that seeks to remedy the perceived shortcomings of liberal democracy. If the first approach is in danger of seeing the path of political development as dictated by the inertia of existing institutions, the second is in danger of being driven by moral teleology. It runs the risk of putting too great a 'shape' on the history of the political process by making certain presumptions about the nature and desirability of democracy and the path of democratic development. This view is useful, however, in that it asks whether the fall of Athenian democracy and the end of popular republicanism in fifteenth-century Italy represent political losses that have not yet been made good. It is a good question, but not one that can be answered simply.

A third view, with which I have greater sympathy, is that lot is a universal problem-solving mechanism, and cannot be confined to the past. According to this approach, if there is a problem which demands an arational solution, and we know the potential of lot, there should be no barrier to using it. Support for this view comes from the fact that lot was revived as a means of selecting public officers in northern Italy in the late Middle Ages without reference to Athenian practice, and from the emergence and endurance of the Anglo-American jury as an institution. If sortition travelled well and found a home in new political settings in the thirteenth and seventeenth centuries there is no reason why it should not do so again. As we saw in the chapter on the French Revolution, the main reasons that sortition was not more widely used was that its potential was not fully understood, and the problems of political consolidation were underestimated. There is thus no unbridgeable gulf between early and later republicanism, just a complex and convoluted learning curve. Linked to this view of lot as a problem-solving mechanism is the idea that it is legitimate to cherry pick political ideas from the past as long as we are aware of how they were understood then, and what they can do for us now.

This is what I would describe as a practical attitude to the past in which past practice is regarded as a legitimate resource for the future. Once we have taken this on board and accepted that sortition *could* have a value for the modern polity, we are faced with the question of *how* we should best understand its possible application. This is, in fact, a huge and complex subject that cannot be fully explored here. The conclusions of the study do, however, furnish us with some basic principles that can act as starting points for further exploration.

My distinction between the primary and secondary potentials of sortition gives us, I would argue, the strongest and clearest guide as to how we can understand its possible application in a modern context. We can think of the secondary principles as linked to those particular political problems for which sortition might provide a solution: problems that present themselves to those involved in politics on a day to day basis, and which arise from one particular aspect or area of the political process. Barnett and Carty's suggestion for a randomly selected House of Lords fits into this category, as do Nilsen's proposals for Iraq, or Barber's advocacy of lot for local council members.[5]

The primary potential, however, is a general expression of the application of sortition in so far as it indicates the potential effect of sortition on the polity as a whole, and in the political sphere as a

[5] See Barnett and Carty (2008); Nilsen (2007); and Barber (1984).

whole, not merely in terms of the particular problem in hand. It tells us that lot can help defend the public nature of the political process. Because we can identify this general or primary potential we can approach the possible modern application of sortition from a more general direction and in terms of more general political aspirations or values. By the same token we can also understand sortition as a potential solution to modern political problems of a more general nature.

In this respect the case for the modern application of sortition has to be based on four main premises. First, that the defence of the public nature of the process of political selection is a desirable aim. Second, the extent to which existing measures and governmental forms adequately address this protection. Third, whether there is another mechanism, existing or to be invented, that can serve the same general purpose and is likely to be more successful in the task. The fourth premise is the extent to which the secondary potentials of sortition can make it more attractive than any rival option. These four premises map out what could be described as the *problematic* of the modern application of sortition: it is the group of related problems that have to be adequately addressed in order to make a general case for application.

While this expresses the necessary issues in general form, the content of this problematic in the current political environment inevitably revolves around the qualities and aspirations of liberal representative democracy. This is not only on account of its ubiquity, but also because liberal representative democracy (a term that encompasses a family of closely related forms) is regarded as a paradigm: a perfected form of governmental best practice. Furthermore (and of considerable importance to our question) of all current polity types, liberal representative democracy also contains the broadest range of mechanisms designed to protect the political process from the exercise of arbitrary or absolute power. From this it is clear that *the general case for the consistent modern application of sortition rests on the extent to which liberal representative democracy is vulnerable to private or covert control over the process by which public officers are selected.* The extent that this vulnerability exists, combined with the extent that we regard such a state as undesirable and the number of other solutions on offer defines the major reason why sortition should be reintroduced. This does not, of course, preclude the introduction of sortition for many of the other good reasons I have explored earlier. This expression of the general case for sortition is the logical outcome of the identification of its primary political potential of sortition as the defence of the public process of selection for office and the projection of this into modern conditions. While it is the culmination of the lengthy historical and analytical work that preceded it, it is also, unfortunately, a question that will have to be addressed elsewhere.

With this unanswered question we reach the end of this particular study, and this particular journey of investigation. As with any exploration of complex historical and political ideas there are as many questions raised as answers supplied, and while I feel I have laid same useful foundations for those who take a serious interest in the subject, there is always more to do. Although I have hinted at some of the reasons why lot was not used in the later republics of France and the United States the full story has yet to be told. In this respect the rise of legitimate political parties would seem to be a significant factor. Likewise the full context of Guicciardini's dialogue remains to be clarified, as does its importance to the ruling élite of sixteenth-century Europe. The extent that sortition was used outside of Italy during the late middle ages is another area where more research could be invaluable, and I have always felt that our political debt to the *popolo* governments has not been properly evaluated. At a more local level I would be interested to know whether Great Yarmouth is an isolated example of Italian-style republicanism on British soil. From a theoretical perspective the relationship between sortition and ideas of equality, impartiality and political power could provide a fruitful cluster of future projects. At the same time, and perhaps with greater urgency, the considerable potential of sortition in the important areas of conflict resolution and political consolidation remains to be explored, both in theory and with reference to current political problems.

This study has taken the form of looking into the past to help solve the problems of the present and the future. This is always a difficult business. I hope, however, that in these pages I have been able to offer the reader a number of new ways of looking at our political inheritance while at the same time stimulating new ideas about the possible shape of our future political world. Whether or not this might involve greater use of sortition is difficult to predict. What I have tried to show in this study is something of the level of responsibility, practical know-how and intellectual sensitivity that would need to accompany such a reintroduction if it is to be purposeful, efficient and successful.

On the Decline of Sortition

I have presented this in an appendix because the question of the decline of sortition was not part of my original study programme. My comments are therefore only a selection of ideas arising from the areas I have studied rather than a coherent argument justified by research undertaken with this end in view.

I mentioned in the concluding chapter that one of the main features in the body of practice of sortition was a distinct break between those polities where it was used extensively and those where it was used only occasionally. I also noted how this division occurs historically at the time when the late medieval and renaissance model of republicanism was in decline and the new model of representative government was emerging. This decline in the importance and frequency of the use of lot is an observable fact of political history. I would be reluctant, however, to attribute it to one causal factor above any other without further work in this area. With this in mind it is still valuable to look at a selection of reasons that might account for it. Some of these are cultural reasons, others as accidents of history, and other reasons I would describe as the actions of individuals who knew what they were doing.

My general orientation has been that the lack of any clearly articulated written rationale for the use of sortition has made it difficult for the practice to make the leap between one era of history or one geographical location and another. This is undoubtedly one reason why those who could have benefited from the use of sortition failed to take it up or even consider it as a viable option. We must also recognise that in some periods and in some cultural milieu sortition simply fell out of favour or was associated with regimes or activities that were the subject of dislike or suspicion. When democracy was thought of as chaotic, brutish and generally undesirable, lot was inevitably tarred with the same brush. The association of lot with chance, divination and gaming also added to the disfavour in which it was regarded, particularly amongst religious groups at the more puritan end of the spectrum. As I suggested in Chapter Five the loss of the lottery element from the Venetian-style ballot could be attributed to the difficulties in transplanting the rituals of the Adriatic republic into the backwoods of Pennsylvania.

To this we can add the idea that in certain periods and amongst certain groups of thinkers the arational was thought of as an irresponsible abdication of individual judgement. This applies to the Dominican tradition of thought (espoused by Savonarola amongst others), the enlightenment tradition we saw expressed by Condorcet and to English Utilitarianism, the philosophy which accompanied the English reform movement. For these schools of thought preference election offered a far more appropriate means of selecting individuals to fulfil special political or governmental roles.

Undoubtedly a factor in the decline of sortition is the replacement of the civic republic, with its emphasis on citizen participation, by liberal representative democracy in which a professional political caste could be hired or fired by public popular majority. We can see some points of origin for this in Guicciardini's Logrongo thesis and in the Venetian division between those who governed and those who voted. With the transition to liberal democracy, however, comes the advent of legitimate political parties—an innovation that would have been unthinkable to the citizen-led, general interest ethos of earlier republicanism. Since sortition was initially introduced to inhibit partisanship it is not hard to understand why it has fallen into disuse in an era that champions the political party.

In respect to the possible conscious suppression of sortition, it is clear that lot had its enemies. These might range from the aristocratic clubs of Athens to the would-be *signore* of an Italian commune or the natural aristocracy of worthy brethren who attended the U.S. Constitutional Convention of 1787. We saw how Guicciardini took sortition seriously enough to explore the arguments for and against its use and to attempt to hide its links with Florentine popular republicanism. We do not know exactly how much his ideas were refined behind the closed doors of subsequent generations of pan-European aristocracy, but if we are looking for an individual responsible for initiating the decline of sortition, Guicciardini must be a prime candidate. On the other hand it would also be true to say that given the potential of sortition to dilute concentrations of power, anyone—democrat or aristocrat—who had an interest in building a power base or faction would be its natural enemy.

Glossary

This glossary is designed to facilitate the reading of the chapters where I have used the original terms rather than their English translations. Their meanings relate specifically to their use in the study and not necessarily to their general or current usage where they might have a different meaning or meanings. Readers who need further details can consult Hansen (1999) for most Athenian, and, Najemy (1982) for most Florentine terms. Other sources are cited with their respective entries.

Accoppiatori: The secretaries in charge of the placing of the names of those elected by the Florentine *scrutiny* into their respective bags ready to be drawn out at intervals as the offices become vacant. (Kent, 1978; Rubinstein, 1966.)

A mano (by hand): The practice, adopted by the Medici, of allowing the secretaries or *accoppiatori* to choose the office holders — i.e., by-passing the random element in the *tratte* or draw. (Kent, 1978; Rubinstein, 1966.)

Anziani (elders): The name given to the highest office-holders in thirteenth-century Italian *popolo* regimes. (Waley 1988; Koenig 1977; Wolfson 1899.)

Areopagos: The aristocratic senate of Ancient Athens.

Arrabbiati: Grouping opposed to Savonarola during the Second Florentine republic. (Roth, 1968.)

Archon: Although the term can apply to any magistrate it is commonly used to describe the nine top executive positions in Ancient Athens.

Arti maggiori, arti minori: Major and minor Florentine guilds. (Becker, 1967.)

Balia: A Florentine extraordinary commission usually used to draw up and pass constitutional measures. *Balia* members were usually appointed.

Benificiati: Those members of Florentine society entitled to membership of the new Grand Council of 1494. (Pesman-Cooper, 1985.)

Bigi: Supporters of the Medici. (Roth, 1968.)

Borsa di speciolata: An additional bag containing the names of those who had received high numbers of votes in the Florentine scrutiny but not sufficient to be included in the main borsi. Those included were to act as reserves. Names were withdrawn from this bag if there were insufficient officers at any time due to the rules xcluding family members to serve together on the same body. The borsa di speciolata as used during the popular regime of 1343.

Borse (sing. borsa): The bags used to contain the names of prospective Florentine office-holders.

Boule: The Athenian Council of 500. (Rhodes, 1972).

Boni homines : The name given to the governing group in the early Italian Communes (prior to the popolo regimes of the thirteenth century). (Waley, 1988).

Borsillino: A smaller bag used in the Florentine selections for office during the latter years of the First Republic. It contained the names of a small group of trusted and experienced individuals and was used to supplement the draws made from the main borsa.

Brevia: A system of selecting electors by lot from the citizen population. It was widely used in the Italian popolo regimes of the thirteenth century. (Wolfson, 1899)

Buoni Uomini: A grouping of twelve selected by the scrutiny to act as an advisory body to the Florentine Signoria.

Busoli, Bussuli (various spellings, often in accusative plural *Bussolos*): Venetian urns or vases used for the secret ballot. These would usually be constructed with two internal compartments. A small cloth pellet would be dropped into one or other of these to signify approval or disapproval of the candidate. (Queller,1986; Wolfson, 1899.)

Capitano del Popolo: A major Florentine officeholder. The name derives from the Primo Popolo regime of 1250–60, but the office was continued even under regimes of a less popular nature.

Cento: The Florentine elected senate of 100 introduced by the Medici. (Kent, 1978; Rubinstein, 1966.)

Ciompi: Florentine textile workers. They featured in an uprising in 1378. (Bruckner, 1968.) Cives*: Citizens.*

Consiglio Grande: The Grand Council. Also known as the Consiglio Maggiori.

Consortieri: Private societies from the late medieval period in northern Italy. These would usually be made up of a number of families who would pool resources in order to build a tower as a symbol of prestige and as a means of defence against other *consortieri*. (Waley, 1988; Pesman-Cooper, 1985.)

Consuls: One of the names given to the top executive officers in the northern Italian city-communes in the early stages of their development. (Waley, 1988.)

Deme: A specially designated locality or ward of Ancient Athens. (Whitehead, 1986.)

Demos: The common people of Athens — i.e. non-nobility. The term is used loosely to mean either the people of Athens as a whole or the poor people of Athens. It is also used in a more precise political sense to describe the people in Assembly — i.e. the citizens.

Dikastai (sing. *Dikastes*): Citizen members of the People's Courts. Although often translated as *juror* or *jury member* the *dikastai* operated in far greater numbers than the jury as we know it and they had no deliberative role. (Hansen, 1990.)

Dikasterion: The Athenian People's Court. (Hansen, 1990.)

Dikē: Justice or 'rightness'. (Introduction by Barker to Aristotle, 1946.)

Divieto: The final stage in the Florentine selection process of *scrutiny and tratte* in which those who failed to qualify for office were excluded. The main reason for disqualification was membership of the same family as another office holder in the same governmental body.

Dokimasia: The process by which the citizenship credentials of Athenian office holders was checked after selection or election but prior to taking office. (Adelege, 1983.)

Eisangelia: The official denunciation of an Athenian magistrate by a citizen that would lead to public prosecution.

Eupatrids (pl.): The Athenian landowning class.

Gens: An Athenian family or kinship grouping.

Gonfalonier of Justice: The highest Florentine civic magistrate, the equivalent of Head of State.

Gonfalonieri of the Companies: Sixteen Florentine office holders who acted as advisors to the *Signoria*. This office was based on the structure of the popular civil militia, and each *Gonfalonier* would come from a designated company that operated in a separate area of the city.

Graphe paranomon: A form of judicial review that operated in Ancient Athens. A citizen could challenge the proposer of any ruling made by the Assembly on the grounds that it contradicted existing law or was against the interests of the *polis*. (Yunis, 1988.)

Helliastic oath: The oath taken by every *dikastes* before he joined the body of 6000 who were entitled to serve in the *dikasterion*.

Hetaireia (pl. *ai*): Aristocratic Athenian political club.

Heliaia: The early name for the People's Courts, as established by Solon.

Hippeis: The second economic stratum of Athenian society, the cavalrymen or knights.

Ho boulemenos: The name given to any Athenian citizen who took a voluntary political initiative. This could involve standing for office, bringing a matter to the Assembly or denouncing a magistrate for misconduct.

Imborsazione: The process of placing the names of those elected by the Florentine *scrutiny* into their respective bags to be drawn out at intervals when the offices in question fell vacant.

Imbroglio: Corruption. Literally 'entanglement'. (Queller, 1986.)

Intelligenze: Illegal Florentine political parties. (Weinstein, 1970.)

Kleroterion (Pl. *Kleroteria*): An Athenian lottery machine. These were slotted wooden or stone displays. The name tickets or plaques of candidates would be placed in the slots and then beans or coloured balls would be drawn to decide which row of names was to be selected. (Dow, 1939; Moore's commentary to Aristotle, 1986.)

Libro D'Oro: The Golden Book which listed the names of all the Venetian nobility or hereditary members of the Grand Council. (Lane, 1973.)

Mercanzia: The five most important Florentine Guilds. (Bruckner, 1962.)

Metic: The Athenian term for a resident foreigner. *Metics* were often wealthy and contributed considerably to the vibrancy of the Athenian economy. They were, however, denied citizen status.

Minus possidentes: French citizens earning less than 1500 L per Annum. (Hammersley, 2005; Lesueur, 1932.)

Monte: A compulsory loan system that became an important part of the Florentine state economy during the First Republic. Under this system the heads of the leading mercantile families were required to lend money to the public funds of the city. This was scarcely an imposition, however, because the rates of interest were extremely high. (Becker, 1968.)

Nomothetai: The Athenian legislative body. This consisted of large numbers of *dikastai* who would listen to arguments for and against any measure before voting for its acceptance or rejection.

Ottimati: Florentine Aristocrats. (Roth, 1968.)

Palleschi: Florentine supporters of the Medici at the time of the Second Republic. (Roth, 1968.)

Parlamento: The name given to the Florentine Assembly of citizens. A *Parlamento* would be called for the simple act of accepting or rejecting any measure.

Parte Guelfa: The only legitimate political party in Florence, the *Parte Guelfa* dates from the factional conflict between the Guelfs and Ghiberlines (supporters of Pope and Empire respectively). During the fourteenth and fifteenth centuries, however, it had become more of a civic society than an active political party in the modern sense. (Bruckner, 1962.)

Pentakosiomedimnoi: The highest economic stratum of Ancient Athens consisting of major landowners and aristocrats.

Phratria (Pl-*ai*, English; *Phratry*): Athenian brotherhood Association.

Piagnoni: Supporters of Savonarola during the Second Florentine republic. (Roth, 1968.)

Plus possidentes: French citizens earning more than 1500L per annum. (Hammesley, 2005; Lesueur, 1932.)

Podesta: The temporary head of state of an Italian city. Usually imported from another locality to ensure some level of impartiality. (Waley, 1988.)

Popolani: The Florentine mercantile ruling class. Distinguished from the *ottimati* or aristocracy by being self-made rather than the descendants of the feudal nobility (many of whom were barred from office by the Ordinances of Justice of 1292). (Becker, 2002.)

Popolo: The name given to popular societies that grew up in northern Italian cities during the thirteenth century. These favoured the rule of law and participatory forms of government, often involving the guilds. *Popolo* governments held power in many cities during this period. (Waley, 1988; Hyde, 1973; Koenig, 1977.)

Pratica (pl. *Pratiche*): Florentine public debates. These were the equivalent to a modern public consultation and participants were usually invited to attend by the ruling *Signoria*.

Primo Popolo: The Florentine popular government that held power between 1250 and 1260. (Davidsohn, 1896; Villani, 1908)

Priors: The name given to individual members of the Florentine *Signoria*. Before the term *Signoria* became popular the collective government of *priors* was known as a *Priorate*.

Prytany (pl. *prytaneis*): A special executive body of the Athenian *boule* drawn from the *boule* members of the same tribe. Each *prytany* would serve for one-tenth of a year in rotation.

Quarantia: The major Venetian judiciary committee of forty. (Queller, 1986; Lane, 1973.)

Remissi: The name given to the Florentine election bags into which the names of those excluded by the *divieto* would be place.

Reggimento: The Florentine ruling group. Used in a more general sense in this study. (Kent ,1978.)

Scrutiny and tratte: The Florentine system for selecting political officers which involved a secret ballot followed by successive drawing of officeholders from special bags as the offices fell vacant in rotation.

Sesto: A division of one sixth of the city of Florence.

Signore: The name given to a single ruler of a northern Italian city. (Waley, 1988.)

Signoria: The collective name given to the top Florentine executive body of six *priors* together with the *Gonfalonier of Justice*. (Increased to eight by the mid-fourteenth century.)

Strategoi: Athenian generals. The board of ten *strategoi* were, strictly speaking, military magistrates and were elected annually by the Assembly.

Thetes: Those of the lowest Athenian economic stratum. Mainly consisting of the urban poor, the *thetes* served as oarsmen in the Athenian navy.

Trittyes: Subdivisions of each Athenian region each making up a third of a tribe. (Traill, 1975.)

Zeugitai: Members of the third property class of Ancient Athens. Every member of the *zeugitai* served as a hoplite or light infantryman and had to have sufficient income to equip himself militarily.

Bibliography

Primary sources

Adams, John (1965), *The Legal Papers of John Adams*, eds. Wroth, L. K. and Zobel, H. B. (Cambridge, Mass.: Harvard University Press).

Aquinas, Thomas, Saint (1954), *Selected Political Writings*, trans. Dawson, J. G.; intro., ed. D'Entreves (Oxford: A.P. Blackwell).

Aristotle (1492), *Politica*, trans. Bruni, L.; commentary, Aquinas, T., Saint (Rome).

Aristotle, (1946) *Politics*, trans. Barker, E. (Oxford: Clarendon Press).

Aristotle (1986), The Athenian Constitution, trans. Moore, J. M. In *Aristotle and Xenophon on Democracy and Oligarchy* (Berkeley: University of California Press).

Aristotle (2000), *Nicomachean Ethics*, trans. Crisp, R. (Cambridge University Press).

Bartolus of Sassoferrato (1997), *On Guelfs and Ghiberlines; Treatise on the Government of a City; Treatise on a* Tyrant, trans. Garnett, G. (University of Oxford).

Beckman, G .M. (1976), *The Statutes at Large of Pennsylvania at the time of William Penn*, vol. 1 (New York & co.??)

Bidwell, W.B. and Janssen, M. eds. (1991-5), *Proceedings in Parliament 1626*, vol. IV (Yale University Press).

Bruni, Leonardo (1986), 'The Constitution of Florence', ed. Moulakis, A., *Rinascimento*, 2nd series, 26 (1986).

Bruni, Leonardo (2001), *History of the Florentine People*, vol. I7, books I–IV, trans., ed. Hankins, J. (Harvard University Press).

Cobbett, W. (1811), *Parliamentary History of England*, vol. VIII (1722–33) (London: T.C. Hansard).

Condorcet (1789), *Examin de cette question. Est-il utile de diviser une Assemblée Nationale en Plusieurs Chambres* (Paris).

Condorcet (1793), *Plan de Constitution présenté à la Convention Nationale* (Convention Nationale France).

Condorcet (1793b), *Plan de Constitution présenté à la Convention Nationale le 15 et 16 Fevrier 1793* (Paris Imp.Nationale: Le 38/1766 (D)).

Condorcet. (1994), *Foundations of Social Choice and Political Theory*, trans., ed. McLean, I., Hewitt (London: F. Edward Elgar).

Connecticut (1750), *Acts and Laws of His Majestie's English Colony of Connecticut* (New London [?]: T. Green).

Contarino, Gaspar (1969), *The Commonwealth and Government of Venice*, original trans. Lewkenor, 1599. (Facsimile edition: Amsterdam and New York: Da Capo Press).

Cooper, Anthony Ashley, 1st Earl of Shaftesbury (1680), *The Fundamental Constitution of Carolina.*

De Tocqueville, Alexis (1966), *Democracy in* America, ed. Mayer, J. P. and Lerner, M., trans. Lawrence, G. (New York, Evanston and London: Harper and Row.

Farrand, M. ed. (1966), *Records of the Federal Convention of 1787*, vol. 2 (Yale University Press).

Gataker, T. (1623), *A just defence of certain passages in a former treatise concerning the nature and use of lots* (London: John Havilland).

Gataker, T. (1627), *Of the Nature and Use of Lots: a treatise historicall and theologicall* (London: John Haviland, first published 1619).

Godwin, W. (1971), *An Enquiry Concerning Political Justice*, abridged and ed. Carter, K., Codell (Kay Cordell) (Oxford: Clarendon Press).

Guicciardini, Francesco (1932), 'Del modo di eleggere gli uffici nel Consigli Grande', in *Dialogo e discorsi del Reggimento di Firenze*. A cura di R. Palmarocchi. Bari Laterza.

Guicciardini, Francesco (1964), *History of Florence*, trans. Grayson, C.; abridged and intro. Hale, J.N. (London: Sadler and Brown Ltd).

Guicciardini, Francesco (1965), *Selected Writings*, trans. Grayson, M.; ed. and intro. Grayson, C. (New York, Toronto, Oxford: Oxford University Press).

Guicciardini, Francesco (1984), *The History of Italy*, trans., ed. Alexander, S. (New Jersey: Princeton University Press).

Guicciardini, Francesco (1994), *Dialogue on the Government of Florence*, trans., ed. Brown, A. (Cambridge: Cambridge University Press).

Guicciardini, Francesco (1997), 'Del Modo di ordinare il Governo Popolare', trans. Price, R. In Kraye, J. ed. (1997), *Cambridge Translations of Renaissance Philosophical Texts* (Cambridge: Cambridge University Press).

Harrington, James (1977). *The Political Works of James Harrington*, ed. Pocock, J.G.A. (Cambridge: Cambridge University Press).

Harrington, James (1992), *The Commonwealth of Oceana and A System of Politics*, ed. Pocock, J.G.A. (Cambridge: Cambridge University Press).

Hawkins, William (1734–5), *Parliament Acts. Statutes at large from the Magna Carta to 7 Geo. II*, 6 vols (London: John Baskett).

Herodotus (1954), *The Histories*, trans. De Selincourt, A. (Harmondsworth: Penguin).

Herodotus (1998), *The Histories*, trans. Waterfield, R. (Oxford World's Classics).

Herty, Thomas (1799), *A Digest of the Laws of Maryland* (Baltimore).

Homer (1987), *The Iliad*, trans. Hammond, M. (Harmondswoth: Penguin Classics).

Jefferson, Thomas (1943), *The Complete Jefferson*, ed. Padover, S.K. (New York: Duell, Sloan and Pearce Inc.).

Jefferson, Thomas (1958), *The Papers of Thomas Jefferson*, vol.15 (New Jersey: Princeton University Press).

Jensen, M., Kaminski, J.P., Saladino, G.J. (1981), *The Documentary History of theRatification of the Constitution* (State Historical Society of Wisconsin).

Kilty, W. (1799), *The Laws of Maryland to which are prefixed the Bill of Rights* (Annapolis: Fredrick Green).

Lanthenas, Fr. (1792), *Des elections et du mode d'élire par listes épuratoives* (Paris).

Leaming, A., Spicer, J. (1758), *The Grants, Concessions and Original Constitutions of the Province of New Jersey* (Philadelphia: Bradford (printer)).

Lesueur, Théodore (1932), *A French draft Constitution of 1792. Modelled on James Harrington's Oceana*, ed. and intro. Liljergen, S. B. (Lund: C.W.Glefrup).

Library of Congress (1907), *Journals of the Continental Congress. 1774-1789*, (Washington: Government Printing Office).

Ludlow, Edmund (1698), *Memoires of Edmund Ludlow Esqu*. (Vivay, Bern).

Machiavelli, Niccolo(1988). *Florentine Histories*, trans. Banfield, L.F., Mansfield H.C. (Princeton University Press).

Machiavelli, Niccolo (1989), *Machiavelli – the chief works and others*, trans. Gilbert, A. (Durham and London: Duke University Press).

Machiavelli, Niccolo (1998), *The Discourses*, trans. Walker, L., ed. Crick, B. (Harmondsworth: Penguin).

Madison, James (1987a), *Notes of debates in the Federal Convention of 1787 reported by James Madison* (New York and London: W. W. Norton and Co.).

Madison, James; Hamilton, Alexander; Jay, John (1987b), *The Federalist Papers* (Harmondsworth: Penguin Classics).

Massachusetts (1814), *The Charters and General laws of the Colony and Province of Massachusetts Bay* (Boston: General Council).

Massachusetts (2000), *Massachusetts General laws Annotated*, vol. 40, ch. 233–6 (West Group).

Mavidal, J. (1862), *Archives Parlementaires de 1787 à 1860*, série 1, vol. LVIII (Paris: Librairie administrative de P. Dupont).

Mill, J.S. (1977), *Essays in Politics and Society*, vols XVIII–XIX, Collected Works, ed. Robson (J.M. Routledge and Keegan Paul: University of Toronto Press).

Mill, J.S. (1978), *Essays in Philosophy and Classics*, vol. XI. Collected Works, ed. Robson (J.M. Routledge and Kegan Paul: University of Toronto Press).

Milton, John (1660). *Readie and Easy Way to Establish a Commonwealth* (London).

Montesquieu (1989), *The Spirit of the Laws*, trans. and ed. Cohler, A., Miller, B.C., Stone, H.S. (Cambridge: Cambridge University Press).

Mont-Gilbert, Francois-Agnes (1793). *Avis au Peuple, sur sa Liberté* (Paris: De L'Imprimerie Nationale).

Morris, Robert (1770), *A Letter to Sir Richard Aston*, 2nd edn (London: Geo. Peach).

Nedham, Marchamont (1650), *The case of the Commonwealth Stated* (London: printed for E. Blackmore and R.Lowndes).

Nedham, Marchamont (1656), *The Excellencie of a Free State or The Right Constitution of a Commonwealth* (London: printed for Thomas Brewster).

Neville, Henry (1698), *Discourses Concerning Government* (London).

New Hampshire (1761), *Acts and laws of His Majestie's Province of New Hampshire in New England* (Portsmouth).

New Hampshire (1771), *Acts and laws of His Majestie's Province of New Hampshire in New England* (Portsmouth).

New Jersey, Statutes (c.1700), *The Concessions and Agreements of the Proprietors, Freeholders and Inhabitants of the Province of West New Jersey in America*.

New Jersey (1800), *Laws of the State of New Jersey* (New Brunswick: William Peterson).

New York (1894), *The Colonial laws of New York from the year 1664 to the Revolution*, vol. III, ed. Commissioners of Statutory Revision (Albany: James B. Lyn, State Printer).

North Carolina (1765), *A Collection of all acts of Assembly of the Province of N.Carolina now in force and use* (Newbern: James Davies).

Paine, Thomas (1795), *Dissertation on the First principles of Government* (London).

Paine, Thomas (1945), *Complete Works*, ed. Foner, P.S. (New York: Citadel Press).

Paine, Thomas (1976), *Common Sense* (Harmondsworth: Penguin Classics).

Patrizzi, Francesco (1594), *De Institutione Rei Publicae* (Argentinae).

Penn, William (1675), *England's Present Interest Discovered* (London: Andrew Sowle).

Penn, William (1982), *The Papers of William Penn*, ed. Dunn, R., Dunn, M. M. (University of Pennsylvania Press).

Pettingal, John (1769), *An inquiry into the use and practice of juries among the Greeks and Romans, from whence the origin of the English jury may probably be deduced* (London)

Plato (1940), *Protagoras*, trans. Wright, J. in Plato and Xenophon (1940)

Plato (1970), *The Laws*, trans. Saunders, T.J. (Harmondsworth: Penguin Classics).

Plato and Xenophon (1940), *Socratic Discourses*, Everyman edn (London: Dent and Sons).

Pseudo-Xenophon (1992), *The Old Oligarch*, trans. Hughes, K.R., Thorpe, M., Thorpe, M.A. Lactor 2 (Cambridge University Printing Services).

Poore, B.P. (1878), *The Federal and State Constitutions, Colonial Charters, and other Organic Laws of The United States, 2nd Edition* (Washington: Govt. Printing Offices).

Rinnuccini, Alamanno (1978), 'De Liberate', trans.Watkins, R.N. In Watkins (1978).

Rous, George (1771), *A letter to the Jurors of Great Britain. Occasioned by the Opinion of Lord Mansfield* (London: G. Peach).

Rousseau, J.J. (1988), *Rousseau's Political Writing*, trans. Bondanella, J.C.; ed. Ritter, A. and Bondarella, J.C. (New York & London: W.W. Norton and Co.).

Savonarola, Girolamo (1978), 'Treatise on the Constitution and Government of the City of Florence', trans. Watkins, R.N. In Watkins (1978).

Scot, George (1685), *The Model of the Government of East New Jersey in America* (Edinburgh).

Sidney, Algenon (1598), *Discourses Concerning Government* (Westminster).

Shaftesbury (1689), *Some Observations Regulating Elections for Parliament* (Found amongst the Shaftesbury Papers).

Sprigg, William (1659), *A Modest Plea for an Equal Commonwealth, Against Monarch* (London: Giles Galveut).

Staughton, George, Nead, Benjamin, M., McCamant, T.(1879), *Charter to William Penn and Laws of the Province of Pennsylvania* (Harrisburg: John Blair Linn).

Stewart, J.H. (1951), *A Documentary Survey of the French Revolution* (New York: Macmillan).

Streater, John (1654), *Observations, Historical, Political and Philosophical upon Aristotle's First book of Political Government* (London).

Streater, John [J.S] (1659), *Government described. Viz what monarchie, aristocracie,oligarchie and demoracie is. Plus a model of the commonwealth or free state of Ragaus* (London).

Testi e Documenti (1961), *Archivio Storico Italiano* 119.

Thucydides (1881), *History of the Peloponnesian War*, trans. Jowett, B. (Oxford: Clarendon Press).

Thucydides (1972). *History of the Peloponnesian War*, trans. Warner, R. (Harmondsworth: Penguin).

Toland, John (1701), *The Art of Governing by Parties* (London: Lintott).

Towers, Joseph (1764), *An Enquiry into the Question whether Juries are or are not Judges of Law as well as Fact* (London: J. Wilkie).

Trott, N. (1736), *The Laws of the province of South Carolina* (Charlestown: Lewis Timothy).

Virginia (1727), *Acts of Assembly passed in to the Colony of Virginia from 1662-1715*, (London: Blasket).

Wallace N. (1921), *Commons Debates for 1629 Critically Edited with an introduction dealing with Parliamentary Sources for the Early Stuarts* (University of Minnesota).

Watkins, R.N. (1978), *Humanism and Liberty. Writings on Freedom from fifteenth-century Florence* (Columbia: University of South Carolina Press).

Wilson, Peter (1784), *Acts of the Council and General Assembly of the state of New Jersey* (Trenton: Issac Collins).

Wilson, James (1967), *Works* (Cambridge, Mass.: Belknap Press, Harvard University Press).

Xenophon (1940), *Memorabilia*, trans. Watson, M.A. In Plato and Xenophon (1940)

Anonymous primary sources

Benefit (post 1688), *The Benefit of the Ballot.*

Chaos (1659), *Chaos–or a discourse wherein is presented the view of a magistrate. By a Well-willer to the Publique Weal* (London: Livewell, Chapman).

Noland (1701), *The Free State of Noland* (London: printed for D. Brown).

Secondary Sources

Adair, D. G. (2000), *he Intellectual Origins of Jeffersonian Democracy*, ed. Yellin (Lexington Books).

Adelege, G. (1983), '*The Purpose of the Dokimasia*', Greek, Roman and Byzantine Studies 24.

Ady, C.M.; Jacobs, E.F. eds (1960), *Italian Renaissance Studies* (London: Faber & Faber).

Aldridge, A.O. (1984), *Thomas Paine's American Ideology* (Newark: University of Delaware Press).

Alengry, F. (1904), *Condorcet, Guide de la Révolution Francais.V* (Paris: Giard et E. Brière).

Allen, J.W. (1928), *The History of Political Thought in the Sixteenth Century* (London: Methuen).

Amar, A.R. (1984), 'Choosing representatives by lottery voting', *Yale Law Journal 93: 7.*

Andrewes, A. (1982), 'The Growth of the Athenian State', *Cambridge Ancient History* III, (Cambridge: Cambridge University Press).

Andrews, C.M. (1912), *The Colonial Period in American History* (New York).

Aston, N. (2004), *The French Revolution. Authority, Liberty and the Seach for Stability* (Basingstoke: Palgrave, Macmillan).

Aubert, V. (1959), 'Chance in Social Affairs', *Inquiry* 2, 1–24

Baczko, B. (1994), *Ending the Terror. The French Revolution after* Robespierre, trans. Petheram, M. (Cambridge: Cambridge University Press).

Bailyn, B. (1992), *Ideological Origins of the American Revolution* (Relknop: Harvard University Press).

Baker, K.M. (1975), *Condorcet: from Natural Philosophy to Social Mathematics* (University of Chicago Press).

Barber, B.R. (1974), *The Death of Communal Liberty* (N.J.: Princeton University Press).

Barber, B.R. (1984), *Strong Democracy: Participatory Politics for a New Age* (Berkeley: University of California Press).

Barker, E. (1913), *The Dominican Order and Convocation* (Oxford: Clarendon Press).

Barnett, A., Carty, P. (2008), *The Athenian Option: An idea whose time is coming* (Exeter: Imprint Academic) [originally published in 1998 by Demos].

Barnett, V. (1974), *Sample Survey, Principles and Methods* (London: Arnold).

Barratt, N. S., Sachse J. F. comp. (1908), *Freemasonry in Pennsylvania 1727–1907* (Philadelphia Press).

Beard, C. A., 'Class Conflict and the Rise of Parties', in Bonomi (1980).

Beatie, J. M. , 'London Juries in the 1690s', in Cockburn and Green (1988).

Becker, M.B. (1967), *Florence in Transition*, vol. I (Baltimore: John Hopkins University Press).

Becker, M.B. (2002), *Florentine Essays*, Collected by Banker, J., Lansing C. (Ann Arbour: University of Michigan Press).

Black, A. (1984), *Guilds and Civil Society in European Political Thought from the Twelfth Century to the Present* (London: Methuen and Co.).

Blanshei, S.R. (1976), ?Perugia 1260–1340.Conflict and Change in a Medieval Italian Urban Society', *Transactions of the American Philosophical Society*, New Series, 66: 2 (1976).

Blythe, J.M. (1992), *Ideal Government and the Mixed Constitution in the Middle Ages,* (Princeton University Press).

Bock, Skinner, Viroli, eds (1990), *Machiavelli and* Republicanism (Cambridge: Cambridge University Press).

Boeckh, A. (1886), *Die Staatshaushaltung der Athener*, I–II , 3rd ed. G. Reimer (Berlin).

Bonomi, P.U., ed. (1980), *Party and Political Opposition in Revolutionary America* (New York: Sleepy Hollow Press).

Bousky, W.M. (1981), *A Medieval Italian Commune. Siena under the Nine 1287-1355* (Berkeley, Los Angeles & London: University of California Press).

Bork, A.M. (1967), *'Randomness in the Twentieth Century'*, *Antioch Review* XVII: 1, Spring (1967).

Boyle, C. (1998), 'Organisations selecting people, how the process could be made fairer by the appropriate use of lotteries', *The Statistician* 47, part 2 (1998), 291–305.

Brock, W.A. (1990), 'Evaluation and Prediction in Economics and Finance', in Casti and Karlquist (1990).

Broome, J. (1984), 'Selecting people randomly', *Ethics* 95 (October), 8–55

Broome, J. (1991), 'Fairness', *Proceedings of the Aristotelian Society* 91, 87–102

Brucker, G.A (1962), *Florentine Politics and Society. 1343-1378* (Princeton, New Jersey: Princeton University Press).

Brucker, G.A (1968), ,The Ciompi Rebellion', in Rubinstein (1968).

Burnheim, J. (1985), *Is Democracy Possible? The Alternative to Electoral Politics* (London: Polity Press).

Bury, J.B. (1900), *History of Greece* (London: Macmillan).

Butters, H.C. (1985), *Governors and Government in Early Sixteenth-Century Florence. 1502-1519* (Oxford: Clarendon Press).

Callenbach, E., Phillips, M.A. (2008), *A Citizen Legislature* (Exeter: Imprint Academic) [originally published in 1985 by Banyan Tree Books/Clear Glass].

Canning, J.P. (1980), ,The Corporation in the thought of the Italian Jurists', *History of Political Thought* 1 (1980).

Carson, L., Martin B. (1999), *Random Selection in Politics* (Westport, Conn. & London: Praeger,).

Casti, J., Karlquist, A. (1990), Beyond Belief, Randomness, Prediction, Explanation in Science (Boca Raton, Sweden: CRC Press).

Chaitin, G.J. (1988), 'Randomness in arithmetic', Scientific American, July (1988).

Chaitin, G.J. (2001), *Exploring Randomness* (London: Springer).

Christophersen, J.A. (1966), *The Meaning of Democracy* (Oslo: Universitetfurlaget).

Clapham, J.H. (1912), *The Abbé Sièyes* (Westminster: P.S King).

Cockburn, J. S., Green, T. A., eds (1988), *Twelve Good Men and True. The Criminal Jury in England 1200-1800* (Princeton, New Jersey: Princeton University Press).

Collier, C., Collier, J. L. (1986), *Decision in Philadelphia* (New York: Ballantine Books).

Conway, F. (1967), *Sampling, an Introduction for Social Scientists* (London: Allen and Unwin).

Coote, A., Stewart, J., Kendall, E. (1997), *Citizens' Juries* (Institute of Public Policy Research).

Cornish, W.R. (1968), *The Jury* (London: Allen Lane).

Cotton, J. (1980), 'The Harringtonian Party (1656–1660)', *History of Political Thought* 1 (1980).

Crook, M. (1996), *Elections in the French Revolution. An Apprenticeship in Democracy1789–99* (Canbridge: Cambridge University Press).

Crosby, N., Kelly.J, Schaefer. P. (1986), 'Citizen's Panels – a new approach to Citizen Participation', *Public Administration Review* 46.

Cunningham, N. E. Jr. (1957), *The Jeffersonian Republicans* (University of North Canada Press).

Curtius, E. (1857–67), *Griechische Geschichte* (Berlin: Weidmannsche Buchhandlung)

Dahl, R.A.(1970), *After the Revolution: Authority in a Good Society* (Yale University Press).

Davidsohn, R. (1896), *Forschungenzurelteren Geschichte Von Florenz* (Berlin: E.S. Mittler und sohn, 1896–1927).

Day, J., Chambers, M. (1962), *Aristotle's History of Athenian Democracy* (Berkeley: University of California Press).

Deming, W.E. (1950), *Some Theory of Sampling* (New York: John Wiley and Sons Inc.)

Dienel, P.C. (1989), 'Contributing to social decision methodology: citizen reports on technological projects', in Vlek, C., Cvetkovich, G. *SocialDecision Methodology for Technological Projects* (Dordrecht, Netherlands: Kluwer).

Dienel, P.C., Renn, O. (1995), 'Planning cells: a gate to "fractal" mediation', in Renn, O.,Webler, T.,Weidemann, P., *Fairness and Competence in Citizen Participation: Evaluating Models for Environmental Discourse* (Dordrecht, Netherlands: Kluwer).

Dennett, D.C. (2003), *Freedom Evolves* (London: Allen Lane).

Devlin, Patrick, Baron. (1966), *Trial by Jury* (London: Methuen).

Diamond, L. (1999), *Developing Democracy* (Baltimore & London: John Hopkins University Press).

Dodds, E.R. (1973), *The Ancient Concept of Progress and other Essays* (Oxford: Oxford University Press).

Dow, S. (1939), 'Aristotle the Kleroteria, and the Courts', *Harvard Studies in Philology* 50.

Doyle, W. (1989), *The Oxford History of the French Revolution* (Oxford: Clarendon Press).

Duruy, J.V. (1892), *History of Greece* (London: Kegan Paul, Trench).

Dutaillis, C.P. (1978), *The French Commune in the Middle Ages*, trans. Vickers, J. (Amsterdam, New York, Oxford: North Holland)

Duxbury, N . (1999), *Random Justice – on Lotteries and Legal Decision-making* (Oxford: Clarendon Press)

Eckhoff, T. (1989), 'Lotteries in allocative situations', *Social Science Information* 28: 1 (March)

Edgar, W. (1998), *South Carolina. A History* (University of South Carolina Press).

Egal, M. 'The pattern of factional development in Pennsylvania N. Y. and Massachusetts', in Bonomi (1980).

Ehrenberg, V. (1966), *Ancient Society and Institutions: studies presented to Victor Ehrenberg on his 75th Birthday* (Oxford: Blackwell).

Ehrenberg, V. (1968), *From Solon to Socrates* (London: Methuen).

Elster, J. (1999), 'Accountability in Athenian politics', in Przeworski A., Stokes S., Manin, B., *Democracy, Accountability and Representation* (Cambridge: Cambridge University Press).

Elster, J. (1989), *Solomonic Judgements* (Cambridge: Cambridge University Press).

Engelstad, F. (1988), 'The assignment of political office by lot', *Social Science Information* 28: 1 (March) 23–50.

Erskine-May, T. (1877), *Democracy in Europe, a history* (London: Longmans, Green).

Eslund, ed. (2002), *Democracy* (Oxford: Blackwell).

Farrar, C. (1988), *The Origins of Democratic Thinking* (Cambridge: Cambridge University Press).

Finer, S.E. (1999), *The History of Government from the Earliest Times*, vol. II (Oxford: Oxford University Press).

Finlay, Robert (1980), *Politics in Renaissance Venice* (London: Ernest Benn).

Finley, M. (1973), *Democracy Ancient and Modern* (London: Chatto and Windus).

Fishburn, P. (1977), 'Lotteries and social choice', *Journal of Economic Theory* 5.

Fisher. H.A.L. (1938), *A History of Europe* (London: Eyre and Spottiswoode).

Fisher, R.A. (1949), The Design of Experiments, 5th edn (Edinburgh: Oliver and Boyd, first published 1935).

Forrest, W.G. (1966). *The Emergence of Greek Democracy* (London: Weidenfeld and Nicholson, London).

Forsyth, M. (1987), *Reason and Revolution: The Political Thought of Abbé Sièyes* (Leicester University Press).

Forsyth, W. (1852), *The History of Trial by Jury* (London).

Fox, J.A., Tracy, P.E. (1986), 'Randomised response a method for social surveys', *Quantitive Applications in the Social Sciences,* Sage.

Frienberg, S.E. (1971), 'Randomisation and social affairs: the 1970 draft lottery', *Science* 171, 255–61

Fustel De Coulanges. N.D. (1864), *The Ancient City*, trans. Small, W (Baltimore: John Hopkins University Press).

Gauci, P. (1996), *Politics and society in Great Yarmouth. 1660-1722* (Oxford: Clarendon Press).

Gilbert, F. (1965), *Machiavelli and Guicciardini. Politics and History in Sixteenth-century Florence* (New Jersey: Princeton University Press).

Gilbert, F. (1977), 'Bernado Rucellai and the Orti Oricellari: a study in the origin of modern political thought', in Gilbert (1977), *History, Choice, Commitment* (Cambridge, Mass.: reprint from: *Journal of the Warburg and Courtauld Institute* 12, 1949).

Gilbert, F. (1968), 'The Venetian constitution in Florentine political thought', in Rubinstein (1968).

Goldie, M. (1980), 'The roots of Whiggism. 1688-94', *History of Political Thought* 1 (1980).

Gomme, A.W. (1962), *More Essays in Greek History and Literature* (Oxford: Blackwell).

Gomme A.W. (1933), *The Population of Athens in the Fifth and Fourth Centuries* (Oxford: Blackwell).

Gobert, J. (1997), *Justice, Democracy and the Jury* (Aldershot: Dartmouth).

Gooch, G.P. (1917), *English Democratic Ideas in the Seventeenth Century* (Cambridge: Cambridge University Press).

Goodwin, B. (2005), *Justice by Lottery* (Charlottesville: Imprint Academic).

Greely, H. (1977), 'The equality of allocation by lot', *Harvard Civil Rights – Civil Liberties Review* 12, 113–41

Green, R.H. (1910), 'Lot meadow customs at Yarnton, Oxon.', *Economic Journal* 20: 77.

Green, T.A. (1985), *Verdict According to Conscience* (University of Chicago Press).

Griffith, G.T. (1966), 'Isegoria in the assembly at Athens', in Ehrenberg (1966).

Grote, G. (1831), *The Essentials of Parliamentary Reform* (London).

Grote, G. (1888), *A History of Greece from the Earliest Period to the Close of the Generation Contemporary with Alexander the Great 1846-56* (London: J. Murray).

Guéniffey, P. (1933), *Le Nombre et la Raison La révolution francais et les élections* (Paris: Editions de l'Ecole des Hautes Etudes en Sciences Sociales).

Hacking, I. (1988), 'Telepathy: origins of randomness in experimental design', *Isis* 79.

Hacking, I. (1990), *The Taming of Chance* (Cambridge: Cambridge University Press).

Hall, M.D. (1977), *The Political and Legal Philosophy of James Wilson* (University of Missouri Press).

Hammersley, R. (2005), *French Revolutionaries and English Republicans – the Cordeliers Club 1790–94* (Boydell Press).

Hampson, N. (1983), *Will and Circumstance Montesquieu, Rousseau and the French Revolution* (London: Duckworth).

Hampson, N. (1991), *St Just* (Oxford: Blackwell).

Handelman. H., Tessler. M., eds (1999), *Democracy and its Limits* (Notre Dame, Ind.: University of Notre Dame Press).

Hansen, M.H. (1990), 'Political powers of the people's courts', in Murray, O., Price, S. eds (1990), *The Greek City from Homer to Alexander* (Oxford: University Press).

Hansen, M.H. (1999), *Athenian Democracy in the age of Demosthenes* (Bristol Classical, first edn 1991.)

Headlam, J.W. (1933), *Election by Lot at Athens* (Cambridge: Cambridge University Press, first edn 1891).

Held, D. (1987), *Models of Democracy* (Cambridge: Polity).

Herlihy, D. (1958), *Pisa in the Early Renaissance* (Yale University Press).

Herlihy, D. (1967), *Medieval and Renaissance Pistoia* (Yale University Press).

Herlihy, D. (1991), The Rulers of Florence' in Molho, A., Raaflaub, K., Emlen, eds. (1991), *City States in Classical Antiquity and Medieval Italy* (Ann Arbor: University of Michigan Press).

Heywood, W. (1910), *A History of Perugia* (London: Methuen).

Hignett, C. (1952), *A History of the Athenian Constitution to the end of the Fifth Century B.C.* Oxford: Clarendon.

Hofstee, W.K.B. (1990), 'Allocation by lot: a conceptual and empirical analysis', *Social Science Information* Vol.29 No. 4.

Holm, A. (1898), *The History of Greece*, trans. Clarke, F. (London: Macmillan).

Honohan, I. (2002), *Civic Republicanism* (London: Routledge).

Hornblower S. (1992), 'Creation and development of democratic institutions in Ancient Greece', in: Dunn, J. ed. (1992), *Democracy: the Unfinished Journey* (Oxford: Oxford University Press).

Hyde, J.K. (1973), *Society and Politics in Medieval Italy. The Evolution of Civil Life1000-1350* (London: Macmillan).

Huntington, S.P. (1991), *The Third Wave* (University of Oklahoma Press).

Inkeles. A. ed. (1993), *On Measuring Democracy* (New Brunswick & London: Transaction).

Jackson, S., Brashers, D.E. (1986), 'Random Factors in ANOVA (Analysis of Variance)', *Qualitative Applications in Social Sciences* 98, Sage.

Jaurès, J. (1972), *Histoire Socialiste de la révolution francais* (Paris: Editions Sociale).

Jensen, M. (1940), *The Articles of Confederation* (University of Wisconsin Press).

Jones, A.H.M. (1957), *Athenian Democracy* (Baltimore: John Hopkins University Press).

Jones J. R. (1961), *The First Whigs. The Politics of the Exclusion Crisis 1678–83* (Oxford: Oxford University Press).

Jones, P. (1997), *The Italian City States – from Commune to Signori* (Oxford: Clarendon Press).

Karston, P. (1967), 'Who was Colonel Sidney? A note on the meaning of Oct. 13th 1691 Penn-Sidney letter', *Pennsylvania Magazine* 91, 193–8.

Keane, J. (1995), *Tom Paine. A Political Life* (New York: Grove).

Kent, D. (1978), *The Rise of the Medici Faction in Florence 1426-34* (Oxford: Oxford University Press).

Kishlansky, M.A. (1986), *Parliamentary Selection* (Cambridge: Cambridge University Press).

Kohl, B.G., Andrews-Smith, A. eds.(1995), *Major Problems in the History of theItalian Renaissance* (Lexington, Massachusetts, Toronto: D.C. Heath and Company).

Kohl, B.G. (1998), *Padua under the Carrara 1318-1405* (Baltimore: John Hopkins University Press).

Kroll, J.H. (1972), *Athenian Bronze Allotment Plates* (Cambridge, Mass.: Harvard University Press).

Kuper, R. (1996), *Citizens' Juries. The Hertfordshire Experience* (University of Hertfordshire Business School).

Landsman, N.C. (1985), *Scotland and its First American Colony. 1683-1765* (New Jersey: Princeton University Press).

Lane, F.C. (1971), 'The Enlargement of the Grand Council of Venice' in Rawe, J.G., Stockdale, W.H. eds. (1971), *Florilegium Historale. Essays presented to Wallace K. Ferguson* (University of Toronto Press).

Lane, F.C. (1973) *Venice, a Maritime Republic* (Baltimore: John Hopkins University Press).

Lansing, C. (1991), *The Florentine Magnates. Lineage and Faction in a MedievalCommune* (New Jersey: Princeton University Press).

Leffevre, G. (1964), *The French Revolution from 1793-1799*, vol. II, trans. Stewart, J.H., Friguglietti, J. (London: Routledge and Kegan Paul).

Lewis, D.M. (1963), 'Cleithenes and Attica', *Historia 12*, 22-40; also in Lijphant A. (1999) *Patterns of Democracy* (Yale University Press).

Lijphant, A. (1999), *Patterns of Democracy* (Yale University Press).

Loraux, N. (1986), *The Invention of Athens* (Cambridge, Mass.: Harvard University Press).

Lokken, (1959), *David Lloyd, Colonial Lawmaker* (Seattle: University of Washington Press).

Luciani, V. (1950), 'Recent Guicciardini studies', *Italica* XXVII (1950) 109–27

MacDowell, D.M. (1978), *The Law in Classical Athens* (London: Thames and Hudson)

Manin, B. (1997), *The Principles of Representative Government* (Cambridge: Cambridge University Press).

Manship, H. (1854), *The History of Great Yarmouth*, ed. Palmer, C.J., Louis, Alfred Meall and Russell Smith, J., (London).

Maples, M. (1957), 'William Penn, Classical Republican', *Pennsylvania Magazine of History and Biography* 81 (April 1957).

Marongiu, A. (1968), *Medieval Parliaments. A Comparative Study*, trans. Woolf, S.J. (London: Eyre and Spottiswoode).

Martines, L. (1968), *Lawyers and Statecraft in Renaissance Florence* (New Jersey: Princeton University Press).

Mathiez, A. (1962), *The French Revolution*, trans. Phillips, C. A. (New York: Russell and Russell).

Mathiez, A. (1975), *La réaction Thermidorienne* (Genèvre: Slat Kine-Megaroitis Reprints).

Maynor, J.W. (2003), *Republicanism in the Modern World* (Cambridge: Polity).

McCormick, R.P. (1964), *New Jersey from Colony to State* (Princeton: Van Nostrand Co.).

McCormick, R.P. (1964), 'New Jersey from Colony to State', *New Jersey Historical Series* 1 (1964).

Meek, C.E. (1978), *Lucca 1369-1400* (Oxford: Oxford University Press).

Meek, C.E. (1980), *The Commune of Lucca under Pisan Rule 1342-69*, The Medieval Academy of America, Speculum Anniversary Monograph (Ann Arbor: University of Michigan Press).

Merriman, R.B. (1911), 'The Cortes of the Spanish Kingdoms of the Late Middle Ages', *American Historical Review* XVI: 3 (April 1911).

Mitford, W. (1786), *The History of Greece* (London: Cadell and Davies).

Morse, S. (1924), *Freemasonry in the American Revolution* Washington D.C.: Masonic Service Association of the United States).

Mueller, D.C., Tollinson, R.D., Willett, T.D. (1972), 'Representative Democracy via Random Selection', *Public Choice* 12, Spring, 57–68.

Mulford, I. (1851), *The Civil and Political History of New Jersey* (Philadelphia: Brown).

Mulgan, R. (1984), 'Lot as a democratic device', *Review of Politics* 46: 4.

Murray, O. (1988), 'Greek forms of Government' in Grant, M., Kitzinger, R. (1988),*Civilisations of the Ancient Mediterranean. Greece and Rome* (N.Y.: Scribner).

Murray, O. (1990), 'Cities of Reason', in Murray, O., Price, S. eds, *The Greek City from Homer to Alexander* (Oxford: Oxford University Press).

Najemy, J.M. (1982), *Corporatism and Consensus in Florentine Electoral Politics, 1280-1400* (Chapel Hill: University of North Carolina Press).

Najemy, J.M. (1991), 'Dialogue of Power', in Emlen, J., Molho, A., Raaflaub, K. eds *City States in Classical Antiquity and Medieval Italy* (Ann Arbour: University of Mitchigan Press).

Najemy, J.M.(1995), 'Guild Republicanism in Trecento Florence', in Kohl, Andrews-Smith, (1995).

Nash, G.B. (1965), 'The Free Society of Traders and the Early Politics of Pennsylvania,' *Pennsylvania Magazine of History and Biography*, vol. 89 (April 1965).

Nash, G.B. (1968), *Quakers and Politics. Pennsylvania 1681–1726* (Boston: Northeastern University Press).

O'Callaghan, J.F. (1975), *A History of Medieval Spain* (Cornell University Press).

Ober, J. (1989), *Mass and Elite in Democratic Athens* (New Jersey: Princeton University Press).

Ober, J. (1998), 'The Athenian Revolution of 508/7 BC', in Dougherty, C., Kuuke, L. (1998), *Cultural Poetics of Archaic Greece* (Oxford: Oxford University Press).

Olson, A.G. (1973), *Anglo-American Politics. 1660-1775. The Relationship between Parties in England and Colonial America* (Oxford: Clarendon Press).

Osborne-Taylor, H. (1925), *The Medieval Mind* (London: Macmillan).

Osgood, H.L. (1924), *The American Colonies in the Eighteenth Century* (Columbia University Press).

Ostrom, E. (1990), *Governing the Commons. The evolution of institutions for collective action* (Cambridge: Cambridge University Press).

Ostwald, M. (1988), 'The reform of the Athenian State by Kleisthenes', *Cambridge Ancient History* IV (Canbridge: Cambridge University Press).

Palmer, C.J. (1856), *The History of Great Yarmouth* (Yarmouth: L.A. Mead & London: J. Russell-Smith).

Palmer, R. (1996), *Athenian Religion, a History* (Oxford: Clarendon Press).

Palmer, R.R. (1953), 'Notes on the use of the term 'democracy' 1789–99, *Political Science Quarterly 68.*

Parker, Robert. (1996), *Athenian Religion, a History* (Oxford: Clarendon Press).

Pateman, C. (1970), *Participation and Democratic Theory* (Cambridge University Press).

Pasquino, P.(1994), 'Emmanuel Sieyès: his constitutional republicanism', in Fontana, B. ed. (1994), *The Invention of the Modern Republic* (Cambridge University Press).

Patrick, A. (1972), *The Men of the First French Republic* (Baltimore: John Hopkins University Press).

Patterson, T.E. (1922), 'The Pennsylvania Method of Drawing a Juror', *Pennsylvania Magazine* 46 (March 1922).

Pesman-Cooper, R. (1985), 'The Florentine Ruling Group under the Governo Popolare 1494–1512', *Studies in Medieval and Renaissance History* 7 (1985).

Pettit, Philip. (1997), *Republicanism* (Oxford: Clarendon Press).

Phillips, Mark. (1977), *Francesco Guicciardini. The Historian's Craft* (Toronto & Buffalo: University of Toronto Press).

Phillips, Mark. (1987), *A Memoir of Marco Parenti* (N.J.: Princeton University Press).

Pirenne, H. (1925), *Medieval Cites. Their Origins and the Revival of Trade* (New Jersey:Princeton University Press).

Pocock, J.G.A. (1975), *The Machiavellian Moment: Florentine Political Thought and the Republican Tradition* (New Jersey: Princeton University Press).

Pocock J.G.A. (1980), 'Civil Wars, Revolution, and Political Parties,' in Bonomi (1980).

Pole J. R. (1996), *Political Representation in England and the Origins of the AmericanRepublic* (London: Macmillan Press).

Polizzotto, L. (1994), *The Elect Nation – the Savonarolan Movement in Florence 1494–1545* (Oxford: Clarendon Press).

Pomfret, J. (1973), *Colonial New Jersey – A History* (New York: Scribner's Sons).

Pope, M. (1989), 'Upon the Country. Juries and the Principle of Random Selection', *Social Science Information* (2 June).

Potter, D. (Goldblatt, Kiloh, Lewis) eds (1997), *Democratization* (Open University Press).

Previte-Orton, C.W. (1926), 'Italian Cities till c1250', in *Cambridge Medieval History* V (Cambridge: Cambridge University Press).

Previte-Orton, C.W. (1935), 'Marsilius of Padua', *Proceedings of the British Academy* 21 (1935).

Queller, D.E. (1986), *The Venetian Patriciate* (Urbana & Chicago: University of Illinois Press).

Raab, Felix. (1964), *The English Face of Machiavelli, a Changing Interpretation. 1500-1700* (London: Routledge and Kegan Paul).

Ramsay, D. (1858), *History of South Carolina* (Charlestown, S.C.: W.J. Duffie).

Remer, G. (1995), 'James Harrington's New Deliberative Rhetoric: Reflection on an Anticlassical Republicanism', *History of Political Thought* XVI, Issue 4 (Winter 1995).

Repp, T. G. (1832), *A Historical Thesis in Trial by Jury, Wager of Law, and other Co-ordinate Forensic Institutions in Scandinavia and Iceland* (Edinburgh: Clark).

Resnick, S.I. (1992), *Adventures in Stochastic Processes* (Boston: Birkhausser).

Rhodes, P.J. (1972), *The Athenian Boule* (Oxford: Oxford University Press).

Rhodes, P.J. (1981), *Commentary on the Aristotelian Ath. Pol.* (Oxford: Oxford University Press).

Rhodes, P.J. (1992), 'The Athenian Revolution', *Cambridge Ancient History* V (Cambridge: Cambridge University Press).

Richard C. J. (1994), *The Founders and the Classics, Greece, Rome, and the American Enlightenment* (Cambridge, Mass.: Harvard University Press).

Ridolfi, R. (1959), *Vita di Francesco Guicciardini*, trans. Grayson, C. (London: Routledge and Kegan Paul).

Riley, P. (1986), *The General Will before Rousseau. The transformation of the divine into the civic* (New Jersey: Princeton University Press).

Robbins, C. (1959), *The Eighteenth-century Commonwealthman* (Cambridge, Mass.: Harvard University Press).

Robbins, F.E. (1916), 'The Lot Oracle at Delphi', *Classical Philology* 11: 3.

Roberts, J.T. (1994), *Athens on Trial. The Antidemocratic Tradition in WesternThought* (New Jersey: Princeton University Press)

Roberts S. K. (1988), 'Juries and the Middling Sort. Recruitment and Performance at Devonshire Quarter Sessions 1649–1670', in Cockburn and Green (1988).

Robey, D., Law, J. (1975), 'The Venetian Myth and the *De Republica Veneta* of Vergerio', *Rinasciamento* 2nd series, 15 (1975) 3–59.

Rosanvallen, P. (1994), 'The Republic of Universal Suffrage', in Fontana, B. ed. (1994), *The Invention of the Modern Republic* (Cambridge: Cambridge University Press).

Rossiter, C. (1966), *The Grand Convention* (New York: Norton).

Roth, C. (1968), *The Last Florentine Republic* (New York: Russell and Russell).

Rubinstein, N. (1954), 'I primi anni del Consiglio Maggiore di Firenze (1494–99), *Archivio Storico Italiano*, n. 403, a cxii, 1954, II, p. 51.

Rubinstein, N. (1966), *The Government of Florence under the Medici.1434-1494* (Oxford: Clarendon Press).

Rubinstein, N. (1968), ed. *Florentine Studies. Politics and Society in Renaissance Florence* (London: Faber and Faber).

Rubinstein, N. (1971), 'Notes on the word Stato in Florence before Machiavelli' in Rawe, J.G., Stockdale, W.H. eds. (1971), *Florilegium Historale. Essays presented to Wallace K. Ferguson* (Toronto: University of Toronto Press).

Russell, C. (1979), *Parliament and English Politics 1621-29* (Oxford: Clarendon Press).

Russell-Smith, H.F. (1914), *Harrington and his Oceana* (Cambridge: Cambridge University Press).

Sandys J.E. (1903–8), *A History of Classical Scholarship from the sixth-century B.C to the End of the Middle Ages* (Cambridge: Cambridge University Press).

Schevill, F. (1904), 'The Podesta of Siena', *American Historical Review* 9: 2 (Jan 1904).

Schevill, F. (1936), *History of Florence* (New York: Harcourt, Brace and Co.).

Schuchard M. K. (2002), *Restoring the Temple of Vision. Cabalistic Freemasonry and Stuart Culture* (Leiden: Brill).

Schwartz, S. (1987), *A Mixed Multitude* (New York: New York University Press).

Sharp, Kevin M. ed. (1978), *Faction and Parliament: Essays in Early Stuart History* (Oxford: Clarendon Press).

Shepherd, W. R. (1896), *History of Proprietary Government in Pennsylvania* (New York: Columbia University Press).

Sher, G. (1980), 'What makes a Lottery Fair?', *Nous* 14.

Shewhart, W.A. (1931), Economic Control of Quality of Manufactured Product (London: Macmillan).

Shuckburgh, E.S. (1894), *History of Rome* (London & New York: Macmillan and Co.).

Shumway, D.B. (1925), 'A rare Dutch Document concerning the Province of
  Pennsylvania in the seventeenth century', *Pennsylvania Magazine* 49: 2 (1925).
Sinclair, R.K. (1988), *Democracy and Participation in Athens* (Cambridge: Cambridge
  University Press).
Sinclair T.A. (1959), *A History of Greek Political Thought* (London: Routledge).
Sirmans, M.E. (1966), *Colonial South Carolina – a political history. 1663-1763* (Chapel
  Hill: University of North Carolina Press).
Sismondi, J.C.L de (1907), *History of the Italian Republics*, Everyman edn (London: J.M.
  Dent and Co., London).
Skinner, Q. (1978), *The Foundations of Modern Political Thought* 1 (Cambridge:
  Cambridge University Press).
Smith, L. Toulmin, Smith, J. Toulmin, Brentano, L. (1870), *English Gilds*, Early English
  Text Society (London: Trubner).
Soboul, A. (1968), *La Première Republique. 1792-1804* (Paris: Calmann-Levy).
Stanley, E.G. (2000), *Anglo-Saxon Trial by Jury* (Woodbridge: D.S. Brewer).
Stapleton, J. (1995), 'Dicey and his Legacy', *History of Political Thought* XVI: 2 (Summer
  1995).
Staveley, E.S. (1972), *Greek and Roman Voting and Elections* (Cornell University Press).
Stephens, J.N. (1983), *The Fall of the Florentine Republic. 1512-1530* (Oxford: Clarendon
  Press).
Stevenson, D. (1988), *The Origins of Freemasonry, Scotland's Century. 1590-1710*
  (Cambridge: Cambridge University Press).
Stockton, D. (1990), *The Classical Athenian Democracy* (Oxford: Oxford University
  Press).
Stone, P. (2007),'Why Lotteries Are Just', *Journal of Political Philosophy* 15: 3, 276–95.
Stone, P. (2007b),'Conceptualizing Lotteries', Working Paper no. 16, *Political Concepts:
  A Working Paper Series of the Committee on Concepts and Methods*, (International
  Political Science Association, September 2007).
Sutherland, K. (2004), *The Party's Over* (Exeter: Imprint Academic).
Sutherland, K. (2008), *A People's Parliament* (Exeter: Imprint Academic).
Sydenman, M.J. (1974), *The First French Republic 1792-1804* (London: B.T. Batsford).
Tabacco, G. (1989), *The Struggle for Power in Medieval Italy. Structures of Political Rule*
  (Cambridge: Cambridge University Press).
Talman, J. L. (1955), *The Origins of Totalitarian Democracy* (Secker and Warburg).
Thirlwall, C. (1846), *History of Greece* (London: John Taylor).
Thomsen, R. (1972), *The Origin of Ostracism*, Humanitas IV (Copenhagen: Gydendal).
Todd, S.C. (1993), *The Shape of Athenian Law* (Oxford: Oxford University Press).
Todhunter, I. (1865), A History of the Mathematical Theory of Probability from the
  time of Pascal to that of Laplace (Cambridge: Macmillan).
Traill, J.S. (1975), *The Political Organisation of Attica*, Hesperia Supplement XIV
  (Princeton, New Jersey).
Tucker, T.J. (1907), *Life in Ancient Athens* (London: Macmillan).
Ullmann, W. (1949), 'The Medieval Idea of Sovereignty', *English Historical Review* 64,
  1–33.
Vaughan-Williams, L. (1994), '*Random Walks, Fair Games and Efficient Markets:
  thedevelopment of an idea*', Nottingham Trent University Occasional Papers in
  Economics 94/5.
Vile, M. J. C. (1998), *Constitutionalism and the Separation of Powers* (Indianopolis: Liberty
  Fund).
Villani, P. (1908), *The Two First Centuries of Florentine History*, trans. Villani, L.,
  (London: Fisher, T. Unwin).
Viroli, M. (1992), *From Politics to Reasons of State* (Cambridge University Press).
Viroli, M. (1998), *Machiavelli* (Oxford: Oxford University Press).

Waley, D. (1952), *Medieval Ovieto. The Political History of an Italian City-state 1157–1334* (Cambridge: Cambridge University Press).

Waley, D (1988), *The Italian City State Republics* (London & New York: Longman).

Wallace, R.W. (1998), 'The Sophists in Athens', in Boedeker, D.D., Raaflaub, K.A. eds (1998), *Democracy, Empire and the Arts in Fifth-century Athens* (Cambridge, Mass.: Harvard University Press).

Weinstein, D. (1970), *Savonarola and Florence* (New Jersey: Princeton University Press).

Weir, R.M. (1983), *Colonial South Carolina. A History* (New York: Kto Press).

Western, J. R. (1965), *The English Militia in the Eighteenth Century* (London: Routledge and Kegan Paul).

Whitehead, D. (1986), *The Demes of Attica* (New Jersey: Princeton University Press).

Whitehead, W.A. (1875), *East New Jersey under the Proprietary Governments* (Newark, New Jersey: Martin R. Dennis).

Williams, D. (2004), *Condorcet and Modernity* (Cambridge: Cambridge University Press).

Wolfson, A. M. (1899), 'Forms of Voting in the Italian Communes', *American Historical Review* V: 1 (October 1899), 1–22.

Woloch, I. (1994), *The New Regime. Transformations of the French Civic Order. 1789–1820* (London: W.W Norton).

Woronoff, D. (1984), *The Thermidorian Regime and the Directory, 1794–9*, trans. Jackson, J. (Cambridge: Cambridge University Press).

Wright, B.F. jr. (1933), 'The Origins of the Separation of Powers in America', *Economica* 40 (May 1933).

Young, W. (1786), *History of Athens, Politically and Philosophically Considered* (London).

Yunis, H. (1988), 'Law, Politics and the *Graphe Paranomon* in Fourth-Century Athens', *Greek, Roman and Byzantine Studies* 29.

Zeckhauseur, R. (1969), 'Majority rules with lotteries on alternatives', *Quarterly Journal of Economics* 83, 696–703.

Unpublished secondary sources

Coleman, E.F. (1987), *Cremona. City and Civic Identity*, D.Phil.Thesis, University of Oxford.

Ellis, E. L. (1961), *The Whig Junto, in Relation to the Development of Party Politics and Party Organisation from its Inception to 1714*, D.Phil. Thesis, University of Oxford.

Fukuda, A. (1992), *James Harrington and the Idea of Mixed Government*, M.Litt. Thesis, University of Oxford.

Kempshall, M.S.(1991), *Bonum Commune and Communis Utilitas*, D.Phil. Thesis, University of Oxford.

Kroenig, J.C. (1977), *The Popolo of Northern Italy 1196-1274*, PhD. Thesis, University of California, Los Angeles.

Nilsen, K. (2000), *European Democracy and Intelligence. A Sociology of Praxis*, PhD. Thesis, University of Ulster.

Nilsen, K. (2004), *Conflict Management and Constitutional Reform.*

Saul, A. (1975), *Great Yarmouth in the Fourteenth Century: A Study in Trade, Politics and Society*, D.Phil Thesis, University of Oxford.

Electronic resources

Nilsen, K.(2007), *Sortition: The Newsletter of the Society for Democracy including Random Selection*. Website: www.sortition.com. See also www.sortition.org.uk [accessed 15 Jan 2007]

Index

Logan (correspondent with William
　　Penn) 161.
London: 178.
Lotteries: form and function: 2-3, 7, 11-29;
　　as a complex phenomena: 8;
　　as a 'non-human' mechanism: 12, 14;
　　design: 7, 19, 94, 120, 148 note 40, 212,
　　　225-7;
　　lottery procedure: 12-14;
　　qualities of lottery decision: 14-16:
　　strong and weak applications: 7, 8, 11,
　　　16-19, 206, 209, 221;
　　process that acts equally: 20;
　　process without responsible agent:
　　　19-20, 34, 47, 47 notes 60 & 61, 49;
　　use in sampling: 23-24;
　　mechanisms:12, 39, 77, 87-8, 101, 139,
　　　144, 147, 155, 156-7, 169, 196-7 (see
　　　Kleroterion);
　　lottery games: 8, 12, 141;
　　lottery voting: 24 note 8;
　　in the design of experiments: 24 note 7.
　　See also **sortition, strong
　　applications, weak applications
　　weighted lottery.**
Lucca: 68, 68 n.1, 76 note 27.
Luck : 91, 121, 129.
Lymington (Hampshire) 162.

Macedonia: 31.
Machiavelli: 6, 98, 99, 104, 100 note 40,
　　117-120, 119 note 70, 123, 134-5, 219,
　　220, 223, 227;
　　History of Florence: 118;
　　*Discourse on the remodelling of the
　　　government of Florence*: 118-120, 198,
　　　219, 220, 223, 227;
　　contrasted with Guicciardini:123.
Madison, James: 168, 169.
Magistrates: See **Athens: selection of
　　magistrates in.**
Magna Carta: 173.
Magnates: 72, 81 note 43, 89 note 67, 112.
Maine: 176.
Manin, B.: 121 note 76, 127 note 98.
Mansfield, Lord: 179.
Manship: 139 note 1.
Markham: 161.
Marpasia: 148.
Marsilius of Padua: 128.
Maryland: 153, 168, 176, 177.
Mason, col.(Virginia delegate to
　　Continental Congress): 168.
Massachusetts: 168, 176 note 144, 177.
McCormack, Richard P.: 157.
Medici: 5, 80, 81, 86 note 57, 91-2, 96, 98,
　　105-108, 109, 110 note 40, 111, 112, 113,

115, 116, 117, 117 n. 63, 118, 120, 121
　　note 72, 129 note 105, 131, 132, 133, 222;
　　Cosimo de: 91, 105;
　　Giovanni de: 118;
　　Lorenzo de: 105;
　　Pietro de: 105, 107.
Mercanzia: 82; Five of: 87.
Metics: 36, 36 n 23.
Minus possidentes: 197.
Mont-Gilbert, F.A.: 194 note 30.
Moore, Sir Thomas: 155.
Morris, Gouverneur: 167, 168.
Morris, Robert: 180, 181.
Military leaders selected by lot: 148.
Militia: 171 note 132, 177 note 149;
　　proposal by Paine: 171-2, 171 note132.
Milton, John: 160 note 98.
Mixed polity: 198. See **Aristotle: mixed
　　government**
Monte: 82.
Montesquieu: 188, 189-90, 191, 211, 218.
Mueller, D.C. et al.: 29 note16.
Municipal Corporations Act 1835: 139.

Napoleon Bonaparte: 209.
National Assembly (France): 191, 193.
National Convention (France): 193, 196,
　　207, 196, 202, 204, 208, 210.
National Executive Council (in Lesueur)
　　197, 199, 212.
National Legislative Council (in Lesueur)
　　197, 199, 212.
Nation state: 228.
Natural aristocracy: 146, 149, 151, 154,
　　193, 195, 198 note 57, 206, 234.
Nedham, Marchamont: 146-7.
New Hampshire: 167, 176 note 144, 177.
New Jersey: 152, 155- 159, 167, 170 note
　　131, 176, 177;
　　jury in: 176;
　　East New Jersey: 153, 153 note 61, 155,
　　　156-9, 176, 184, 218, 220, 223; Court
　　of
　　Appeal in: 157, 176;
　　West New Jersey: 155, 161, 163.
New republican agenda: 229.
New York: 157, 176 note 144, 178.
Nilsen, K.: 231, 217 note 3.
Noland: 152 note 60.
Nomination: 86, 87, 113, 144, 152, 155,
　　158, 162, 163, 164, 196;
　　in Florentine *scrutiny*: 86, 87, 88, 89 note
　　　67, 92, 93;
　　for Florentine *Consiglio Grande*: 110,
　　　115;
　　in Venice: 101, 102, 104;
　　in Lesueur proposals: 196;